The Master Musicians

New Series Edited by Eric Blom

DEBUSSY

DEBUSSY

by

EDWARD LOCKSPEISER

Illustrated

London   J. M. Dent and Sons Ltd.
New York   E. P. Dutton and Co. Inc.

93028

Master school of music association

MORSEMUS.

ML
410
D28
L8

783.2
D28
L9

2148
76

J'ai la fureur d'aimer.   Qu'y faire?   Ah, laisser faire!

PAUL VERLAINE.

PREFACE

DEBUSSY once said that at the age of sixty he would write his memoirs. But he died in 1918 at fifty-five, and a definitive biography has not yet been written. Several authors have written an account of his life, but they have dealt mainly with exterior facts. One of these accounts, by M. Louis Laloy, has special value as having been written with Debussy's approval. It is an early work, however, and necessarily incomplete. Following this, the most authoritative French study that has appeared is M. Léon Vallas's *Claude Debussy et son temps*. Yet here again, as M. Vallas states in his preface, 'the personal life, rich in piquant anecdotes, of a great artist whose extreme and unrestrained sensibility forced him into certain positions which it is not our business to judge,' is intentionally left aside.

The task of writing Debussy's intimate life has therefore been largely work on virgin soil. I am deeply indebted to the work of M. Vallas, which all students must now take as their starting-point, but I have gone chiefly to Debussy's published letters, a list of which, scattered in journals and reviews, will be found in Appendix D. Many of these have not been used in any previous biography and appear here, in English, for the first time.

I have to thank Debussy's pupil and stepson, M. Raoul Bardac, for allowing me to publish the letters addressed to him and for the photographs facing pages 84 and 108; Debussy's sister, Mlle Adèle Debussy, and his friends, M. Nicolas G. Coronio, the late Paul Dukas, MM. Robert Godet, Louis Laloy and Gabriel Pierné, for valuable conversations; Count

Bennigsen for searching his family records concerning Debussy's visits to Russia; Countess Bennigsen for the translations of the correspondence of Mme von Meck on pages 12-15; M. Gilaiev for information concerning Debussy's early unfinished Symphony; the committee and secretary of the Royal Philharmonic Society for communicating the letters in Appendix E; and M. Henry Prunières for the illustration facing page 188.

I have, however, reserved the right to interpret any information that has been given to me in my own way.

The musical quotations from the works entitled *Fantoches, Mazurka, Danse, Pour le piano (Sarabande), Ariettes oubliées (C'est l'extase* and *Green), Chansons de Bilitis (La Flûte de Pan* and *Le Tombeau des Naïades), Prélude à l'Après-midi d'un faune, Nocturnes (Nuages* and *Fêtes)* are printed by permission of the publisher and proprietor, M. Jean Jobert, 44 Rue du Colisée, Paris; *Paysage sentimental,* by permission of Les Éditions de la Sirène Musicale; and *Mandoline, Le Balcon, Pour ce que plaisance est morte, Ballade de Villon à s'amye, Estampes (Pagodes* and *Soirée dans Grenade), Images (Reflets dans l'eau, Hommage à Rameau* and *Poissons d'or), Children's Corner (Doll's Serenade* and *Golliwog's Cake-walk),* the Quartet, *La Mer,* and *Pelléas et Mélisande,* by permission of MM. Durand et Cie, publishers and proprietors, 4 Place de la Madeleine, Paris.

E. L.

May 1936.

CONTENTS

LIFE

CHAP. PAGE

I. CHILDHOOD—1862–1873 3

II. AT THE CONSERVATOIRE—1873–1884 . . 9

III. ROME—1885–1887 23

IV. PARIS—1887–1892 34

V. EARLY ACQUAINTANCES—1887–1892 . . 41

VI. THE TEN YEARS OF 'PELLÉAS'—1892–1902 . 51

VII. THE HEDONIST 65

VIII. TWO YEARS—1902–1904 75

IX. THE YEARS OF 'DEBUSSYISM'—1904–1913 . 85

X. THE WAR—1914–1918 97

XI. THE ABANDONED OPERAS—1902–1918 . . 102

WORK

XII. THE SONGS 111

XIII. THE PIANO WORKS 133

XIV. THE CHAMBER WORKS 151

XV. THE ORCHESTRAL WORKS 166

XVI. THE CHORAL AND DRAMATIC WORKS . . 187

XVII. THE LITERARY WORKS 213

XVIII. DEBUSSY'S INFLUENCE 225

Contents

APPENDICES   PAGE

A. CALENDAR 235

B. CATALOGUE OF WORKS 247

C. PERSONALIA 260

D. BIBLIOGRAPHY 267

E. UNPUBLISHED LETTERS 274

F. ACHILLE-CLAUDE DEBUSSY: MANUSCRIPT MEMOIR
   BY NICHOLAS VON MECK IN THE TCHAIKOVSKY
   MUSEUM AT KLIN (U.S.S.R.) 279

INDEX 282

LIST OF ILLUSTRATIONS

DEBUSSY AT ROME, AGED TWENTY-FOUR .	*Frontispiece*
DEBUSSY AT EIGHTEEN	*facing page* 13
STÉPHANE MALLARMÉ *(from the Portrait by Manet)*	,, ,, 37
LETTER TO ERNEST CHAUSSON . . .	,, ,, 54
DEBUSSY WITH HIS FIRST WIFE, PAUL POUJAUD, PAUL DUKAS AND PIERRE LALO, ABOUT 1902	,, ,, 73
DEBUSSY AND HIS SECOND WIFE, EMMA BARDAC	,, ,, 84
DEBUSSY, AND LOUIS LALOY FLYING A KITE	,, ,, 108
UNPUBLISHED SKETCHES FOR 'LA CHUTE DE LA MAISON USHER'	,, ,, 188

LIST OF ILLUSTRATIONS

...

LIFE

CHAPTER I

CHILDHOOD—1862–1873

'SEE how easily they are mistaken,' Debussy once said to a journalist in Vienna. 'Some think I'm a melancholy northerner, others that I'm from the south, from Provence, the country of Daudet—*tireli, tirela*! Well, I'm just a native of Saint-Germain, half an hour from Paris.'

Until Léon Vallas published his researches this was virtually all that was known of Debussy's ancestry. It now appears that through a line of farmers, small landowners and labourers his family goes back to one Valentin de Bussy, born in the village of Courcelles-sous-Grignon in Burgundy at the end of the seventeenth century. Five miles from this village, at Bussy-le-Grand, is the ancient Burgundian seat of the Counts de Bussy. No definite link between Debussy's ancestors and their neighbours of noble blood is known to exist, although one fact in support of a possible relationship between them may be mentioned. Roger de Rabutin, Count de Bussy, the distinguished soldier and writer, better known as Bussy-Rabutin, the cousin of Mme de Sévigné, was said to have had that prominent forehead which was one of Debussy's most striking features. He lived at Bussy-le-Grand during the second half of the seventeenth century and was notorious for his exploits with women.

Debussy's ancestors left Burgundy at the time of the Revolution and settled near Paris. His grandfather was a carpenter. His father, Manuel-Achille, was born at Montrouge in 1836, tried his hand at a number of things, and eventually settled

3

down as an accountant in a firm in Paris. On 30th November 1861 he married, at Levallois, then a village on the outskirts of Paris, a Parisian, Victorine Manoury,[1] six months his junior. The next day the young couple moved into a little brown-faced house, number 38 Rue au Pain, at Saint-Germain-en-Laye, taking over the china shop on the ground floor.

Little is known of this modest couple. From one or two stray remarks of Debussy's boyhood friends we gather that Manuel Debussy was fond of music, particularly of *opéra-comique,* and appears to have had a brother who was a conductor, possibly of a military band, somewhere in the provinces. Henry Prunières writes that Manuel Debussy boasted 'of only the most superficial education,' yet 'pretended to the widest interests. He frequented playhouse galleries, saw all the most successful pieces, read the most popular books, talked of them at length, and fancied himself as a musical connoisseur.' His son, however, used to refer to him as 'le vieux galvaudeux' (the old waster). Of Mme Debussy we are told that she was highly emotional. One fact is certain: the first eight years of their married life were passed under great financial strain.

The year after they were married, on 22nd August 1862, was born their first child, named after his father and paternal grandfather, Achille-Claude. Our information concerning his early childhood is still scanty; but there is one matter which I am able to elucidate. Vallas mentions that he was not baptized until 31st July 1864, that is, almost two years after his birth, and adds:

His baptismal certificate bears two names which he declared later were unknown to him: those of his godfather, Achille-Antoine Arosa, and his godmother, Octavie de la Ferronière. The identity of the financier, Arosa, will be disclosed some day, and Octavie de

---

[1] Mlle Adèle Debussy, the composer's sister, has informed me that her maternal grandmother was likewise from Burgundy.

la Ferronière will be despoiled of the high-sounding name she assumed; we shall ascertain what relationships, legal or otherwise, united the two people who held Achille-Claude at the baptismal font: then only shall we know the exact circumstances of his child-hood. We do not propose to reveal here any further particulars on the subject.[1]

It is hardly to be wondered at that this mysterious reference caused some people to doubt the legitimacy of Debussy's birth. If the doubt still exists (as I believe it does) it must be said that Vallas subsequently stated that no such idea was ever in his mind, and that there is absolutely no foundation for questioning that Achille was the son of Manuel and Victorine Debussy. The truth of the matter is that 'Octavie de la Ferronière' was Manuel's sister, her real name being Mme Roustan (*née* Debussy). The benefactress of the Debussy family, she was able to secure through her relationship with Arosa, then a fairly well-to-do bachelor, material support and guidance for a child whose parents were living almost in misery. To this poor, struggling couple Arosa, a man of taste and distinction, appeared, in fact, to be almost a fairy godfather.[2]

Achille was the eldest of five children. Within two years a girl, Adèle, was born, and the Debussys, not having made a success of the china business, gave up their shop and moved first to Clichy and then to Paris, where they lived in the Rue Pigalle. Three boys were born within a short time and Mme Debussy, doubtless for financial reasons, entrusted all her children, except Achille, to the care of her sister-in-law.

Achille—it was only in later years that, finding this name 'quite ridiculous,' he reversed the order of his Christian names and was known to his friends as Claude—stayed with his mother. She was, we are told, 'passionately fond of him.' He never went to school. She taught him to read and write,

[1] Translation by Maire and Grace O'Brien.
[2] Information kindly supplied by M. Paul Arosa.

but such elementary education as he received from her was far from complete, and his spelling was faulty even at the age of thirty. According to his sister, he was (at about the age of eight) 'uncommunicative and closed in upon himself, liking neither his lessons nor his games. . . . He would spend whole days sitting on a chair thinking, no one knew of what.' He was much attracted by tiny ornaments and engravings and had a passion for collecting brilliantly coloured butterflies, which he arranged in zigzags on the walls of his room. At one time, it is said, he thought of becoming a painter.

Of a few years later we have these illuminating glimpses from Gabriel Pierné:

He was a gourmet, but not a gourmand. He loved good things to eat and the quantity mattered little. I remember very well how he used to delight in a cup of chocolate which my mother invited him to take at the Café Prévost, and how, at Bourbonneux's (a famous *pâtisserie*) he used to choose some delicate little pastry from a case specially reserved for the *produits de luxe,* while his friends were more likely to be content with something more substantial. This poor boy, who had come from a most ordinary class of society, had in everything the taste of an aristocrat. He was particularly attracted to minute objects and delicate and sensitive things. My father had a beautifully bound set of *Le Monde illustré.* When Achille came to the house we used to look at the pictures with delight. He preferred those which took up little space and were surrounded by a huge margin. One day he persuaded me to help him cut out these pictures to put on our walls. The crime was soon committed, and I remember that Debussy went off with reproductions of famous pictures, by Meissonier in particular, surrounded by these huge margins.

When Achille was seven, his brother Eugène died of meningitis and he and his sister were taken to Cannes by their aunt. He wrote to Jacques Durand in 1908:

I remember the railway passing in front of the house and the sea stretching out to the horizon. You sometimes had the impression that the railway came out of the sea or went into it—whichever you like. Then there was the Route d'Antibes, where there were so many roses. I never saw so many all together in my life. I hope the railway is still there, so that you will be able to come back, and also the roses, because there is no better way of decorating streets. With a Norwegian carpenter who used to sing—Grieg, perhaps— from morning till night I close my memoirs.

In Cannes it was Mme Roustan who first had the idea that her nephew should be taught music and accordingly arranged for him to take piano lessons from an old Italian teacher named Cerutti. Of these early lessons we know nothing beyond this bare fact mentioned in the early biography of Louis Laloy. It seems that his career was determined by a meeting in Paris some time later. Through Charles de Sivry he came into contact with Mme Mauté de Fleurville, a former pupil of Chopin, and the mother of Mathilde Mauté, the unfortunate wife of Paul Verlaine. 'He must become a musician,' she said, having heard him strum on an old piano; and she offered herself as a pianoforte teacher. Manuel Debussy, who up till this time had thought of sending his son into the navy, decided thereupon that he should become a virtuoso, and in the traditional manner of fathers of promising musicians imposed on him long hours of daily practice.

In his correspondence with Durand, Debussy twice mentions Mme Mauté de Fleurville. On 27th January 1915, when he was working on an edition of Chopin, he wrote: 'It is a pity that Madame Mauté de Fleurville, to whom I owe the little I know about the piano, is dead. She knew many things about Chopin.' And on 1st September of the same year:

With all respect to his great age, what Saint-Saëns says about the pedal in Chopin is not quite right, for I remember very well what Madame Mauté de Fleurville told me. Chopin wanted his pupils to study without using the pedal and only to use it sparingly when performing. It was this use of the pedal as a kind of breathing that I noticed in Liszt, when I heard him in Rome.[1]

Such are the available facts of Debussy's childhood. Living apart from his brothers and sister, never having gone to school and continually in the company of his mother, he was not a happy child and had little opportunity of acquiring any sense of sociability. His father was not the kind of man to deal with such introspection as this upbringing tended to breed; and the narrowness of his mother's mind soon became apparent. When at the age of eleven he was admitted to the Conservatoire, his awkward ways and unsociable manner, not to mention his poor education, hardly made him attractive to his fellow-students.

[1] In her *Mémoires* Mathilde Verlaine tells that her mother frequented the highest circles of Paris society. She was an extremely kind-hearted woman, often engaged in charity work, and she had known intimately the greatest artistic celebrities of her day, among them Balzac, de Musset and Wagner. Mathilde, to whom Verlaine dedicated *La Bonne Chanson*, was a child of her second marriage with Mauté, 'de Fleurville' being an assumed part of the name.

CHAPTER II

DEBUSSY entered the Paris Conservatoire in 1873 and remained there eleven years.

The first class in which he was enrolled was the so-called *solfège* class for which this school is famous. At no other institution is the course in ear-training so rigorous. Students are required not merely to sing at sight and to transpose easily, but to analyse and to reproduce any harmonic or contrapuntal texture before they acquire, in the study of harmony, the rule-of-thumb methods of putting parts together. Lavignac, the master, was an erudite musician who incidentally introduced Debussy to the music of Wagner by playing over to him, one winter evening, the overture to *Tannhäuser*. Whatever it meant to the young boy, he must have been completely unaware of the great conflict that Wagner was later to cause in his musical development, from which ultimately his very personal style evolved. Debussy remained in Lavignac's class four years and at the annual examinations was awarded the third, second, and finally the first prize.

In the piano class which he attended at the same time the teacher was Marmontel. Debussy was not, in his opinion, one of the best pupils of his class. 'He doesn't like the piano much, but he does like music,' Marmontel once said. In 1877, however, Debussy won the second prize with the first movement of Schumann's G minor Sonata, and his parents were still able to hope for the career of a virtuoso. But the following two years were disappointing. He received no award at either of the annual examinations, and all such hopes were abandoned.

Debussy's first musical leanings, as recorded by his friend Paul Vidal, reveal the almost forgotten Paris musical world of the eighteen-seventies as dominated by *opéra-comique*. Offenbach, Pessard and Delibes—such were the composers who were then in vogue. In Marmontel's class they played a great deal of Chopin and Schumann and various works of Stephen Heller and Alkan. Debussy liked Berlioz immensely and also Lalo, whose *Namouna* brought from him such a manifestation of enthusiasm at the Opéra that he was ordered to leave the theatre. He was very fond of Ernest Guiraud, his future teacher of composition, of Pessard, whose *Capitaine Fracasse,* a popular light opera, delighted him, of Delibes and Saint-Saëns. César Franck he liked to a certain extent. Beethoven he abhorred—but only, as he said, for the reason that Marmontel had given the sentimental words: 'O mère, douleur amère,' to the rondo of the 'Pathetic' Sonata.

In the harmony class the teacher was Émile Durand. According to Maurice Emmanuel, who is the authority for Debussy's studies at the Conservatoire, his instruction in harmony was 'second-rate.' Durand, writes this author, 'liked neither music, teaching, nor his pupils. . . . If, when the class was over, one of the pupils would play over to his friends some composition he had attempted, Durand would slam the lid of the piano on his fingers and say: "You'd do better to work at your progressions!"' However, from the four years, 1876 to 1880, that Debussy spent in this class date his first known compositions. They consist of several songs on poems of Théodore de Banville and two songs, now lost, entitled *Madrid, princesse des Espagnes* and *Ballade à la lune.* Of these we might possibly form some idea from the following anecdote told by Vidal, which at least throws an interesting light on his early musical taste:

As I kept on worrying him to play me his new works, which he hadn't the time or the inclination to write down, he played the joke on me of making me learn by heart a set of songs by Pessard, *Les Joyeusetés de bonne compagnie,* which he sang to me pretending they were his.

Chanson d'un fou, a song recently published under Debussy's name, is actually not by Debussy at all, but a song of this set by Pessard.[1]

By 1880 he had received no awards in Durand's class, and without some recommendation in harmony it was not allowed to proceed to one of the composition classes. The first prize in Auguste Bazille's score-reading class which he obtained in the summer of 1880 enabled him, however, to do this. But here we must interrupt the account of his studies at the Conservatoire to relate an important episode of his early life. During the summer of 1880, when he was first assured of following the career of a composer, he made the acquaintance of the patroness of Tchaikovsky, Nadezhda von Meck.

Let us picture the young Debussy, shy and clumsy, as his friends remember him then, in the company of this Russian 'grande dame.' She was a woman of fifty and a multi-millionaire. Her husband had died in 1876, leaving her with eleven children. In the same year she developed that strange passion for the personality of Tchaikovsky which forbade her ever to make his acquaintance and which she sublimated in the love-letters she incessantly wrote him over a period of sixteen years. She was an accomplished pianist, cultured and widely read. She had known the Rubinsteins well and several of her children had taken lessons from Liszt. After the death of her husband she retired almost completely from society, giving herself up to a passionate cult of the music of Tchaikovsky, whom she maintained with a handsome allowance.

[1] See Catalogue of Works (Appendix B).

Here, in her letters, is the first reference to Debussy. It is dated 10th July 1880, from Interlaken:

Two days ago a young pianist arrived from Paris, where he has just graduated at the Conservatoire with the first prize in the class of M. Marmontel.[1] I engaged him for the summer to give lessons to the children, accompany Julia's singing and play four hands with myself. This young man plays well, his technique is brilliant, but he lacks any personal expression. He is yet too young, says he is twenty, but looks sixteen.

He was, in fact, eighteen. At the end of July Mme von Meck travelled with Debussy and five or six of her children from Interlaken through the south of France to Arcachon. On 7th August she writes:

Yesterday for the first time I played our Symphony [i.e. Tchaikovsky's No. 4] with my little Frenchman. So to-day I am in a terrible state of nerves. I cannot play it without a fever penetrating all the fibres of my being and for a whole day I cannot recover from the impression. My partner did not play it well, though he read it splendidly. That is his only, though very important, merit. He reads a score, yours even, *à livre ouvert*. He has another merit, which is that he is delighted with your music. Theoretically he is Massenet's pupil and naturally considers Massenet the great luminary. But yesterday I also played your suite with him and he was enchanted with the fugue, saying: 'Dans les fugues modernes je n'ai jamais rien vu de si beau. M. Massenet ne pourrait jamais rien faire de pareil.' He does not care for the Germans and says: 'Ils ne sont pas de notre tempérament, ils sont si lourds, pas clairs.' On the whole he is a typical Parisian boulevard product. It seems he is eighteen and has already graduated at the Conservatoire *avec premier prix*. Blessed are those who study at the Paris Conservatoire. He composes very nicely, but here too he is the true Frenchman.

---

[1] As we have seen, the first prize he received in 1880 was from the score-reading class of Bazille. Either Debussy had misinformed her or she was misled by the fact that Marmontel had recommended him.

DEBUSSY AT EIGHTEEN, DURING HIS
STAY AT FLORENCE WITH MADAME VON MECK

Debussy was never, as far as is known, a pupil of Massenet.
He might have been an *auditeur* in Massenet's class or, what
is more likely, he might have learnt to consider Massenet as
the 'great luminary' in the harmony class of Émile Durand.
Massenet was the most popular master at the Conservatoire
and, as the songs, *Nuit d'étoiles, Beau soir* and *Fleur des blés*
clearly show, Debussy in his younger days was certainly one
of his disciples.

At the beginning of September we find the von Mecks and
Debussy in Florence. The earliest mention of Debussy's compositions is in a letter of 8th September from the Villa Oppenheim:

I shall send you for your appreciation a little composition—one of
many—by my little pianist, Bussy [writes Madame von Meck to
Tchaikovsky]. This youth intends to become a composer and
writes very nice things, but they are all echoes of his professor,
Massenet. He is now writing a trio. It is very nice but it is
again reminiscent of Massenet. He score-reads and accompanies
singing perfectly. . . .

Many of these early pieces passed into the hands of members
of the von Meck family and either disappeared at the time of
the Revolution or have otherwise remained unpublished. The
little composition sent to Tchaikovsky was the recently discovered *Danse bohémienne* published by Schott. Tchaikovsky
remarked that it was 'a very nice little thing, but altogether
too short. Not a single thought is developed to the end, the
form is bungled and there is no unity.' An accurate criticism,
though no doubt disheartening for Debussy, who might have
shared some of his hostess's feelings for Tchaikovsky.

It appears that in Florence Debussy was required to play
in the household trio with the violinist Pachulsky and the
cellist Danilchenko.[1] We gather that they were on intimate

[1] On seeing a photograph of this household triumvirate, Tchaikovsky remarked: 'Bussy has something in the face and hands that
vaguely recalls Anton Rubinstein in his youth. God grant that his

terms with the children. A song called *Rondeau* on word
of Alfred de Musset that Debussy wrote in 1882 bears th
dedication: 'Pour mon ami Alexandre de Meck. Souven
bien affectueux.' Pachulsky married Julia and Maximilia
de Meck remembers that Debussy fell in love with his sister
Sophie, and asked her to marry him. She was then age
sixteen and flatly refused.

On 29th September Mme von Meck informs Tchaikovsk
that her 'little Frenchman' has finished his Trio. 'I ar
sorry not to be able to send it to you for your criticism, but h
is leaving shortly and would not have the time to copy it out
This is no doubt the Trio in G mentioned by M. Vallas i
Claude Debussy et son temps. It has remained unpublished an
is dedicated in affectionate terms to his harmony master, Émil
Durand. His earliest publication seems to have been a
arrangement, made at his hostess's request, of the Spanish, Italia
and Russian dances from Tchaikovsky's ballet *The Swan Lak*

No doubt the eighteen-year-old Debussy fully appreciate
the agreeable duties of his post and the opportunities to wor
at the Villa Oppenheim. 'Just imagine, that boy crie
bitterly when he left me,' writes Mme von Meck on 31s
October. 'Naturally I was deeply touched—he has a ver
faithful heart. He would not have gone at all were it nc
that his masters at the Conservatoire disapproved of hi
request for a prolongation of leave.'

The following spring he sought to renew his engagement
Mme von Meck was then in Russia. On 12th May 188
she wrote to Tchaikovsky from Brailov in the Ukraine: 'M

---

lot be as happy as that of the "king of pianists."' It was the presenc
of these musicians at her house that first caused Mme von Meck t
suggest to Tchaikovsky that he should write a trio. 'Why have you
never written a single trio?' she writes on 18th October 1880. 'Ever
day I regret it, for every day trios are played to me and I alway
complain that you have not written one.'

ttle Frenchman is anxious to come here. I shall not have
ne heart to refuse him though I have a pianist, the elder
'achulsky.' Here, then, we are able to elucidate some of the
mystery of Debussy's early visit to Russia—an episode which
is more imaginative biographers have not failed to dwell upon.

We know now the circumstances and the date. Debussy
rrived in Russia early in July 1881. It is not clear whether
e first went to Brailov and from there journeyed with Mme von
Meck to Moscow, or whether he met her in Moscow. At all
vents she was in Moscow from the middle of July till the end
f September, and at least part of this time he was with her.

Unfortunately the references to Debussy in her corre-
pondence of these months are few. There is mention of
is having played certain scores of Tchaikovsky's, but the
etters of this period deal almost entirely with family matters
nd business worries and give little indication of the life
Debussy led in Moscow or the music he heard. From a
etter of 11th September 1881 we learn of a journey that he
nade with Nicholas von Meck to Gourievo near Moscow to
lay Tchaikovsky's fourth Symphony at the house of Countess
Alexandra Bennigsen (*née* von Meck). How long he stayed
n Russia after this visit cannot be ascertained. The next
nd last mention of him is in a letter of 24th November 1881
om Florence, in which Mme von Meck says:

When Bussy was with me I often translated [the words] for him,
o that he should better grasp the significance of the music. I gave
im the score of the *Maid of Orleans* and he also asked me for your
verture of *Romeo and Juliet*. I miss him awfully, he played me so
nuch of your music.

Such is the information to be gained from Mme von Meck's
orrespondence. Her last surviving son, Maximilian de Meck,
as informed me that Debussy spent three summers with his
amily, and it may well be that more details will be found in
olumes of this correspondence, to be published later. We

might then hear about the *Symphonie en si* which Debussy dedicated to his hostess, a movement of which, for piano duet, was recently discovered in a Moscow market and published by the Soviet State Publishing Company.[1]

Debussy's acquaintance with Russian music other than that of Tchaikovsky would appear, from this correspondence, to have been very limited. Balakirev was the only member of the 'Kutchka' whom Mme von Meck admired. Rimsky-Korsakov she found 'lifeless,' Cui 'perverted' and Moussorgsky 'quite finished.' Borodin 'never had much brain and overstepped his mark.' But she loved Napravnik and loved Anton Rubinstein 'very much,' and her love for Tchaikovsky was in her 'flesh and blood.'

Raymond Bonheur, a student at the Paris Conservatoire remembers, however, that Debussy brought back from Russia an old opera of Rimsky-Korsakov and some songs of Borodin. The song, *Paysage sentimental,* written by Debussy in 1880, the year of his visit to Florence, shows even then an acquaintance with Borodin. And there are passages reminiscent of Borodin and Rimsky-Korsakov in other works of his belonging to this period (notably in *La Belle au bois dormant* and *Le Triomphe de Bacchus,* both written between 1880 and 1883). But not of Tchaikovsky! According to M. Laloy's biography Debussy became well acquainted with the Tsigansky songs in the Moscow cabarets—a point that is always brought up in discussing his early musical development.[2] On this Mme von

[1] In a private collection in Leningrad there are two unpublished pieces signed: 'Debussy, Moscow 1884.'

[2] According to Count Bennigsen, a grandson of Mme von Meck, Debussy might have been initiated into Moscow cabaret life by Vladimir von Meck, Mme von Meck's eldest son. A popular man in Moscow society in the eighties, it was he who played such havoc with his mother's fortune that in 1892 she was brought to the brink of ruin and saw herself forced to discontinue Tchaikovsky's allowance.

Meck says nothing. Jean Lépine mentions that in 1880 Mme von Meck introduced Debussy to Wagner at Venice. According to the same author, in Moscow he knew Borodin. Paul Vidal mentions that during these journeys he heard *Tristan* for the first time, at Vienna. Wagner, Borodin, the Tsigansky folksongs in Moscow—here was indeed music that might have weaned him from his devotion to Massenet. Can it be that Mme von Meck, with her infatuation for Tchaikovsky, concealed from him any preference for such music that Debussy might have shown? The scarcity of references to him during his visit to Moscow would thus have some significance.

Meanwhile, at the Conservatoire, after a brief venture into the class of César Franck, with whom he was quite unable to agree, he had enrolled in the composition class of Ernest Guiraud.

Guiraud had been a great friend of Bizet and had known Berlioz. He had written a number of operas, classed in style with those of Massenet, and a treatise on orchestration which in spite of its age is still considered a work of great value. To judge from certain accounts of M. Emmanuel, Debussy at this time was beginning to see the insufficiency of the music of Massenet and Delibes and was attracted to Guiraud, not because this master was in any way opposed to the aesthetic of Massenet—for he was not—but because of a certain liberal-mindedness and tolerance.

One winter evening of 1883 [M. Emmanuel recounts] Debussy went to the Erard to imitate the sound of the buses going down the Faubourg Poissonière. He played a sort of chromatic groaning, to which his friends and a few people who had stayed on from other classes listened mockingly. 'Look at them,' Debussy said, turning round. 'Can't you listen to chords without knowing their names? . . . Listen, and if you can't make it out go and tell the director I am ruining your ears.'

At the piano we heard groups of consecutive fifths and octaves;

sevenths which instead of being resolved in the proper way actually led to the note above or weren't resolved at all; shameful 'false relations'; chords of the ninth on all degrees of the scale; chords of the eleventh and thirteenth; all the notes of the diatonic scale heard at once in fantastic arrangements. . . . And all this Claude called 'le régal de l'ouïe' [a feast for the ear]. Delibes's class [of which M. Emmanuel was a member] shook with amazement and fear.

His reputation as an 'eccentric' and a 'troublesome propagandist' was investigated by the registrar.

This austere gentleman, Émile Réty, wondered how Guiraud could have any esteem for such a pupil. To Claude, caught in the very act of abusing the harmony treatise, he said one day: 'So you imagine that dissonant chords do not have to be resolved? What rule do you follow?' 'Mon plaisir!' Debussy replied. . . . And Réty turned away, pale with indignation.

Now there is nothing extraordinary in a composer of worth flouting accepted canons. The history of music, it has been said, is the history of the infraction of the rule. But what we may notice are the exact words of Debussy's reply to Réty: 'Mon plaisir,' and the description of his improvisations as 'le régal de l'ouïe.' For here is a clear indication of that sensualism which played such an important part in his psychology and which, at the time of his studies with Guiraud, must have ruthlessly revealed the shortcomings of his former models from the school of Massenet.

The years 1881–4 were spent in preparation for the *Grand Prix de Rome.* Of his life outside the Conservatoire during these years we know that he was the accompanist to a choral society, *La Concordia,* and became intimately associated with its president, Charles Gounod. This post he received through the recommendation of Vidal. Vidal also recommended him as accompanist to the singing teacher, Mme Moreau-Sainti, where he met Mme Vasnier, an accomplished singer and a very beautiful young woman, who becomes another important figure in his early life.

Mme Vasnier was the wife of an architect very much older than herself. Their flat in the Rue de Constantinople and their summer house at Ville d'Avray provided just that intellectual background that Debussy missed in his home. M. Vasnier suggested books that he should read and became his guide in matters literary and artistic. From Théodore de Banville and Paul Bourget, favourite poets of his earlier days, he progressed to Verlaine and Mallarmé. From this time dates the first version of *Fêtes galantes,* on the poems of Verlaine, a *Chanson espagnole* for two voices, sung by Debussy and Mme Vasnier at a fancy-dress ball, a *Rondel chinois,* 'from contemporary manuscripts,' and a *Nocturne* and *Scherzo* for piano and violin (played at a concert of the violinist Maurice Thiéberg in 1882 'with the gracious aid of Mme Vasnier and Monsieur Achille de Bussy'). Besides these, which have all disappeared except the *Fêtes galantes,* there is, in a private collection, an album of songs bearing the following dedication:

To Madame Vasnier

These songs which she alone has made live and which will lose their enchanting grace if they are never again to come from her singing fairy lips.

The eternally grateful author.

M. Prunières, who writes authoritatively on this period, has spoken of Mme Vasnier as Debussy's 'first great love.' It appears that her husband, almost twice her age, regarded the affair as one that could not come to much harm. Whether he knew that Mme Vasnier became Debussy's mistress, as she did, we do not know. At any rate Debussy seems to have been absolutely guileless in the matter and later, when he was at Rome, wrote him the most sincere and affectionate letters. A curious episode!

Debussy

Let us here quote from an article on Debussy by Mlle Marguerite Vasnier:

Debussy at eighteen was a big beardless boy with clearly marked features and thick black curly hair which he wore flat on his forehead. In the evening when his hair was untidy, suiting him much better, my parents said he was like a type of medieval Florentine. His face was very interesting. His eyes especially were striking. His personality made itself felt. His hands were strong and bony and his fingers square. His playing at the piano was powerful but it could be extremely tender. . . .[1]

As he had little support [from his family] he asked my parents if he could come and work at our house, and henceforth he was admitted as one of the family. I can still see him in the little *salon* in our flat on the fifth floor of the Rue de Constantinople, where for five years he wrote most of his compositions. He used to come nearly every evening and often in the afternoon, leaving the music he wrote on a little table. He composed sometimes at the piano, on a curious old Blondel, and sometimes walking about. He would improvise for a long time and then walk up and down the room humming, either with a cigarette in his mouth or rolling one in preparation. Then, when he was sure, he wrote. He made few corrections but he spent a long time getting it right in his head or at the piano before writing. He was not easily satisfied with his work.

---

[1] It is curious to note how Debussy's youthful playing struck his contemporaries. As we have seen, Mme von Meck found that he lacked 'any personal expression.' Gabriel Pierné has described his playing in Marmontel's class as 'very strange. I don't know whether it was because of his clumsiness or his shyness, but he used literally to throw himself on the keyboard and exaggerate his effects. He seemed to be in a rage with the instrument—ill-treating it with his impulsive movements and breathing nervously when he came to the difficult passages. These faults gradually became less noticeable and there were moments when he produced surprising effects of sweetness. With all its faults his playing was very individual.'

M. Emmanuel says that he played Beethoven 'heavily'—hardly the word one would have expected.

Then there is this interesting glimpse:

He was very quick to take offence and extremely sensitive. The slightest thing put him in good humour or made him sullen or angry. He was very unsociable and never hid his displeasure when my parents invited friends, for he did not often allow himself to be with strangers. If people dropped in and were fortunate enough to please him, he could be amiable and would play and sing Wagner or he would imitate or caricature some modern composer. But when he didn't like any one he showed it. He was original though rather unpolished, but very charming with people he liked.

Of his visits to the Vasniers at Ville d'Avray Mlle Vasnier writes:

The singing-classes were over and Debussy used to come every morning and leave at night by the last train. He worked a lot and sometimes we would take long walks in the Parc de Saint-Cloud or have endless games of croquet. He was quite skilful but he was a bad loser. . . . In the evening he would accompany my mother. Generally they went over his songs, which they studied together. . . . On rainy days we played cards. He was always a bad player and when he lost he got into a terrible humour, particularly as any money he won had often to be spent on the train journey home. To get him into good spirits we used to put a packet of tobacco under his serviette at the dinner table—and then he was so pleased! But of course he was only nineteen or twenty.

The *Premier Grand Prix de Rome* was awarded to Debussy in 1884 for his cantata *L'Enfant prodigue*. That he stayed on at the Conservatoire after gaining only the second prize at the competition of 1883 was largely due to the Vasniers' influence. Of the twenty-two out of twenty-eight academicians who voted in favour of *L'Enfant prodigue* the principal voice was that of Gounod. He did not hesitate to express the opinion that it was the work of a genius.

Many years later Debussy recalled his impressions:

I was on the Pont des Arts awaiting the result of the competition and watching with delight the scurrying of the little Seine steamers. I was quite calm, having forgotten all emotion due to anything Roman, so seductive was the charm of the gay sunshine playing on the ripples, a charm which keeps those delightful idlers, who are the envy of Europe, hour after hour on the bridges.

Suddenly someone tapped me on the shoulder and said breath-lessly:

'You've won the prize!'

Believe me or not, I can assure you that all my pleasure vanished! I saw in a flash the boredom, the vexations inevitably incident to the slightest official recognition. Besides, I felt I was no longer free.'

In those words may be seen the saturnine recluse fleeing the tawdriness of public life, from which in later years he was never able quite successfully to escape. And little by little, as is often the way with intensely warm-hearted people, he obscured himself from the outside world by a screen of bristling irony. Here is perhaps the key to Debussy's per-sonality—irony and sensuousness, the one eating into or overriding the other. He was a hedonist—like Verlaine and like Wagner. But the life of a hedonist is a short one; and we had better praise it while it lasts.

---

¹ *Monsieur Croche the Dilettante-hater*. Anonymous translation. (London, 1927.)

CHAPTER III

ROME—1885–1887

ON 27th January 1885, in accordance with the regulations for holders of the *Prix de Rome,* Debussy, much against his will, left for the three years' sojourn at the Villa Medici in Rome. His life here is told for us in his letters, chiefly to M. Vasnier.[1] The following is the first, written on the way to Rome, from Marseilles:

DEAR MONSIEUR VASNIER,

I have not much to say to you because I don't want to tell you how sad I am. I'm trying to show courage and even, if necessary, to forget you. No, it's not ingratitude; besides, I wouldn't be able to. I shall write to you at greater length from Rome. Believe me to be your sincere friend,

ACH. DEBUSSY.

Give my regards to Madame Vasnier and kiss Marguerite and Maurice for me.

A few days later we have a long letter to M. Vasnier giving his first impressions:

Here I am in this abominable Villa. I can tell you that my first impressions are not very favourable. It's awful weather—rainy and windy. There was no need to come to Rome to have the same weather as in Paris, especially for any one with such a grudge against Rome as I have.

My friends came to meet me at Monte Rotondo, where the six of us slept in one dirty little room. If only you knew how changed they are! None of their good-hearted friendly ways of Paris. They're

---

[1] The letters to Mme Vasnier have been destroyed.

stiff and impressed with their own importance—too much *Prix de Rome* about them.

In the evening when I arrived at the Villa I played my cantata, which was well received by some, but not by the musicians.

I don't mind. This artistic atmosphere and camaraderie that we are told about seem to me very exaggerated. With one or two exceptions, it is difficult to talk to the people here, and when I hear their ordinary conversation I cannot help thinking of the fine talks we used to have which opened my mind to so many things. Then the people here are so very egoistic. I've heard the musicians demolishing each other—Marty and Pierné against Vidal, Pierné and Vidal against Marty, and so on.

Ah! When I got back to my enormous room, where you have to walk a league from one piece of furniture to another, I felt so lonely that I cried! I'm so used to your friendship and to your asking me about my work. I shall never forget all you have done for me and the place I had in your family. I shall do all I can to prove to you that I am not ungrateful. So please don't forget me, for I feel I am going to need you.

I've tried to work but I can't. You know how much I love music and how much this state of mind annoys me. This is not the life for me. Their happiness isn't mine. It's not pride that makes me hate this life. I can't get used to it. I have no feeling for it and I haven't the necessary indifference.

Yes, I fear that I shall have to return to Paris earlier than you think. It may appear silly, but what is there to do? I don't want to make you cross and I should be very sorry to try your friendship. But whatever you think, you can't accuse me of lacking courage. I'm rather unwell—Rome again—my beastly heart doesn't seem to be working properly. I rack my brain to work, but nothing comes of it except a fever which knocks me down completely.

I was so pleased to get your letter, and if I'm not asking too much, I know how little time you have, send me a long letter to remind me of the pleasant talks we used to have.

Very affectionately,

Your devoted

ACH. DEBUSSY.

Give my best regards to Madame Vasnier. How is Marguerite? Is she still working at my songs? I like Marguerite very much and I would like her to become an accomplished musician. That would please you and me too, for at least I should have done something worth while. A kiss for her and also for that silly little Maurice.

Here he paints himself as very desolate. But before long he began to work and for a time his correspondence is mainly concerned with projects for compositions which he was required to send periodically to Paris. The first of these was *Zuléïma,* a work for chorus and orchestra on a text from Heine's *Almanzor.* Some work was done on it but it was quickly put aside. The subject is 'too old and fusty,' he wrote in a letter of 4th June 1885.

These great silly verses, which are only great in their length, bore me, and my music would be stifled by them. Then there's another thing: I don't think I shall ever be able to put music into a strict mould. I'm not speaking of musical form; it's a literary question. I shall always prefer a subject where, somehow, action is sacrificed to feeling. It seems to me that music thus becomes more human and real and one can then discover and refine upon a means of expression.

A very interesting glimpse of the musician's development. Shortly after, he intends to send to Paris a stage work, *Diane au bois,* on a comedy by Théodore de Banville, which he had begun in Paris and which Guiraud had advised him 'to keep for later' or 'he would never have the *Prix de Rome.*' He explains to M. Vasnier his particular liking for Banville:

Diane isn't a bit like the poems that are generally used for these *envois,* which are really only highly polished cantatas. Thank God! I had enough of one of them and I think I should take advantage— as you would say—of the only good thing there is at the Villa, the liberty to work and do something original instead of always keeping to the old paths. I'm sure that the Institut won't be of my opinion. Their way, of course, will be the only right one! But I'm too fond of my freedom. At least if they don't allow me to go where I like, I can think and do what I like. All I can say is that I can't write the kind of music they would approve. Now, I don't know if I'm big enough to do what I have in mind. Anyhow, I'll do all I can to make some of them content, the rest can go hang.

That explosive manifestation of freedom is followed by a request to have a long letter from M. Vasnier 'to enlarge the doors of my prison.' 'I think it is very good,' he concludes, 'for such an unpractical fellow as myself to have stuck it here these few months.'

The arrival of a new director at the Villa Medici gives us occasion to quote a remark illuminating Debussy's early atti-tude to Wagner. The new director, Hébert, was an able painter, a disciple of Ingres and a good amateur violinist. 'He loved music passionately,' Debussy recollects some twenty years later,

but Wagner's music not at all. At that time I was a Wagnerian to the pitch of forgetting the simple rules of courtesy, nor did I imagine that I could ever come almost to agree with this enthusiastic old man who had travelled through all these emotions with his eyes open, whereas we hardly grasped their meaning or how to use them.[1]

'A Wagnerian to the pitch of forgetting the simple rules of courtesy'! Debussy's early acquaintance with Wagner has not been, and probably cannot now be, fully investigated. It is often held that his great *engouement* for Wagner came at the time of his visits to Bayreuth in 1888 and 1889. But apparently he was very well acquainted with Wagner in Rome and as ardent a Wagnerian then as ever. Augustin Savard, a friend at the Villa Medici, recollects his living apart, 'playing the score of *Tristan* in his room,' and Vidal has recorded a per-formance they heard together of *Lohengrin* at the Teatro Apollo. But whatever the extent of his admiration he realized from the

[1] *Monsieur Croche the Dilettante-hater.*

first the distance that lay between the Wagnerian conceptions and his own. Referring in a letter of 19th October 1886 to *Diane au bois,* he points out to M. Vasnier that it would be 'ridiculous' to take Wagner as a model. 'I should like to keep the melodic line lyrical,' he explains, 'and not allow the orchestra to predominate.' Those are words which might have been written by Berlioz.

In the summer of 1885 Debussy was invited to spend a short time in Fiumicino at the seaside villa of Count Primoli. 'There weren't any people or casinos,' he writes. 'I was able to be by myself as much as I wanted, knowing no one and only speaking when I wanted something to eat—which was nuisance enough. . . . I worked I should almost say well.' But such contentedness lasted only a short time. The following month M. Vasnier is implored to sanction a return to Paris:

> I really believe that to make me stay here a second year would be doing me no good whatever. It would only make me dislike the place more and I should no longer be able to work with the ease I once had. You can't say, I hope, that I haven't tried to settle down here. This year has been lost. So I intend to leave at the end of the year and I ask you, Monsieur Vasnier, knowing that I can count on you as a friend, not to think that I am acting unwisely, for I am not doing this for myself but for my future.

Beyond the grant of the *Prix de Rome* Debussy had, as far as we know, no means of support. Doubtless M. Vasnier pointed this out in his reply, for the next letter, of 24th November, although full of resentment against his 'life of a non-commissioned officer with full pay,' makes no mention of leaving.

> I went to hear two masses [he says in this letter], one of Palestrina, the other of Orlandus Lassus, in a church called S. Maria dell' Anima. I don't know if you know it—it is stuck away among some awful little streets. I like it very much, as it is very simple and pure in style, unlike so many others with their array of

sculptures, pictures and mosaics, all so theatrical. The statue of Christ in these churches looks like a lost skeleton that wonders how it got there. The Anima is the only place to hear such music, which is the only church music there is for me. That of Gounod and company seems to come from some kind of hysterical mysticism and has the effect of a sinister farce.

The two above-named people are masters, especially Orlandus, who is more decorative and more human than Palestrina. The effects he gets from his great knowledge of counterpoint are amazing. You perhaps don't know that counterpoint can be the nastiest thing in music, but in their work it is beautiful.

Beyond this sixteenth-century music and *Lohengrin*, mentioned previously, we know that Debussy heard the first performance in Italy of Beethoven's second Symphony and the 'Emperor' Concerto, played by Sgambati. He also made careful studies of the ninth Symphony and of the organ works of Bach.

In the course of his stay he travelled to other towns in Italy and became acquainted with certain of his older Italian contemporaries. Leoncavallo, whom he knew slightly, introduced him to Boito in Milan. From the account of their meeting by André de Ternant, Boito appeared to Debussy to be more of a literary man than a musician. His study, littered with magazines, books and newspaper cuttings, showed no sign of any musical activity, and when at length Boito came in he explained to his visitor that he had been giving a lecture on the English Lake Poets. He talked of his own music, with which he was generally displeased, and of the possibility of adapting opera librettos from the plays of Shakespeare and Goethe, which he thought afforded excellent material. His belief, however, was that it was most worthy to write, not for the theatre or the church, but for the concert-room.

With an introduction from Boito Debussy set out to meet Verdi at Sant' Agata. 'He found Verdi in his shirt-sleeves,'

M. de Ternant writes, 'busy planting salads with the assistance of a small boy.' He was a jovial and good-natured man and knew France well. But he had no inclination to discuss his contemporaries. He felt he had made enough enemies. He passed a few remarks about Ambroise Thomas, Gounod and Wagner, but was careful to conceal his own feelings. After lunch Verdi returned to his garden, in which he was seemingly more interested than in talking about music.

Then there was Liszt, who came often to the Villa Medici and knew Pierné and Vidal well. Debussy met him at the house of Sgambati.

The great Hungarian musician [writes M. de Ternant] was accompanied by his intimate friend, Cardinal von Hohenlohe, who was a generous patron of classical concerts in Rome. The prince-cardinal, after being introduced to Debussy, graciously requested, in honour of the young holder of the *Grand Prix de Rome* and as a compliment to French musical art, that Liszt and Sgambati should play Saint-Saëns's Variations for two pianos on a theme of Beethoven (Op. 35). This was the last time Liszt touched a piano in Rome. He left the Eternal City on the following day, and never returned to Italy. Debussy said it was the greatest musical treat of his life, and when he related the incident to Saint-Saëns, the French composer was much affected and warmly embraced him.

On another occasion Debussy and Vidal played to Liszt the *Valses romantiques* for two pianos by Chabrier. Liszt died the following year and—who knows?—possibly only just missed counting Debussy as the last of his discoveries.

At the beginning of 1886 Debussy became very weary of life at the Villa, and one day burst out crying, threw himself at Hébert's feet, threatening to kill himself if he were not allowed to leave. Questioning the genuineness of this scene, M. Prunières tells us that old friends of Debussy remember how he used to play the *commediante-tragediante*. 'Do you want me to cry?' he would say. Whereupon he would pour forth a flood of tears followed by a burst of laughter. 'Furthermore,' M. Prunières pertinently remarks, 'we know that he had been reading with fervour the memoirs of Berlioz.'

However, he left, and in February he suddenly appeared in Paris. M. Vasnier apparently convinced him of good reasons to return, for in April he was back in Rome; but with the same distaste for the Villa and still feeling 'that majestic ennui which is part of the air one breathes.' He had been counselled to visit the museums. 'Well, I shall go to see them,' he wrote. 'I know you won't like the "well." It is that of a desperate man dragged to the Sistine Chapel as to the scaffold.' The museums in Italy meant little to him. He liked best the frescoes of Signorelli in the cathedral at Orvieto, and in architecture the less imposing things like the delightful Villa Pia in the gardens of the Vatican. Michelangelo's 'Last Judgment' in the Sistine Chapel, when finally he did see it, he abhorred.

In a letter shortly after his return he mentions a visit of Gounod, who knew Hébert well and was at the Villa Medici as a *Prix de Rome* during the directorship of Ingres. Here is Debussy's comment:

Hébert told me that he [Gounod] is coming to Rome this winter. Together they will not be at all funny. What with Hébert pontificating almost as much as Gounod, you can imagine the grandiose ideas and hollow speeches we shall hear! By the way, the interest the Héberts show in me is a nuisance. They wish to make things more pleasant for me but actually they are making them more disagreeable. I suppose you'll say that I haven't changed, but if they were in Paris I should probably like them very well; here they are nothing more than jailers.

And so the second year passed. By October 1886 all he had written was one scene of *Diane au bois* and the beginning of *Zuléima*. With *Diane* he was poorly satisfied and *Zuléima*, he wrote, was 'too much like Verdi and Meyerbeer.' Towards the end of 1886 we have a series of letters to a certain Émile Baron, a stationer and bookseller in the Rue de Rome in Paris. These are at first of a rather different tone. Debussy tells him of the Roman men and women who pass before his window and of the long processions of priests, 'some of whom, dressed in black, are like curious black radishes, and others, in red, like roguish pimentos.' The winter was particularly cold. 'You mentioned in your letter how much you wanted to go to a town where it was always spring,' he wrote.

Well, don't come to Rome, because at present this town, reputed to be so sunny, is like Moscow, all covered with snow and freezing cold. The Romans don't seem to be able to make it out. The coats they wear are too short in any case, and they don't seem to be able to get used to proper overcoats. But the snow gives a very pretty colour to the ruins. It shows up their severe contours and makes them look clean. They are a thousand times better than with that perpetual blue sky and their usual pipeclay colour.

But before long he confides his difficulties to Émile Baron as previously to M. Vasnier. He is unable to write music 'to order'; and it is now Émile Baron who is 'about the only one' to whom he can 'speak of such things, feeling sure of being understood.' 'I have had enough of music and of the sameness of this scene,' he says, exasperated. 'I want to see some Manet and hear some Offenbach. That may sound paradoxical, but I must tell you that breathing the air of this place puts the most ridiculous ideas into one's head.'

By February of the following year a new work, *Printemps*, was well advanced. He writes of this to Émile Baron:

The work I have to send to Paris is giving me a lot of trouble and causes me to lead a life compared to which convicts have a leisurely time. The idea I had was to compose a work in a very special colour which should cover a great range of feelings. It is to be called *Printemps*, not a descriptive *Printemps*, but a human one.
I should like to express the slow and miserable birth of beings

31

and things in nature, their gradual blossoming and finally the joy of being born into some new life. All this is without a programme, for I despise all music that has to follow some literary text that one happens to have got hold of.[1] So you will understand how very suggestive the music will have to be—I am doubtful if I shall be able to do it as I wish.

Printemps and *Zuléïma* were the works he finally chose as his *envois*. *Zuléïma* has been lost. *Diane au bois* he never finished. Although he chose the text of Banville himself, he subsequently found it unsuitable. Possibly he had outgrown this favourite poet of his Conservatoire days, for his acquaintance with literature had grown. He knew the Goncourts, was very much attracted to Flaubert and had taken parts, with Vidal and Xavier Leroux, in reading the plays of Shakespeare. It was in Rome, furthermore, that he first became acquainted with the new Symbolist magazines, *La Revue indépendante* and *Vogue,* sent to him by Émile Baron, from whom, too, he received the newly published works of Jean Moréas and Rabbe's translation of Shelley. In the new spirit that was breaking through, music, he felt, had not found its level. He tells Émile Baron:

I believe that the public, apart from the shopkeepers who form the larger part of it, have had enough of cavatinas and *pantalonnades* which show up the singer's fine voice and form. It is curious that the literary movement has found such support—the new forms of the Russian novelists, for instance (I wonder they haven't placed Tolstoy higher than Flaubert), while there is no sign of music changing at all. A dissonant chord would almost cause a revolution.

This letter foretelling the great changes that were shortly to come belongs to the early part of 1887. Before the spring, after only two years at the Villa Medici, instead of the statutory

[1] An opinion that he would certainly not have held later.

32

three, Debussy returned definitely to Paris. To M. Vasnier, two days before his departure, he wrote his final decision:

> You know when I work how doubtful I am of myself. . . . When something of mine pleased you it gave me courage. Here I should never have that. My friends make fun of my sadness and I should never get any encouragement from them. If things don't go better I know that many people will give me up. But I'd rather do twice as much work in Paris than drag out this life here. . . .
>
> I am leaving on Saturday and shall arrive in Paris on Monday morning. Don't, I beg of you, be too hard with me. Your friendship will be all I have.
>
> Believe me,
A. Debussy.

His friendship with the Vasniers after his return lasted only a short time.

> When he finally came back [writes Mlle Vasnier] the former intimacy was no longer the same. He had evolved and so had we. We had moved and had made new acquaintances. Reticent and unsociable as he was, he no longer felt at home. However, he often used to come in the evening and play what he had written away from us. . . . He would come to ask advice and even material aid, for, not living with his family and not yet known, he had somehow to live. . . . Then, little by little, having made new acquaintances himself, he no longer came and we never saw him again.

That is the last record of Debussy's relations with the Vasniers.

CHAPTER IV

PARIS—1887–1892

WITH Debussy's return to Paris in the spring of 1887 we enter upon a period of approximately five years where comparatively few facts concerning his private life are available. His published correspondence of these years amounts to no more than two or three letters; recollections of his friends are now curiously vague; and where we should expect to find a glimpse of some psychological value—from the members of certain literary circles he soon began to frequent—we are offered little more than the bare facts of his relations with them. These are lacunae, however, of which we may well take advantage; for it is just at this period that a view of the changing artistic ideals of the Paris world will tell us most about the elements in Debussy's musical formation.

The first thing to be noticed in that Paris world of 1887 is the swing away from the cold observation of fact that characterized the output of all those—Naturalists, Realists, *Parnassiens*—who proceeded from the philosophy of Auguste Comte. In much the same way as the last war brought a craving for sound and colour in their more sensuous and primitive appeals, the Franco-Prussian war had annihilated, for the time being, all desire on the part of artists and thinkers to approach the world in any calculating, scientific manner. 'In face of the unknown,' wrote M. André Barre, 'let us rather have a poet than a scientist.' That might have been the slogan of the new idealism. Flaubert, Taine and Renan were dethroned in favour of Edgar Allan Poe (first translated by Baudelaire), the English Pre-Raphaelites and certain of the Russian novelists. A translation of *Is Life Worth Living?* by William Hurrell Mallock, a penetrating English writer on religion and philosophy, ran into a great number of editions and preceded a vogue for spiritualism. In face of these influences the Age of Reason seemed imperilled. 'Jeune homme,' said Renan to Déroulède, 'la France se meurt, ne troublez pas son agonie.' The death-blow came with the popularization in Paris of the music of Wagner.

The new art was a sensuous, hedonistic art, and as such sought expression most naturally in music. I will here mention a little anecdote. Once at a gathering of poets Debussy heard the line of Jean Moréas:

Et toi, son cou, qui pour la fête tu te pares?

'Cou qui—te tu te,' he repeated. The assonance he thought ugly. 'Musicien!' shouted Moréas derisively. 'Et vous jouez aussi de la flûte?' For this Moréas might well have been hounded out as a cretin. For the days were over when a literary critic could baldly declare: 'La musique est un bruit désagréable que l'on fait exprès.' That could be said in the days of Berlioz, but not of Debussy. Paul Valéry, writing of his contemporaries in the eighties, emphasizes that 'poetry felt itself insufficient before the power and resources of the orchestra.'

What has been called Symbolism [he explains] can be quite simply resumed in the desire common to several families of poets . . . to take back from music what they had given it. The secret of this movement is nothing other than this. . . . We were fed on music and our literary minds only dreamt of extracting from language almost the same effects that music caused on our nervous beings. . . . Certain people who had preserved the traditional forms of French verse endeavoured to eliminate descriptions, judgments, morals and arbitrary definitions; they purged their poetry of almost all those intellectual elements which are outside the sphere of music. Others gave to all objects infinite meanings, implying some hidden metaphysic. Their means of expression was delightfully ambiguous. . . . Everything was allusion. Nothing was content to be. In those mirrored realms everything thought, or at least everything appeared to think. . . . Further, some magicians, more self-willed and disputatious, challenged the old prosody. For some, coloured hearing and the art of alliteration appeared to have no secrets. They deliberately transposed orchestral timbres into their verse. . . . Others cleverly sought out the naïvety and spontaneous grace of old folk verse. . . . It was a time of theories and inquiries, of interpretations and excited explanations. A ruthless youth discarded the scientific dogma that was beginning to go out of fashion. They saw order and perhaps truth in the cult of a unification of the arts. It would have needed little more for some kind of religion to have become established.[1]

This cult of music was not a cult of Massenet or Gounod. It was the cult of Wagner. Wagner fell upon the Paris of the eighties, dominating the entire world of literature and art. He even penetrated spheres of religious and intellectual thought.

The craze began with the Wagnerian concerts of Charles Lamoureux in 1882. The curious fact is that Wagner was at first more appreciated in literary than in musical circles. The *Revue wagnérienne,* a monthly journal that appeared between 1885 and 1888, far from containing any musical analyses, was almost exclusively devoted to studies of Wagner by literary men. The editor, Édouard Dujardin, was a writer who was also the editor of the Symbolist magazine, *La Revue indépendante.* Victor Wilder wrote on the ritual of the *Meister-singer,* Huysmans on the overture to *Tannhäuser,* Swinburne on the death of Wagner and Teodor de Wyzewa on Wagnerian painting. This was not, as might be imagined, painting for the scenery of Wagner's dramas, but painting such as that of Degas, G. Moreau, Odilon Redon, Fantin-Latour, supposedly inspired by the ideals of Bayreuth. In the number for January

[1] Paul Valéry, Preface to *La Connaissance de la Déesse,* by Lucien Fabre. (Paris, 1920.)

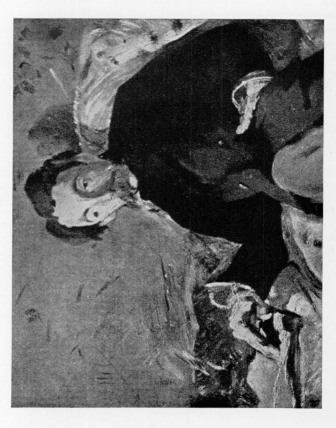

STÉPHANE MALLARMÉ

1886 six sonnets in praise of Wagner appeared by the foremost
Symbolist poets, among them René Ghil, Paul Verlaine and
Stéphane Mallarmé. The extent to which the musicians were
as yet untouched by this Wagnerian cult is seen in the fact
that during these years, 1885-8, Gounod was engaged on his
last sacred works while Massenet was writing *Werther*.

The outstanding example of this literary Wagnerism—by
which Debussy was as much affected as by the music of
Wagner itself—is the case of Stéphane Mallarmé.[1] Here, in
a translation by A. I. Ellis, is his sonnet to Wagner:

This silence now is death's fast gathering gloom, whose pall
Blots out our 'household gods' with fold on silken fold,
And they, as sink in gloom the walls that them uphold,
Suddenly shall to utter dark's extinction fall.
Triumphant play of word that held us once in thrall,
Dead hieroglyphs, wherein they feel, the herd unsoul'd,
As with a pulse of wing the thrill they crave from old—
In inmost cupboard-void let us entomb them all.
From out the glorious stress of powers contending flung
And primal clash of splendour, lo! there hath upsprung
To yon slope fore-ordained to be their imag'd shrine
Trumpets of blaring gold on page eterne aswoon—
Wagner, his path to heav'n with his own radiance strewn,
That ev'n the ink finds speech in breath's sobs sibylline.

It is obvious, from this abdication of poetry in favour of music,
that Mallarmé was as much concerned with the musical

[1] André Cœuroy traces the first sign of Wagnerism in French
literature to a tale of provincial life by George Sand. Basing her
argument on an article by Wagner on *Freischütz,* published in the
Gazette musicale about the time of his visit to Paris in 1839, she
doubts the success in France of any popular mysticism. Other
writers who were attracted to Wagner before the Symbolists were
Théophile Gautier, who wrote on *Tannhäuser* in 1857, and Gérard
de Nerval, Champfleury and Baudelaire, who wrote on *Lohengrin*
in 1859.

rhythm and euphonic interrelation of words as with their actual significance. Hence his abstruseness (which makes him almost untranslatable) and his conception of Symbolism: 'To evoke in a deliberate shadow the unmentioned object by allusive words.' We are surely here very near Debussy's shadowy Mélisande.

Not all the Symbolists, however, were so directly concerned with Wagner as Mallarmé, although in Symbolist poetry as a whole there is an almost abnormal craving for the sensuousness of sound as also for the sensuousness of colour. Verlaine in his *Art poétique* demands:

> De la musique avant toute chose.

Colour, he specifies, should be represented by 'rien que la nuance,' for

> . . . la nuance seule fiance
> Le rêve au rêve et la flûte au cor!

René Ghil, inspired by Rimbaud's famous sonnet, *Les Voyelles,* beginning:

> A noir, E blanc, I rouge, U vert, O bleu,

worked out an elaborate system of 'verbal orchestration.' Flutes approximated to the sound *ou,* piccolos to *û,* trombones to *ô,* horns to *eu* and *eur,* and so on. A whole group of young poets considered that by this means poetry and music could be fused into one. Music of colour, music of words—such were the slogans of the day. The character of Jean des Esseintes, in Huysmans's *A rebours,* with his curious hankering after orange (the colour of 'men of a hectic, over-stimulated constitution') and his 'mouth-organ'—a liqueur-chest in which each liqueur corresponded in taste with the sound of a particular instrument —was perhaps less of a satire on the intellectuals of that age than is generally supposed!

So much for the literary movements. When Wagner opened the eyes of the musicians—and it is curious that before the later eighties the Wagnerian influence in French music is hardly discernible—their enthusiasm bordered on delirium. At Bayreuth during the prelude to *Tristan,* Chabrier burst into tears and Guillaume Lekeu was carried out fainting. French opera as Massenet or Chabrier had conceived it gave way to such pseudo-Wagnerian works as Bruneau's *Le Rêve* (1888), Magnard's *Yolande* (1890), d'Indy's *Fervaal* (1896) and Chausson's *Le Roi Arthus* (1899). The most pitiful example of them all is *Gwendoline.* It is by that most jovial of French composers, Chabrier.

But there was another world of curiosity. In the *Revue wagnérienne* of 8th February 1886 there appeared a letter from St. Petersburg by one Wladimir Iznoskow, who had been asked to write about the Wagnerian movement in Russia. He gave instead an account of the Russian 'nationalist' composers who wished to reform opera but whose ideals, he pointed out, differed from those of Wagner in that they did not write their own librettos nor did they believe in keeping the main musical interest in the orchestra pit instead of on the stage. He then went on to explain the differences between the Russian and the Wagnerian conception of opera with a few not very enthusiastic words about the champion of Wagner in Russia, Serov. That, if we except César Cui's *La Musique en Russie,* published in 1881 (without any intention to proselytize), was the first instance of the coming conflict between the interests of Wagner and of the Russians.

It was not long before this conflict became apparent. At the *Exposition Universelle* of 1889 singers, dancers and national orchestras from Africa, Arabia, the Orient, Scandinavia and Russia introduced their primitive and exotic musics. The dancing of the Javanese Bedayas to the music of their national *gamelang* incited comparisons with the flower-maidens of *Parsifal*! Concerts were given by Hungarian gipsies and Roumanian laouters. Spanish folk music vied with choirs from Finland, the music of Norway and tribal dances of African negroes. In the summer of this year the whole musical universe passed through Paris.

At this exhibition, rather appropriately, Rimsky-Korsakov conducted two historical concerts of Russian music. One or two short works of the Russian 'nationalists' had already been played in France, but virtually nothing had been heard of Balakirev, Rimsky-Korsakov or Moussorgsky. 'The young French and Russian schools,' wrote Julien Tiersot in *Le Ménestrel,* 'straight away greeted each other and fraternized.' And, he added significantly, 'I believe that the future belongs to them both.' From this year dates what has been called the Franco-Russian musical alliance.

Such was the background of Debussy's life in Paris from his return from Rome until the beginning in 1892 of *L'Après-midi d'un faune* and *Pelléas et Mélisande.*

The action of these various movements is told in his works. The passing vogue for the Pre-Raphaelites is reflected in *La Damoiselle élue* (1888); in the *Cinq Poèmes de Baudelaire* (1887-9) the fight against Wagner is at its keenest; the Russians are the real heroes of such compositions of about the year 1891 as the *Ballade,* the *Mazurka* and the *Rêverie*; and in 1893 Oriental elements from the Javanese *gamelang* take root in the Quartet. Yet, from under all these extraneous influences and in spite of France's comparatively poor musical heritage—had not even Berlioz described himself as 'un musicien aux trois quarts allemand'?—there emerged in *L'Après-midi d'un faune* one of the most beautiful of all French creations. In reply to Renan's pessimistic remark Déroulède could have pointed to nothing better than this.

CHAPTER V

EARLY ACQUAINTANCES—1887–1892

DEBUSSY, on his return from Rome, made many acquaintances in the literary circles of Paris, but approached terms of intimacy with few. One would have thought that at the bookshop of the *Revue indépendante,* or at the gatherings of Mallarmé, where he met Whistler and Verlaine, Stuart Merrill and Jules Laforgue, Henri de Régnier and Pierre Louÿs, he would have found just that support and understanding he had missed at the Villa Medici. But the reason he did not one may well imagine. Once in later years he was invited to the house of Marcel Proust. He declined, but with a strange explanation: 'Vous savez, moi, je suis un ours.' From this description of himself, given with such charming frankness, one suspects that he was more conscious of the shortcomings of his early education than his friends have given us to believe; and a certain sensitiveness on this point must have prevented him from frequenting the company of Mallarmé and his admirers, to whose sensibility he was instinctively drawn. Alone among these poets, Pierre Louÿs, several years later, became an intimate friend; and it is significant that in speaking of this friendship Paul Valéry should have remarked that Louÿs was 'the director of Debussy's literary conscience.'

His relations with the musicians were scarcely more fortunate. Some deep emotional support in spite of (or possibly because of) his reclusion was in any case necessary to him at all times of his life. An intimate friendship with Paul Dukas and Raymond Bonheur, both students at the Conservatoire,

41

lasted only a short time. With Gounod he parted company in disagreement, it appears, over *Lohengrin,* a work which Gounod could not abide. 'Pour toi, pour toi, pour toi,' he angrily replied as his young friend spoke of it admiringly. With Chabrier, whom Debussy knew only slightly, there must have been great disappointment. Chabrier's capitula-tion to Wagner in *Gwendoline* and the establishment among his friends of 'Le Petit Bayreuth' could hardly have met with the approval of one who had taken such delight in the real, sprightly Chabrier. Somewhere between the attitudes to Wagner of Chabrier and Gounod Debussy felt his own to lie. But before attempting to discover this we must follow him again on his journeys abroad.

In 1887, the year of his return to Paris, he set out for Vienna to meet Brahms. Debussy and Brahms! Is there not in the juxtaposition of these names all the future antagonism between the musical worlds of France and Germany? A meeting between the musical lion of Vienna, austere and unapproach-able, and the twenty-five-year-old Debussy, 'passionate and turned in upon himself, with something feline and something of the gipsy about him,' as Henri de Régnier remembers him, was not to pass off easily. Here is the account of their meeting by A. de Ternant:

Debussy wrote a letter to Brahms and received no reply. He called twice at his house. On the first occasion he was informed that the Master was unwell and on the other that he was engaged. At last the wife of one of the secretaries of the French embassy promised to help him in his difficulty. She was a Hungarian by birth, though married to a French diplomat, and had been in her younger days to some extent a pupil of Brahms. . . . It was not long before Debussy received an invitation to luncheon from the lady and she stated that there would be only three persons present, viz., the Master, Claude Debussy and herself.

After the introduction Brahms growled out: 'Are you the young Frenchman who wrote to me and called twice at my house?'

Debussy bowed graciously. 'Well, I will forgive you this time,' exclaimed Brahms, 'but don't do it again.' During the luncheon Brahms did not utter a single word, but after drinking several glasses of French champagne at the end, he said it was the 'most glorious wine in the world,' and quoted the lines from Goethe's *Faust*:

> 'One cannot always do without the foreigner
> But give him to me in the shape of wine.
> A true-born German hates with all his heart
> A Frenchman—but their wines are excellent.' [1]

That—we hope—was Brahms in one of his grosser moods. Debussy was at least tactful enough not to allow publication of this until after his death. But let us continue with M. de Ternant's account:

Franco-German wars were inevitable, Brahms said, but French and German art would always flourish and would be, until the Day of Judgment, the glory and wonder of the world. He was quite aware of the fact that the French musical public considered him the most German of contemporary composers. The brilliant French nation was correct in its judgment and he was heartily thankful. He was proud to be a German composer. A musician who abandoned his nationality in art would never leave any permanent mark on the history of the music of his country. There was no excuse for the imitation of foreign music.

But under all this Brahms eventually showed his more tender self. He told Debussy of his great admiration for Bizet, whom 'he would have gone to the end of the earth to embrace,' and that he had heard *Carmen* twenty times. The following day Debussy was invited to dine with him in town and to a

---

[1] This is not a very accurate translation, at least of the second line. Brander's lines (in Auerbach's cellar) are:

> 'Man kann nicht stets das Fremde meiden,
> Das Gute liegt uns oft so fern.
> Ein echter deutscher Mann mag keinen Franzen leiden,
> Doch ihre Weine trinkt er gern.

performance of the favourite *Carmen*. Together they visited the Conservatorium and the graves of Beethoven and Schubert. 'Before leaving Vienna,' M. de Ternant's account concludes, 'Debussy called at the house of Brahms. He was "at home" this time, and wishing Claude *bon voyage* and a successful career, the great German master embraced the young French-man like a son. He said a "crusty" old bachelor has quite as much fatherly feeling as a more fortunate married man.'

After Vienna, Bayreuth. In 1888 and 1889 Debussy attended the Bayreuth Festival performances of *Parsifal, Meister-singer* and *Tristan und Isolde*. In conversation with his old master, Guiraud, after the second of these visits he recounted his impressions. He argued that Wagner was less of an innovator than he was generally considered to be; that Berlioz was less strictly tonal than Wagner; that Wagner's harmony was an amplification of Mozart's; that his music was very moving, 'mais que ça chante trop.' 'So you are a liberal Wagnerian,' said Guiraud. Debussy pointed out that he saw no reason to imitate what he admired—which was the point of that letter to M. Vasnier from Rome in which he spoke of maintaining the lyrical atmosphere and not allowing the orchestra to predominate. In truth the earnest sensuousness of Wagner's music corresponded very nearly to his own ideal, yet there arose the problem of reconciling this sensuousness with that lyrical clarity which French composers have always trea-sured. Guiraud questioned him on his own choice of a libretto. 'I would seek a poet,' he said, 'who would merely hint at things and would allow me to graft my thought on his; whose characters belong to no time or place and who would allow me, here and there, to show more art than he.' An extra-ordinary prediction of his choice of Maeterlinck's *Pelléas et Mélisande*. Meanwhile the *Cinq Poèmes de Baudelaire,* written between 1887 and 1889, show that he was well in Wagner's grip.

The Deviation from Wagner—Erik Satie

Another approach to the aesthetic problems that beset him during these years may be found in his relations with that fantastic composer, almost unheard of in England nowadays —Erik Satie. Erik Satie, by reason of the weird eccentricities, both in his music and in his personal life, earned for himself the reputation of a musical exhibitionist. No doubt he provides first-rate material for the psycho-analyst; but by his pert little compositions he kept alive the breeziness of the *opéra-comique* at a time when the very foundations of French music were threatened by the Wagnerian tidal-wave. He went on, in fact, where Chabrier gave in.[1]

Satie, when Debussy met him in 1891, was employed as a pianist at the 'Auberge du Clou' in Montmartre. In his jocular style he once gave in a lecture an account of their early relations:

When I first met Debussy he was full of Moussorgsky and was very deliberately seeking a way that wasn't very easy to find. In this problem I was well in advance of him. I was not weighed down with the *Prix de Rome,* nor any other prize, for I am a man like Adam (of Paradise) who never won any prizes—a lazy fellow, no doubt.

I was writing at that time *Le Fils des étoiles* on a libretto by Joseph Péladan, and I explained to Debussy the need a Frenchman has to free himself from the Wagnerian venture, which didn't respond to our natural aspirations. I also pointed out that I was in no way

---

[1] The stories about Satie could profitably fill a small book. Once, for instance, he set out to give a piano recital wearing a fireman's helmet. His mother, who was an Englishwoman, died when he was very young and he was always horribly lonely. In illustration of this his biographer, P. D. Templier, quotes a very charming little note to a friend, written from the country in a northern *patois* which I cannot refrain from reproducing here: 'J'étais ici, tout seul avec mi. Faudraut voir m'figure triste. Personne ne pensau à mi, sauf vous et trois cents amis. J'arrivau l'soir à m'maison, toute vide. Le piano m'regardaut, l'pauvre fieu; il n'savaut pas.'

anti-Wagnerian but that we should have a music of our own—i possible without any *Sauerkraut*.

Why could we not use the means that Claude Monet, Cézanne Toulouse-Lautrec and others had made known? Why could w not transpose these means into music? Nothing simpler. . . .

That was the origin of a departure which brought results tha were safe enough and even fruitful. Who was to show him examples? To reveal new treasures? To suggest the ground to be explored? To give him the benefit of previous considerations Who? I shan't reply, for I no longer care.

There is a slight suggestion in those last words that Satie was imperfectly briefed to prove his case. At any rate no one knows what 'new treasures' he revealed to Debussy nor what ground he suggested to be explored. As for there being 'nothing simpler' than to transpose into music the painting technique of Claude Monet, Cézanne and Toulouse-Lautrec, that is an abstract consideration by which, as far as we know, Debussy was never consciously affected. What attracted him to Satie was no doubt the fact that even in his small way he was able to stand up to Wagner. And during those most critical years for French music this must indeed have been encouraging.

Their relationship, which lasted nearly thirty years, was a curious one and has often been discussed. There are some who consider Satie a precursor of Debussy; and others who see in him nothing but *cocasserie*. It has been established that Satie's *Sarabandes*, written in 1887, contain the first examples of certain harmonic procedures (unresolved ninths in particular) which later became associated with Debussy. But to argue from this that Satie was an important influence on Debussy is an exaggeration. For a view of their personal and musical relationship, the following account by Louis Laloy is the most convincing that I have come across:

Debussy introduced me to him, and we sometimes met at his

ible, exchanging a few cattish remarks and side-glances which
rather amused Debussy. In his relationship with Satie there were
violent outbursts of temper, yet their friendship remained indis-
oluble. It was like one of those family hatreds, where all patience
is lost by the continual grating of each other's faults, but where there
nevertheless remains an underlying sympathy. They might have
been two brothers placed by circumstances in different positions,
the one rich and the other poor: the former gracious and open-
hearted, but conscious of his superiority and always ready to make
it felt, the other sadly appearing as a wag, paying his share by
cracking jokes for the entertainment of his host, and hiding his
humiliation. They were always on their guard, but they couldn't
help loving each other dearly.

Satie himself endorsed this when he once wrote: 'If I didn't
have Debussy . . . I don't know what I'd do to express my
wretched thoughts—if I am still able to express them.' And
through this remark one can see the truth of another statement of Laloy's: that 'Satie's great admiration for Debussy
compelled him to lie low, and when he did venture into
composition, to give his work the appearance of a joke.'

Satie's reference to Moussorgsky brings us to the very con-
troversial question of Debussy's acquaintance with *Boris
Godounov*. In 1909 Debussy supplied the information to his
biographer, M. Laloy, that he had been introduced to the score of
Boris by an old gentleman whose name, we have since come to
know, was Jules de Brayer, at one time the organist at Chartres
Cathedral. In the following year Debussy returned, according
to M. Laloy, to Bayreuth, but came back 'undeceived.' He
then 'endeavoured to explain to his old friend that one could
not admire at the same time two such opposed forms of art.
Being an ardent Wagnerian, this friend would hear nothing
of it; and they parted.' From this account there has grown
up the legend that *Boris Godounov* revealed to Debussy, in a
flash, the fallibility of Wagner and delivered him, so to speak,
from the clutches of Klingsor.

In the first place, as we have seen, Debussy was perfectly aware of the Wagnerian menace long before he had known *Boris*. But even if he had not been, *Boris* was not the work to wean him from a devotion to Wagner—as certain French critics have supposed it did. In a letter of 6th February 1911 he says: 'I do not consider the *placage* in *Boris* any more satisfactory than the persistent counterpoint in the *Meistersinger* finale'; by which he clearly implies that the rough-hewn brusque qualities of Moussorgsky are as far from French lyrical ideals as any Wagnerian ponderousness.

In point of fact, the score of *Boris* that Debussy saw had passed into the hands of Jules de Brayer from Saint-Saëns, who had brought it back from his journey to Russia in 1874, the year it was first played at the Maryinsky Theatre in St Petersburg. Brayer admitted, in a letter of 1896 to Pierre d'Alheim, that the only person in Paris beyond himself on whom this score (the only one then in France) had made a favourable impression was Debussy's intimate friend, the Swiss journalist Robert Godet. Debussy's name is not even mentioned in this letter, yet the score had been lent to him as long ago as 1889. This is not to say that Debussy did not find much to admire in Moussorgsky. But according to M. Godet his full appreciation of *Boris* did not come until the Moussorgsky concerts of Pierre d'Alheim in 1896—that is, four years after *Pelléas* was begun. We know now that the great impression of 1889 was not of *Boris*, but of the pentatonic music of the Javanese *gamelang*, the dancing of the Bedayas and the Annamite theatre at the *Exposition Universelle*.

It is unfortunate that the work in which we might best study Debussy's state of musical development, immediately before the composition of *L'Après-midi d'un faune* and *Pelléas et Mélisande*, is not available. About 1890 Debussy began an opera entitled *Rodrigue et Chimène*. The libretto, based on *Las Mocedades del Cid* by Guillem de Castro, was prepared for him by Catulle Mendès, the librettist of Chabrier's *Gwendoline*. Three scenes were drafted, but they have remained unpublished. In January 1892 Debussy wrote to Robert Godet: 'I'm anxious to let you hear the two acts that are finished, for I fear that I have been victorious over myself.' Victorious over himself! Had he succumbed to the dreaded Wagnerian influence? According to M. Vallas the style of these sketches recalls, among other things, *Tristan, Götterdämmerung* and *Parsifal*.

Rodrigue et Chimène was abandoned like *Diane au bois*. Debussy was thirty, and nothing of his had been heard beyond one or two songs or pianoforte pieces and the compulsory performance of the *Prix de Rome* cantata, *L'Enfant prodigue*. Of the music he wrote during the five years following his return from Rome, he was satisfied with very little. *La Damoiselle élue* (on the translation by Gabriel Sarrazin of Rossetti's *The Blessed Damozel*) was finished in 1888 and constituted the last of the *envois de Rome*. The *envois,* with *Zuléima* and *Printemps,* were then ready for the traditional concert of the works of each holder of the *Prix de Rome* at the Salle du Conservatoire. But that concert never took place. Behind the reasons given for its abandonment one can see that Debussy was not in the least anxious to present to the public works that he considered experimental or transitional. Alone of the *envois de Rome, La Damoiselle élue* achieved some success later. *Printemps* was forgotten for seventeen years; *Zuléima* was destroyed. The *Fantaisie* for piano and orchestra, of the year 1889, was to have been played at a concert of the Société Nationale in 1890. But at one of the rehearsals Debussy removed the parts from the stands himself and wrote to the conductor, Vincent d'Indy, that it had been withdrawn. At about the same time he wrote to his friend, Robert Godet:

Such music as mine has no other aim than to become part of things and people. That you have accepted it is a more lovely glory than any approval from the elegant people who kow-tow to

E 49

the Wagnerian Monsieur Lamoureux with his eyeglasses an
hieratic forefinger. . . .

And in 1893 to Ernest Chausson:

Here I am, just turned thirty-one and not quite sure of m
aesthetic. There are still things that I am not able to do—crea
masterpieces, for instance, or be really responsible—for I have th
fault of thinking too much about myself and only seeing realit
when it is forced upon me and then unsurmountable. Perhaps
am rather to be pitied than blamed. In any case I am writing yo
this expecting your pardon and your patience.

Chausson replied that in his opinion Debussy knew perfectl
well what he wanted; the truth of which we shall immediatel
see.

CHAPTER VI

THE TEN YEARS OF 'PELLÉAS'—1892–1902

ONE summer evening of 1892 Debussy bought, on the Boulevard des Italiens, the newly published drama of Maeterlinck, *Pelléas et Mélisande*. The thought of setting to music certain scenes occurred to him straight away, and within a short time he had communicated to his friend Godet a number of sketches and themes. The following May, a performance of the play at the Théâtre des Bouffes-Parisiens decided him to take it as a text for an opera.

Pelléas occupied Debussy over a period of ten years, between the ages of thirty and forty. As the only one of his numerous projects for operas that ever materialized, it stands out, flanked on one side by a period of some fifteen years of experiment, and on the other by a similar period of growing disillusionment, as the central work of his life.

We will follow its composition in the delightful series of letters to Ernest Chausson. The first reference is in a postscript to a letter of 6th September 1893:

LATEST NEWS

. . . .

C. A. Debussy finishes a scene of *Pelléas et Mélisande* ('A fountain in the park,' Act IV, scene iv), on which he would like to have the opinion of E. Chausson. It has been suggested to run excursion trains between Paris and Royan [where Chausson was staying], in view of this event, of which there is no further need to mention the importance.

But the following month he discovered he had been too hasty. On 2nd October:

I was in too great a hurry to crow about *Pelléas et Mélisande,* for after a sleepless night, in which I began to see things clearly, I had to admit that what I had got wasn't right at all. It's like a duet by Mr. Anybody-you-like; and then the ghost of old Klingsor, alias R. Wagner, appeared at a turning of one of the bars, so I tore the whole thing up and struck off on a new line with a little compound of phrases I thought more characteristic—trying to be as Pelléas as Mélisande. There is music behind all those veils by which she hides herself from even her most ardent worshipper. I've got something which will please you perhaps—the others don't care about. Quite spontaneously I have used silence as a means of expression (don't laugh). It is perhaps the only means of bringing into relief the emotional value of a phrase. If Wagner used silence, I should say it was only in an extremely dramatic way, rather as it is used in certain other dubious dramas in the style of Bouchardy, d'Ennery [1] and others!

At about this stage, permission being required for use of the libretto, Henri de Régnier wrote to Maeterlinck:

My friend, Achille Debussy, who is a musician of the most clever and delicate talent, has begun some charming music for *Pelléas et Mélisande,* which deliciously garlands the text while scrupulously respecting it. Before going further with this work, which is no inconsiderable, he would like authorization to continue. [2]

And, with Pierre Louÿs, Debussy set out to meet Maeterlinck at Ghent. On the way they stopped at Brussels.

The person I was most interested to see there [runs an undated letter of 1893 to Chausson] was Ysaÿe, whom I called on first

---

[1] Joseph Bouchardy (1810–70) and Adolphe Philippe d'Ennery (1811–99), popular dramatists known for the facile effectiveness of their technique. D'Ennery was the librettist of Massenet's *Le Cid.*

[2] Translation by Janet Flanner.

You won't be very surprised to hear that he actually shrieked with joy on seeing me, hugging me against his big chest and treating me as if I were his little brother. After which reception I had to give him news of every one and particularly of you, of whom, unfortunately, my only knowledge was from letters. And then music, and music till we went mad with it. That memorable evening I played in succession the *Cinq Poèmes* [of Baudelaire], *La Damoiselle élue* and *Pelléas et Mélisande*. I got as hoarse as if I had been selling newspapers on the street. *Pelléas* softened the hearts of certain young people, English, I believe; as for Ysaÿe, he became delirious. I really can't repeat what he told me! He liked your Quartet too and is getting some people to work at it.

I saw Maeterlinck, with whom I spent a day in Ghent. At first he assumed the airs of a young girl being introduced to her future husband, but after some time he thawed and was charming. When he spoke of the theatre he seemed a very remarkable man. As for *Pelléas,* he authorized me to make any cuts I like and even suggested some very important and useful ones himself. He says he knows nothing about music and when he comes to a Beethoven symphony he is like a blind man in a museum. But really he is a very fine man and speaks of extraordinary things in a delightfully simple way. When I thanked him for entrusting me with *Pelléas* he insisted that it was he who should be grateful to me for setting it to music. As my opinion was the very opposite I had to use what little diplomacy nature has endowed me with.

So, you see, it was a more profitable journey than the journey of Urien.[1]

We hear nothing more of *Pelléas* until the following year, when, probably from the first days of 1894, we have this charming glimpse:

DEAR FRIEND,

It's Mélisande's fault—so will you forgive us both? I have spent days in pursuit of those fancies of which she is made. I had no

---

[1] Allusion to *Le Voyage d'Urien* (published in 1893), one of the first works of André Gide.

courage to tell you of it all—besides, you know what such struggles are. I don't know if you have ever gone to bed, as I have, with a strange desire to cry, feeling as if you had not been able to see during the day some greatly loved friend. Just now I am worried about Arkel. He is from the other side of the grave and has that fond love, disinterested and far-seeing, of those who will soon disappear —all of which has to be said with *do ré mi fa sol la si do*. What a job!

I shall write to you at greater length to-morrow. This is just for you to know that I am thinking of you and to wish you good day.

CLAUDE DEBUSSY.

The letter of 8th January is probably of the following day, and here it is all gloom: 'The colour of my soul is iron-grey and sad bats wheel about the steeple of my dreams. My only hope is in *Pelléas et Mélisande,* and God only knows if that won't end in smoke.'

Meanwhile he was making some reputation as a Wagnerian pianist. On 5th May 1893 his former collaborator, Catulle Mendès, gave a lecture at the Odéon on *Rheingold* and *Walküre* illustrated at two pianos by Debussy and Raoul Pugno. A letter to Chausson of 21st May reveals a barbed tongue:

I'm rid of the *Rheingold*. This is a nuisance so far as the gold is concerned, but it is good to have done with the Rhine. The last performance was a terrible bore. Catulle Mendès spoke on the *Walküre* in such a way that the mothers who had naïvely brought their daughters were frightened away by the wicked priest's fiery words. The month of May, it appears, is henceforth to be the month of the *Walküre,* for some simple-minded people believe that this work announces the spring of a new music and the death of the old worn-out formulae. It's not what I think, but that doesn't seem to matter.[1]

---

[1] Debussy could be equally sarcastic about the Russian composers. In a letter of 1893 to Chausson he says: 'I suppose we shall hear a lot of the Russians now because of patriotic feeling. When Admiral

Cher Ami

C'est la Faute à Mélisande !

et pardonnez-moi à tous les deux ?

J'ai froid des journées à la poursuite de ce
"rien" dont elle est fait (Métif-del et je manquais
parfois de courage pour me raconter tout cela,
ce sont d'ailleurs des luttes que vous connaissez
mais, je ne sais pas si vous êtes canoté comme
moi, avec une vague envie de pleurer, un peu
comme si on avait peur de voir dans la
journée quelqu'un de très aimé.

Maintenant c'est Arkel qui me tourmente.
celui-là, il est d'outre-tombe, et il a cette
tendresse désintéressée et prophétique de ceux qui
vont bientôt disparaître et il faut dire tout cela
avec, do, ré, mi fa, sol, la, si, do,,!!! Quel métier ?

Je vous écrirai plus longuement demain aujourd'hui
c'est un simple bonjour, et pour vous dire
que je pense bien à vous,

Claude Debussy

LETTER TO ERNEST CHAUSSON

At the very time he was struggling away from Wagner in *Pelléas* he received engagements to play *Tristan* and *Parsifal* at the piano in Paris society. It appears that Chausson put this work in his way to supplement his meagre income from lessons and transcriptions for publishers. Robert Godet has said that in the art of rendering the difficult Wagnerian scores at the keyboard he was unsurpassed even by Mottl. I will quote here an illuminating passage from a letter of 5th February 1894 to Chausson from his brother-in-law, Henri Lerolle:

Debussy played the first act of *Parsifal*. It went off very well and I think the people liked it, although some of them said they couldn't hear the words. I'm not surprised! You know how he articulates. We consider ourselves fortunate if he sings anything but *tra ta ra ta ta*. *Parsifal* is very lovely, especially the religious part. But poor Debussy came to the end of his tether. I thought he'd never go through with it. Directly it was over I took him aside in a room at the back and gave him something warm. I thought he'd collapse. The fact is that he plays and sings with such energy! He assured me that if I hadn't been there to turn over the pages, at a certain moment he would have closed up the score and gone off. The next time there will be an interval for a cigarette in the middle of the second act, and then every one will be happy. Our good Debussy does this playing for the same reason that a man carries a trunk—to earn a few coppers. But I believe he is happy to think that we were able to get about a thousand francs for him.

One day in the spring of 1895 Debussy told Godet that *Pelléas* was finished—'this morning, to be historical.' But within a short time it was taken up again, pondered afresh,

---

Avellan was here it's a pity they didn't invite him to a concert. The bard Tiersot would certainly have said a few words of welcome.' Admiral Avellan was an admiral of the Russian fleet who made an important visit to Paris in 1893 at the time of the Franco-Russian Alliance.

revised and altered. The following year Ysaÿe, having attempted to get the work produced at the Théâtre de la Monnaie at Brussels, suggested a concert performance of certain parts. Debussy was opposed to this in much the same way that Wagner would have opposed a concert performance of *Tristan*. A letter of 13th October 1896 to Ysaÿe begins:

DEAR GREAT FRIEND,

I was most touched by your kind letter and your friendly anxiety for *Pelléas et Mélisande*. The poor little creatures are so difficult to introduce into the world, for with a godfather like you the world doesn't want to have anything to do with them.

Now I must humbly tell you why I am not of your opinion about a performance of *Pelléas* in part. Firstly, if this work has any merit, it is in the connection between the drama and the music. It is quite obvious that at a concert performance this connection would disappear and no one could be blamed for seeing nothing in those eloquent 'silences' with which this work is starred. Moreover, as the simplicity of the work only gains significance on the stage, at a concert performance they would throw in my face the American wealth of Wagner and I'd be like some poor fellow who couldn't afford to pay for 'contra-bass tubas'! In my opinion Pelléas and Mélisande must be given *as they are,* and then it will be a matter of taking them or leaving them, and if we have to fight, it will be worth while.

In 1897 a second version was finished which Pierre Louÿs had the greatest difficulty in persuading his friend not to destroy. The same year it was accepted by Albert Carré for performance at the Opéra-Comique. But it was not given until five years later. It was not only that the management, although they had accepted it, were diffident about producing a work of such novelty (Carré, with as little success as Ysaÿe, had at first suggested special performances in concert form); Debussy was continually taking back his score for improvement. Of the work in its final stages we know only that André Messager, who conducted the first performance, was its champion and that Debussy initiated him into each section of the work as he rewrote it. But even on the eve of the rehearsals there were sections that had still to be revised.

Let us now review Debussy's other musical activities during these years. The first time an important work of his was performed was on 8th April 1893. Gabriel Marie conducted *La Damoiselle élue* at a concert of the Société Nationale. Charles Darcours, in the *Figaro,* described it as 'very sensual and decadent,' and prophesied that 'this subcutaneous injec-tion may possibly produce dangerous eruptions among the small fry of the future.' The same year, on 29th December, the string Quartet was played at another concert of the Société Nationale by a quartet led by Ysaÿe. Guy Ropartz, in the *Guide Musical,* referred to it as 'a very interesting work in which the predominant influence is that of young Russia'; and the Belgian musician, Maurice Kufferath, remarked on the 'sus-tained harmonies that evoke a memory of the *gamelang.*' But on the whole the reception was not very favourable. Chausson was apparently displeased with it; and Debussy wrote to him:

> I must tell you that I was for some days very grieved by what you said of my Quartet, for I felt that it had only made you like *certain things* in me which I had wished you not to see. Well, I'll write another for you, really for you, and I'll try to bring more dignity to the form.

No knowledge of this work has come to light, but the existing Quartet is still called '1er Quatuor.'

A year later, on 22nd December 1894, came the first per-formance of the *Prélude à l'Après-midi d'un faune,* conducted, again at the Société Nationale, by Gustave Doret. This work, inspired by Mallarmé's eclogue, was originally to have extended beyond the *Prélude* to an *Interlude et Paraphrase finale.* Of these sections we know only that they were announced, but not given, at a concert in Brussels on 1st March 1894. Possibly Debussy incorporated whatever sketches he had made in other works.

Here is the programme of the concert at which *L'Après-midi d'un faune* was first performed:

La Forêt	Glazounov
Suite serbe	J. Bordier
La Vague et la cloche	Henri Dupuis
L'Enterrement d'Ophélie	A. Bourgault-Ducoudray
Troisième Concerto pour violon	Saint-Saëns
Prélude à l'Après-midi d'un faune	C. A. Debussy
Prière	Guy Ropartz
Rédemption, fragment symphonique	César Franck

Again there was no enthusiasm in the press. In the majority of cases it was coupled with the *Prière* of Ropartz as merely 'interesting.' Nor, apparently, did it receive any more whole-hearted recognition at a subsequent performance at the Concerts Colonne the following year. On this occasion Ignace Philipp, the famous piano teacher, wrote in *Le Ménestrel*: 'The *Prélude à l'Après-midi d'un faune* of M. Debussy is finely and delicately orchestrated; but one seeks in vain any heart or any strength. It is precious, subtle and indefinite in the same way as the work of M. Mallarmé'—and he continued with a very enthusiastic account of César Franck's *Psyché*.

In a letter to G. Jean-Aubry of 25th March 1910 Debussy recalls the impressions of Mallarmé:

I used to live then in a little furnished flat in the Rue de Londres. . . . Mallarmé came in with his prophetic air and his Scotch plaid around him. After listening to it he remained silent for a long time; then said: 'I didn't expect anything like that. This music draws out the emotion of my poem and gives it a warmer background than colour.' And here are the lines that Mallarmé wrote on a copy of *L'Après-midi d'un faune* which he sent me after the first performance:

> 'Sylvain d'haleine première,
> Si ta flûte a réussi
> Ouïs toute la lumière
> Qu'y soufflera Debussy.'

The opinion of most musicians, however, was more akin to the caustic expression of Saint-Saëns in his *Rimes familières*:

> Je deviendrais vite aphone,
> Si j'allais en étourdi
> M'égosiller comme un faune
> Fêtant son après-midi.

Before *L'Après-midi* was completed Debussy had begun the *Nocturnes*. In its original form this was a work in three movements for violin and orchestra intended for performance by Ysaÿe. In a letter to Ysaÿe of 22nd September 1894 we read:

I am working at three *Nocturnes* for violin and orchestra. The orchestra of the first part consists of strings; of the second, flutes, four horns, three trumpets and two harps; of the third, of both of these groups. It is, in short, an experiment with the different combinations that can be obtained from one colour—like a study in grey in painting. I hope this will appeal to you, for the pleasure it might give you is what I am most concerned with. I am not forsaking *Pelléas* for this—and I must say that, the further I go, the more depressed and anxious I become. . . .

Two years later, on 13th October 1896, Ysaÿe is begged to accept, in the place of excerpts for concert performance of *Pelléas,* 'three *Nocturnes* for violin and orchestra written for Eugène Ysaÿe, a man I love and admire.' And he continues: 'Indeed, these *Nocturnes* can only be played by him. If Apollo himself were to ask me for them I should have to refuse him! What do you say to that?' The following year they were recast for orchestra. Why was the original form abandoned? Following the correspondence of 1896, the next and last published letter to Ysaÿe is of 30th December 1903, two years after the first performance of the work in Paris. Ysaÿe had decided to conduct it at Brussels. Debussy wrote: 'I needn't tell you of my joy. My only regret is that, for the most wretched reasons, I shan't be able to be there to hear what I am sure will be *the performance I have dreamed of.*'

Whilst the *Nocturnes* were being recast, Debussy again entertained a number of projects for works that never materialized. In the letter to Ysaÿe of 13th October 1896 (from which I have already quoted) we read: 'It is probable that by December I shall have finished a work I am doing [1] on a poem of D. G. Rossetti—*La Saulaie.* It is an important work and written in the light of my latest discoveries in musical chemistry.' *La Saulaie* was a translation, made by Pierre Louÿs, of Rossetti's *Willowwood.* Of the music nothing is known.

He also planned to write a stage work on a libretto of Pierre Louÿs called *Cendrelune.* But he suggested so many alterations in Louÿs's text that Louÿs finally gave up all hope of collaboration. He wrote to Debussy:

Write *Cendrelune* yourself. You are perfectly capable of it. You have made so many changes in the little thing that it has become quite foreign to me. As it stands I can't go on with it. The religiousness, the triumph of the lily over the rose and of Chastity over Love—all that means nothing to me. I can't do anything at all along a direction where I have no idea of my bearings. . . .

Then there was to have been a *Daphnis et Chloé.* Of 17th January 1896 we have this letter:

MY DEAR PIERRE,

I have received from Mr. Houston Chamberlain an offer to write a ballet on *Daphnis et Chloé.* Although this man has given his name to a filter, his ideas appear to me confused.[2] Ask him to come with you to-morrow, I really need more details. He doesn't even mention how or where the ballet is to be given. Is it to be for xylophone, banjo or Russian bassoon? And then just imagine

---

[1] In the original, 'une chose que j'ai faite,' meaning, no doubt, the piano score.

[2] Allusion to the *Filtre Chamberland,* a filter for water.

that he's no further than Wagner and still believes in the recipes of that old poisoner!

Your invulnerable
CLAUDE.

Some work was done on this, for in March of the following year Louÿs is begged for advice on 'Daphnis who isn't getting on and Chloe who takes after him.' But after this we hear nothing more. Houston Stewart Chamberlain was apparently no more successful with Debussy than that other Wagnerian champion, Catulle Mendès, had been.

It is perhaps significant that at the time these projects were being abandoned Debussy was sufficiently interested in the *Deux Gymnopédies* of his friend Erik Satie to make an orchestral version of them, performed at the Société Nationale on 20th February 1897. From the spring of the same year date the three songs on texts from Louÿs's book, *Chansons de Bilitis*. Bilitis, 'born at the beginning of the sixth century preceding our era, in a mountain village on the borders of Melas towards the east of Pamphylia,' was the perfect hedonist. Here, in an anonymous translation (published by the Fortune Press), is the text of the second of Debussy's songs, *La Chevelure*:

He told me: 'To-night I dreamed. I had your hair around my neck. I had your locks, like a black necklace, round my neck and over my breast. I caressed them, and they were mine, and we were tied for ever thus by the same hair with mouth upon mouth, like two laurels, which have but a single root. And little by little it seemed to me that our limbs were so melted together that I became you and you entered, like a dream, into me.' When he had finished he laid his hands softly on my shoulders and looked at me with a look so tender that I lowered my eyes, trembling.

For some time Debussy appears to have been peculiarly loath to allow the performance of these songs. On 16th October 1898 he wrote to Louÿs:

So M. A. Ségard is going to give a lecture on the *Chansons de*

Bilitis. Therein, in beautiful language, is all that is ardently tender and cruel in acts of passion; so true, in fact, is this that the most craftily voluptuous of people are obliged to admit the childishness of their play by the side of this terrible, fascinating Bilitis.

Now will you tell me what my three little bits of music can bring to a straightforward reading of your poems? Nothing. My dear fellow, I will even say that my music, blundering in, would divide the listeners' excitement. Really, what is the point of harmonizing the voice of Bilitis in major or minor, since she is the possessor of the most persuasive voice in the world? You will ask me why I wrote the music. Aha! old fellow, that's another point. . . . The music is for other occasions. Now you must listen to me—when Bilitis appears, let her speak unaided.

I needn't mention other, quite material difficulties, such as finding some young person who, out of consideration for our pale aesthetic figures, would be willing to consume herself in the study of these songs for a mere thank you. Then there's that shameful habit I have of scattering whole handfuls of wrong notes about whenever I play before more than two people.

Well, I have said all; and I hope you will understand. I don't wish to shirk, but to help you.

With all my affection,
CLAUDE DEBUSSY.

The *Chansons de Bilitis* were first sung by Blanche Marot at the Société Nationale on 17th March 1900. The same year, on 9th December, the Concerts Lamoureux gave the first and second parts of the *Nocturnes* and on 27th October of the following year the complete triptych. The reception was most enthusiastic. Meanwhile, at the *Exposition Universelle* of 1900, official performances had been given of *La Damoiselle élue,* the Quartet and the *Chansons de Bilitis.* Debussy at last gained recognition. On 1st April 1901 he accepted, for a period of six months, the post of music critic to the *Revue Blanche.* It was decided to give *Pelléas et Mélisande* at the Opéra-Comique in 1902.

In these ten years Debussy's unobtrusive emergence changed

the whole face of French music. As we now see, his extraordinary innovations opened up an entirely new world. But
it is not only the positive value of these innovations that we
have to consider. To Debussy alone French music owes its
release, on the one hand, from the yoke of Wagner and, on
the other, from the triviality of the *opéra-comique*. Two other
composers, Vincent d'Indy proceeding from César Franck
and Gabriel Fauré from Saint-Saëns, endeavoured to establish
the lines of a national music; but in both cases German means
were only imperfectly adapted to French taste. Debussy once
humorously said that the only true French composer was one
Paul Delmet, a well-known *chansonnier* in a Montmartre
cabaret.

But at the close of the century Debussy's achievement was
by no means fully appreciated. In a report on French music
in 1900 presented to the Minister of Fine Arts, Alfred Bruneau
praised the *Nocturnes* and *L'Après-midi d'un faune,* but considered that a more precious achievement was Charpentier's
opera, *Louise.* It is curious to note that *Louise* was greatly
admired by Richard Strauss and that in the early years of the
present century Charpentier was of all French musicians the
most liked in Germany. Debussy's opinion of *Louise* is
expressed in a vituperative letter of 5th February 1900 to
Pierre Louÿs. As a conclusion to this chapter and as a reply
to this German preference it is worth quoting in full:

DEAR PIERRE,

I have been to the show of the Charpentier family, so that I am
in just the right state of mind to appreciate the forcefulness of your
letter. It seems to me that this work had to be. It supplies only
too well the need for that cheap beauty and idiotic art that has such
an appeal. You see what this Charpentier has done. He has
taken the cries of Paris which are so delightfully human and picturesque and, like a rotten 'Prix de Rome,' he has turned them into
sickly cantilenas with harmonies underneath that, to be polite, we

will call parasitic. The sly dog! It's a thousand times more conventional than *Les Huguenots,* of which the technique, although it may not appear so, is the same. And they call this Life. Good God! I'd sooner die straight away. What you have here is something of the feeling after the twentieth half-pint, and the sloppiness of the chap who comes back at four in the morning, falling all over the baker and the rag-and-bone man. And this man imagines he can express the soul of the poor!!! It's so silly that it's pitiful.

Of course M. Mendès discovers his Wagner in it and M. Bruneau his Zola. And they call this a real French work! There's something wrong somewhere. It's more silly than harmful. But then people don't very much like things that are beautiful—they are so far from their nasty little minds. With many more works like *Louise* any attempt to drag them out of the mud will completely fail.

I assure you that I'd very much like *Pelléas* to be played in Japan, for our fashionable eclectics might approve of it—and I can tell you that I should be ashamed.

Thank you for your kind and lovely letter, and *à bientôt,* eh?

Your

CLAUDE.

CHAPTER VII

THE HEDONIST

BEFORE going on to the production of *Pelléas* let us stop here to consider the man.

As an introduction we can do no better than give the following portrait by André Suarès of Debussy as he remembers him about 1900:

At first sight there was nothing striking about him. He was not tall and appeared to be neither particularly robust nor delicate. He had a certain look of solidity about him although he was rather languid. He was well-covered, not to say stout, the lines of his figure all merging into each other. His beard was soft and silky, his hair thick and curly. His features were full, his cheeks plump. He had a bantering manner, but beneath there was a subtle shrewdness. He was an ironic and sensual figure, melancholy and voluptuous. His complexion was of a warm amber brown. Highly strung, he was master of his nerves, though not of his emotions—which must have affected him profoundly, especially as he tried to conceal them. In love's retreat and night's inveigling sweetness he must have known some passionate hours.

Irony was part of his nature, as indeed was his love of pleasure; he had a mischievous sense of humour and acknowledged a love of good living. He had a barbed tongue, a certain carelessness of speech and something rather affected in his gestures; his enthusiasms were controlled, his taste unfailing, and though appearance often suggested the contrary, he was very simple. Debussy was as much a bohemian of Montmartre as he was a man of the world. In his reclusion there was something feline. With all his apparent sensuality there was no sign of brutality, though there might have been a capacity for violence. . . . The shape of his head showed great obstinacy of mind.

All who saw him were impressed by his face and head. Casella writes: 'The enormous forehead bulged forwards, while there seemed something missing at the back of the huge skull.' Another observer, Ugo Ojetti, speaks of his 'box-like head,' and Cyril Scott of his 'somewhat Christ-like face, marred by a slightly hydrocephalic forehead.' I do not know what justification there is for saying that the shape of his fore-head was due to hydrocephalus. To my knowledge, only one other person has hinted that he was afflicted with this disease. This was the playwright Georges Feydeau, who spoke of Debussy as 'a sort of dark, bearded hydrocephalic.' [1] In England the resemblance to Rossetti was everywhere noticed.

Casella's recollections continue:

His colour was sallow; the eyes were small and seemed half-sunk in the fat face; the straight nose was of the purest classical Roman type; in the thick and jet-black hair and beard fifty years had here and there sown a silver thread. As always with artists of the finer sort, the hands were most beautiful. Debussy's voice was un-prepossessing, being hoarse (and this was aggravated by the abuse of tobacco), and he spoke in an abnormal, nervous, jumpy way. His dress was scrupulously cared for in every detail. His walk was curious, like that of all men who have a weakness for wearing womanish footgear. [2]

By the side of this we may place a comparison of Debussy and Maeterlinck. Georgette Leblanc, observing them to-gether, notes that they were both of a saturnine disposition, but points to interesting differences.

Debussy's reserve was physical [she writes]. In him one felt a painful sensitivity and even something morbid which was biding its time. In Maeterlinck the physical and moral balance made itself felt at once. His timidity was the result of his nature and character.

---

[1] His brother Eugène, it will be remembered, died at an early age of meningitis.

[2] Translation by Richard Capell.

The musician suffered from the little things of life. The poet refused to endure them. With him the 'Do not enter' sign meant 'Do not disturb me.' . . . With Debussy it seemed to mean 'Do not make me suffer.'

Both had an unquiet look in their eyes, but of a definitely different nature: in the poet's glance it was clear and hurriedly questioning; in Debussy's it took on a fixed intensity that awaited no answer. What was most noticeable in the musician was his body, built for strength and yet apparently uninhabited by it.[1]

Yet with all his reserve no one felt more than Debussy the need for moral and emotional support. He was certainly not the type of recluse who could stand alone. His intimate letters express an overflowing warmth of feeling that seems now to have gone from our steely world. Yet he was always sure to bargain for some deep-seated attachment, as if the affection received should always tally with that bestowed.

Here are two characteristic extracts. The first is from a letter of about 1890 to Robert Godet:

I am so glad, dear friend—just allow my little sensibility to speak awhile—yes, I am so glad of our friendship, over which thoughtless pride had cast its shadow—and I am glad too that such pain as we have known has been shared. All this is perhaps an old-fashioned way of looking at life. But then, fortunately, we are not 'modern'!

And the other from a letter to Ernest Chausson of 4th June 1893:

Ah, my dear friend! What a Sunday! A joyless Sunday it was without you. Had you been here the atmosphere would have been a delight to breathe, for I must tell you that if I already loved you very much, the few days I spent in your company have made me for always your devoted friend. But I will not try to express my emotions here. However lyrical I might become I should not do myself justice.

---

[1] Translation by Janet Flanner.

Yet this is not so laughable as you might think. It was so good to feel that I belonged somehow to your family and that I was part of you all. But am I not going too far, and won't you feel my friendship to be rather a nuisance? I wish so much to please you that sometimes I imagine things that, decidedly, are crazy.

Beautiful as such feelings of friendship are, there is no hiding, in this insufficiency—for it was an insufficiency—what is conventionally called a weakness of character. One day, in the last years of his life, having missed an appointment, he wrote to his publisher, Durand: 'There are moments in life when to have missed a friend is as awful as the worst catastrophe. I went back to my house like a man condemned to live!—full of resentment.' The letters to Pierre Louÿs reveal in even stronger terms his insatiable desire for sympathy. According to Paul Valéry Debussy found in Louÿs 'the most precious support in his career, in all ways, at all times and in all difficulties.' And indeed he made full use of this support. Here is an extract from a letter written some time in 1898. Its pathetic tone is indicative of a state of mind that was perhaps not exceptional:

I really do need your affection, I feel so lonely and helpless. Nothing has changed in the black background of my life and I hardly know where I am going if it is not towards suicide—a senseless ending to something that might have turned out better. I've got into this state of mind from continually fighting against silly and despicable impossibilities. You know me better than any one and you alone can take it upon yourself to tell me that I am not altogether an old fool. . . .

As one would imagine, Debussy was an atheist. As a boy at the Conservatoire he told his friends that he lacked the necessary religious feeling to set to music Lamartine's *Invocation,* required of him at a preliminary examination for the *Prix de Rome*. He might at one time have taken part in the spiritualist séances at Bailly's offices of *La Revue indépendante,* but rather because it was a fashion than to find some form of religious expression. To quote Jean Lépine: 'His atheism was sensual and instinctive. To find support for his lack of belief there was no question of devoting himself to any serious study as Voltaire, Renan and Anatole France did. Nor did he seek any philosophic system to defend himself. Quite simply he experienced no desire for a religion.' And what interests us particularly: 'It is unlikely that these problems presented themselves with sufficient force for him to seek a satisfactory solution.' (It is impossible not to suspect that it was this lack of any religious feeling that drove him away from César Franck's class at the Conservatoire). His young friend, René Peter, tells us that he was very superstitious and 'would not go to bed without first thoroughly blowing his nose and then placing his slippers so that the toes pointed outwards. (Not to do this was to tempt Providence.)'

René Peter has also written about Debussy's reactions to certain political movements. At the end of the last century the Dreyfus affair divided the whole of France. Debussy was only mildly interested. In keeping with most of his friends, he instinctively took sides with the nationalists. Peter persuaded him to hear Anatole France and Jean Jaurès speak in favour of Dreyfus at the meetings in Montparnasse; but he was little impressed. Yet at this period of his life he was anything but the fierce chauvinist he is generally thought to have been. In 1897 *Messidor,* an opera by Alfred Bruneau on a libretto by Zola, Dreyfus's most ardent supporter, was produced at the Opéra. Partly for political reasons, it was a failure. In a letter to Louÿs Debussy leaves no doubt as to his feelings on the intermingling of politics and art:

I haven't got any further than you with the score of *Messidor,* for life is short and I'd rather go to a café or look at pictures. How do you expect people so ugly as Zola and Bruneau to be capable of anything but the second-rate? Have you noticed, in their two articles, the deplorable use they make of patriotism? It might be bad, but in any case it's French!!! By George! We've only got one musician who's really French, and that's Paul Delmet. He's the only one who has caught the melancholy atmosphere of the faubourgs and the wholehearted sentimentality round where that burnt grass is by the fortifications.[1] The best disciple of this master is Massenet.[2] The others with their social preoccupations and their claim to put life into chords of the seventh are just a lot of dreary fatheads. If, indeed, they have any view of life at all, it is through their last laundry bill.

Until the production of *Pelléas,* Debussy's material position was always insecure. On his return from Rome he contrived to make a living as a pianoforte teacher and by making transcriptions for the publishers Fromont and Durand. His compositions were only a source of revenue for a short time. About 1895 Georges Hartmann, a publisher later associated with Fromont, secured the rights on all his work for five hundred francs a month. But Hartmann died in 1900, leaving him without any hope of securing a similar contract from another publisher. 'He was sent to me by Providence,' he told Pierre Louÿs, 'and played his part with a grace and charm quite rare among the philanthropists of art.' In 1893 he contemplated taking a post as a conductor at Royan, and on two occasions he attempted to establish connections in London.

Debussy first came to London when a young boy and heard *H.M.S. Pinafore* at the Strand Opera Comique. He paid another visit on his return from Rome in 1887, this time to investigate the rights of *The Blessed Damozel.* Berthold Tours introduced him to Novello's, but to no material advantage. In 1895 he came again and stayed for three weeks near Belsize Road at the house

[1] Meaning the outlying, poorer districts of Paris.

[2] The point here is that the *chansonnier,* Paul Delmet (1862–1904), was a pupil of Massenet.

of a French professor. On the way over he met Saint-Saëns, who introduced him to Parry at the Royal College of Music. But again, as one might in this case well imagine, to no avail. Debussy could hope for even less success in London than in Paris. It was long before he could reap any material benefit from his works. His royalties amounted to less than £10 a month, even when he was over forty.

He had, however, an extravagant way of living and that lack of any practical sense which has long become an indispensable feature in the picturesque portrayal of a musician. One day when he went out with his last twenty francs to try and borrow from his friends he came back without a sou and with a porcelain cat he had seen in a shop-window. Still, this was a far cry from the stupendous extravagances of Wagner. And the difference between the ways of living of the two musicians was characteristic in other respects. The *faculté maîtresse* of both men was their love of sensual pleasure. But while Wagner collected forty silk dressing-gowns, the French musician was content to steal a friend's tie because it was of his favourite green. And in their dealings with women there was something of the difference between the gorging Tristan and the more hesitant Pelléas.

We have already noted Debussy's early love-affairs with Sophie von Meck and Mme Vasnier. About 1888 he took unto himself a mistress, nicknamed Gaby.

The most remarkable thing about the appearance of this pretty blonde [writes René Peter] was the strikingly green colour of her eyes. I don't know where Claude met her; scandalmongers — but we shan't listen to them—said in some frivolous place. She was certainly the least frivolous blonde I ever came across. Her chin was forceful, she was strongly built and looked at you as resolutely as a cat.

Beyond which our knowledge of her relations with Debussy is limited. During the period of about ten years that they lived

71

together in the Rue de Londres and the Rue Gustave-Doré, Debussy inscribed to her a sketch for *L'Après-midi d'un faune* and his unfinished opera, *Rodrigue et Chimène*. But she did not hold his whole affection during this time. About 1893 he was engaged for a short time to a young singer, Thérèse Roger. And about five years later he had a violent romantic affair with a young society woman. This gives us occasion to quote an illuminating passage from a letter of 9th February 1897 which Debussy sent to Louÿs, then in Algeria:

I've had some troublesome business in which Bourget seems to have joined forces with Xavier de Montépin [1]—which may not be altogether impossible. Gaby, with her steely eyes, found a letter in my pocket which left no doubt as to the advanced state of a love affair with all the romantic trappings to move the most hardened heart. Whereupon—tears, drama, a real revolver and a report in the *Petit Journal*. Ah! my dear fellow, why weren't you here to help me out of this nasty mess? It was all barbarous, useless and will change absolutely nothing. Kisses and caresses can't be effaced with an india-rubber. They might perhaps think of something to do this and call it The Adulterer's India-Rubber!

On top of it all poor little Gaby lost her father—an occurrence which for the time being has straightened things out.

I was, all the same, very upset and again very sad to feel you so far away, so hopelessly far away that I hadn't the strength to pick up my pen and write to you. I didn't think I could give you the right feeling of the thing. For writing is not the same as looking into the face of a friend. You will think perhaps: 'It's his own fault.' Well, there you are. I am sometimes as sentimental as a *modiste* who might have been Chopin's mistress. I must say that my heart is still capable of fluttering instead of getting on quietly with its own business. . . . Now don't let us speak of this any more, and believe me to be still your fine strong Claude.

---

[1] Xavier de Montépin (1826–1902). Popular author of serial stories and melodramas.

DEBUSSY WITH HIS FIRST WIFE, PAUL POUJAUD (*left*), PAU
DUKAS (*right*) AND PIERRE LALO (*seated*), ABOUT 1902

Slightly before this he had made the acquaintance of Rosalie Texier.

She had come from the department of Yonne [writes René Peter], a pretty girl, pale complexion, a small mouth and her hair then rather dark brown. She came to earn her living at a Paris dressmaker's. Her first meeting with Debussy, brought about by friends of whom I was one, brought little sign of affection from either of them. Claude found her pretty but peevish; he even used to imitate her little ways. But she was a charming girl and took it very good-naturedly. Gaby, however, liked her very much. Then we lost sight of the three of them. No one could have foreseen that what, in the eyes of us all, was hardly the beginning of a relationship, was one day to come to a formal and happy ending.

For on 19th October 1899 they were married, Debussy having to give a piano lesson in the morning to have enough to pay for a wedding breakfast at the Brasserie Pousset. From a letter he wrote to Godet on 5th January 1900 he certainly appeared to have no illusions about his wife's intellectual capacities:

I must tell you straight away of what has happened. Two things: I've moved and I'm married. Yes, my dear friend, and please remain seated. Mlle Lily Texier has changed her disharmonious name to Lily Debussy, much more pleasant-sounding, as every one will agree. She is unbelievably fair and pretty, like some character from an old legend. Also she is not in the least 'modern-style.' She has no taste for the music that Willy[1] approves, but has a taste of her own. Her favourite song is a roundelay about a grenadier with a red face who wears his hat on one side like an old campaigner —not very provoking aesthetically.

A year later we may judge of his feelings from an inscription on the manuscript of the *Nocturnes*:

This manuscript belongs to my little Lily-Lilo. All rights

---

[1] i.e. Henri Gauthier-Villars, the critic.

reserved. It is proof of the deep and passionate joy I have in being her husband. Claude Debussy. At the peep of January 1901.

Finally there is a glimpse of the unaffected person she must have been in an unfinished play, *Les Frères en art,* which Debussy wrote with René Peter. Here Maltravers, impersonating Debussy, says to a character impersonating Lily:

You don't pretend to be a Muse who frightens the sparrows away. You don't do your hair like the women in the frescoes. You have a lovely perfume and you are as sweet as a peach without ever reminding me of the latest success from Houbigant's. You dress up very little, which gives you so much more time, but which is also rather my fault.

While it lasted, their relationship was satisfying and simple.

CHAPTER VIII

TWO YEARS—1902–1904

IT was decided to give *Pelléas* at the Opéra-Comique in 1902, and rehearsals began on 13th January. But it was only in March that the date of the dress rehearsal was fixed for 27th April and the first public performance for three days later. Debussy was taken by surprise, for during the rehearsals a number of revisions were recommended and orchestral interludes were seen to be necessary to allow time for the scenery to be changed. Many passages were thus not completed until the last moment. Robert Godet mentions that during these months he had 'to settle affairs with the legatee of one of his patrons (i.e. Georges Hartmann) and this exposed him to daily summonses for debts he could not repay.' To complicate matters still further a quarrel broke out between Debussy and Maeterlinck. For a time it was thought that the whole production would be wrecked.

So much scandal went about as the result of this quarrel that it is difficult to reconstruct the episode truthfully. Here is, I think, the most authoritative version, by Georgette Leblanc, Maeterlinck's wife, around whom the affair centred. The scene is in the Rue Raynouard in Passy at the end of 1901:

Debussy came to play his score. The position of the piano forced him to turn his back to us and permitted Maeterlinck to make desperate signs to me. Not understanding music in the least the time seemed long to him. Several times he wanted to escape, but I held him back. Resigned, he lit his pipe.

At this first hearing of *Pelléas* many of its beauties escaped me, but with the prelude for the death of Mélisande I felt that special, that unique emotion we undergo in the presence of a masterpiece. . . . It was late. Two candles outlined Debussy's silhouette. Maeterlinck was half asleep in his arm-chair. Before my eyes the high windows framed the soft blue of growing night.

Just before he left we talked of the casting. I longed to play the part. Maeterlinck urged it. Debussy said he would be delighted. It was decided that I should begin to study Mélisande immediately. We arranged for the first rehearsal.

There were two or three rehearsals at my house and two at his, the fifth floor in the Rue Cardinet, where he lived in an extremely modest apartment. . . .

My work with Debussy was progressing, when one day Maeterlinck read in a paper that another artist had been engaged to create Mélisande and that she was rehearsing with him. That Debussy should do such a thing surprised me, as he was not a man to pay meaningless compliments. My enunciation gave him a pleasure that he constantly commented upon. Was it not the poem of *Pelléas* that had inspired him? Had he not followed it word for word as no other composer had ever done before? No, certainly the quarrel was not between him and me. It came from the Opéra-Comique and my disagreeable adventure connected with *Carmen*. . . .

Maeterlinck, thus betrayed by Debussy, referred the case to the Society of Authors, thinking that he was legally within his rights. He was mistaken, first because the law gives precedence to the musician rather than to the author, and furthermore because in his preliminary authorization he had added a gracious clause: 'The piece may be played where, how and when you like.'

Justly annoyed to find himself stripped before the law, Maeterlinck brandished his cane and announced to me that he was going to 'give Debussy a drubbing to teach him what was what.'

My love had none of the stoic quality of the heroines of antiquity. This threat of a beating terrified me, and I clung to Maeterlinck, who jumped briskly out of the window. (Our ground-floor flat in the Rue Raynouard was half-way up the slope of the street. We had to go down through the garden in order to reach the

76

porte-cochère and then climb the hill. We often went out through the window.) I waited in agony, convinced of disaster. I did not picture Debussy with his tragic mask of a face taking kindly to a reprimand.

I watched the deserted street for Maeterlinck's return. Finally he appeared at the top of the hill, brandishing his cane to heaven with comic gestures.

The story was pitiable. As soon as he entered the *salon* he had threatened Debussy, who dropped into a chair while Mme Debussy distractedly ran toward her husband with a bottle of smelling salts. She had begged the poet to go away and, my word! there was nothing else to do.

Maeterlinck, who did not like musicians any more than music, kept saying as he laughed: 'They're all crazy, all off their heads, these musicians!'

This scarcely reassured me. I thought that after Maeterlinck had left Debussy would arise from his chair in terrible wrath. Perhaps his seconds would call on us the next day.

As for Maeterlinck, he found it only just to attack the management of the Opéra-Comique.[1]

Whereupon Maeterlinck wrote a letter, dated 14th April 1902, to *Le Figaro,* in which, besides opposing the substitution of another singer for Georgette Leblanc in the part of Mélisande, he says:

> They have managed to exclude me from my work, and from now on it is in the hands of the enemy. Arbitrary and absurd cuts have made it incomprehensible. They have retained passages that I wished to suppress or improve as I did in the libretto which has just appeared and from which it will be seen how far the text adopted by the Opéra-Comique differs from the authentic version. In a word, the *Pelléas* in question is a work which is strange and almost hostile to me; and deprived of all control over my work, I can only wish for its immediate and decided failure.
>
> M. MAETERLINCK.

---

[1] Translation by Janet Flanner.

The question of a duel did arise, possibly as the result of this letter, and Albert Carré and Robert de Flers both offered to take the place of Debussy. But eventually the affair blew over, although Maeterlinck was for a long time deeply hurt by the way in which he considered his wife had been slighted. He heard only one act of Debussy's work, many years later in New York.

The part of Mélisande was thus given to Mary Garden, a young Scotch-American girl who, ironically enough, had made a romantic début some years previously in the opera which was an object of Debussy's special hatred—*Louise.* Here is the cast of the first performance:

Mélisande	Mary Garden
Geneviève	J. Gerville-Réache
Pelléas	Jean Périer
Golaud	Hector Dufranne
Arkel	Félix Vieuille
Yniold	Blondin

Scenery painted by Jusseaume and Ronson
Conductor   André Messager

Several things combined to make the dress rehearsal a rather painful experience. At the doors a 'Select Programme' was sold, in which the plot was maliciously ridiculed. Maeterlinck's letter had afforded just the opportunity to laugh a new work off that a certain section of the Paris musical public always awaits, and during the performance there was the uproar that, ever since Victor Hugo's *Hernani,* traditionally accompanies the first production of a great work in France. The storm broke forth in the second act at the words of Mélisande, 'Je ne suis pas heureuse.' At mention of the words 'petit père,' in the scene between Golaud and Yniold, the house set up peals of laughter. At one point in this scene the uproar almost brought the curtain down. 'Sont-ils près du lit?' asks Golaud; and with the sweetest innocence Yniold replies: 'Je ne vois pas le lit.' At the request of a government official this passage, as well as Yniold's scene with the sheep in the same act, was cut at the first public performance and has never been restored.

The reception in the press was divided. Romain Rolland in the Berlin paper, *Morgen,* had no hesitation in proclaiming that *Pelléas* 'was one of the three or four outstanding achievements in French musical history.' Gaston Carraud in *La Liberté* made a pertinent comparison when he spoke of Debussy taking his place 'more definitely even than Wagner among the sensualists in music of whom Mozart was the greatest.' Some weeks later he enlarged on the connection with Mozart in the journal, *Minerva*:

M. Debussy is really a classical composer. I am not speaking paradoxically. After the unbridled romanticism to which music has fallen a prey, he has the lucidity, the tact, the restraint and the sense of proportion that characterize the classical composers. He has the same controlled emotion as they; he has their charm and dignity of expression, their scorn of emphasis, exaggeration and mere effect.[1]

The notice in *Le Journal* was by Catulle Mendès, Debussy's former collaborator in *Rodrigue et Chimène*. He wrote:

Every artist has noted the collaboration [of Debussy and Maeterlinck] with great pleasure. By their delicate and subtle sensibility, the similarity of their emotions and dreams, their fraternity, one might say, they seem as well matched as possible. One expected —what is so rare in an opera-house—a really homogeneous work, as if inspired by one man and in which the spoken drama would of itself develop into a musical drama.

If our hope was not always deceived, it was too seldom realized. There was often disagreement, sometimes divorcement, just when we expected that perfect concord more indispensable in this work than in any other.

---

[1] Translation by Maire and Grace O'Brien.

Mendès then goes on to speak of 'Debussy's persistence in getting music out of unmusical phrases,' and amazingly concludes: 'We came away from this performance with two desires—one, to hear the score in the concert-hall without the singers, and the other, to see the play of Maeterlinck without music, on the dramatic stage.'

One other criticism may be quoted as expressing a curious view shared by not a few people. It is by Camille Bellaigue and appeared in the *Revue des deux mondes*.

I remember when we were both students at the Conservatoire. When M. Debussy used to play the piano he used to puff on the strong beats of the bar. We used to poke fun at this habit of his. He has certainly got over it. In his rhythm now there are no accents. In his structureless art the abolishment of rhythm goes hand in hand with the abolishment of melody. . . . After hearing the work one feels the uneasiness and agony of the hero who sighs: 'Il ne me reste rien si je m'en vais ainsi. Et tous ces souvenirs c'est comme j'emportais un peu d'eau dans un sac de mousseline.' But there is something more and something worse. Art such as this is unhealthy and harmful. I know that there are distinguished and pure-minded people who have no use for music and who not only do not like it but are afraid of it, for, as they say, it strikes at their very being, weakens and dissolves their conscience. When it comes to music such as this they are quite right. It dissolves us because it is itself in a state of dissolution. Its hardly perceptible vitality tends to the lowering and the ruin of our existence. It contains germs, not of life and progress, but of decadence and death.

This reminds one unmistakably of the theories of Max Nordau, who, in his once-famous book, *Degeneration,* so bitterly attacked the Impressionists and Symbolists. The director of the Conservatoire, Théodore Dubois, so feared the nefarious influence of *Pelléas* that he forbade students of the composition classes to hear it.

Within a short time *Pelléas* became a great box-office

success. But one performance was dissatisfying, and Debussy characteristically wrote to Messager:

I suppose I had to expect the consequences of such excitement —I fell into an awful state of depression. The performance last Saturday didn't go off very well. All sorts of silly little things happened which really had nothing to do with me. There'll be another performance next Thursday unless something unfortunate happens in the meantime. I am quite incapable of putting a good face on things when I am discouraged, as you know.

The following performance was again a success. There was then a question of giving the part of Pelléas to a woman.

It may seem strange, but it's not altogether silly [Debussy wrote to Messager]. Pelléas has not the ways of making love of a hussar, and when he finally does resolve upon something his plans are so quickly checked by the sword of Golaud that the idea might be worth considering. I must admit that I would rather like to see . . . Without speaking of the change in sex there would be a change in the scheme of timbres which worries me rather. Perhaps I am more curious about it than genuinely interested. I will await your advice.

The idea was dropped.

In the course of the year, the musical historian Jules Combarieu, then an official at the Ministry of Education, proposed Debussy for the decoration of the Croix d'Honneur. He accepted it, but only, as he told Louis Laloy, 'for the joy it will give my old parents and all those who love me.'[1] He soon found life in the public eye, which the success of his opera had brought him, distasteful. In June, at the end of the Paris season, he wrote to Godet:

It is I, Claude Debussy, and I am none the prouder for being he. You will never know what remorse I feel for this unmention-

---

[1] Paul Valéry's comment in a letter of congratulation was: 'Every real artist has the power, some day, to decorate the government.'

able behaviour to you—you whom I love with all my heart! Truth to tell, I am tired out. It is like neurasthenia—a fashionable illness to which I thought I was immune. Apparently the mental and nervous strain of these last months have got the better of me, for I couldn't even think of writing to Godet. I have just now a moment when I feel less fagged and I beg you not to think too badly of me and to believe that there's nothing rotten in the state of Denmark. As for your article, I can hardly thank you, it would almost be an insult. Besides, I did not need to be reminded of your sensitive understanding and your scrupulously loyal love of beauty. . . . To come back to the story, I must tell you that the dress rehearsal has given me the most wretched trouble. What I foresee is that I shall continually be pushed into public life. I am not really made for that kind of thing and all I shall be is my clumsy self. . . .

Well, I am anxious to see these performances of *Pelléas* over. It's time they were. They are beginning to take it for one of the repertory works. The singers are beginning to improvise and the orchestra are getting heavy. They'll soon be thinking more of *La Dame blanche*. . . . But I think I've got some way of getting the orchestral score published.

I will write to you shortly when I am in less of a hurry. I want this to reach you as soon as possible.

Then he retired for the summer to the home of his parents-in-law at Bichain in Burgundy. *Pelléas* was given in the autumn and again during the following year. The Opéra-Comique, he told Durand in 1903, 'is absurdly taking up all my time, and this life of the theatre disgusts me and deadens me.' The two years from the summer of 1902 to the summer of 1904 were, however, remarkably fruitful. They saw the appearance of a number of piano works—the *Estampes, D'un cahier d'esquisses* and *L'Isle joyeuse,* the second series of the *Fêtes galantes* on the poems of Verlaine, the *Danse sacrée et danse profane* for harp and orchestra, and the beginning of the second large orchestral triptych, *La Mer.*

The first mention of the last work is in a letter to Durand of 12th September 1903. Its three movements are here referred to as *Mer belle aux îles sanguinaires, Jeux de vagues* and *Le Vent fait danser la mer.* In a letter to Messager of the same date we read:

> You perhaps do not know that I was destined for the fine life of a sailor and that it was only by chance that I was led away from it. But I still have a great passion for the sea. You will say that the ocean doesn't wash the hills of Burgundy and that what I am doing might be like painting a landscape in a studio. But I have endless memories and, in my opinion, they are worth more than reality, which generally weighs down one's thoughts too heavily.

An opinion revealing an attitude to nature that has certainly nothing pantheistic about it.

At the beginning of 1903 he was appointed music critic to the daily paper *Gil Blas,* and in April came to London to notice the *Ring* at Covent Garden. The rest of the year passed without any noteworthy happenings. Performances took place and his reputation seemed assured. If there was no great improvement in his material position, it at least promised to be more secure. Then, in the summer of 1904, came the great turning-point in his life. Debussy left his wife for Mme Bardac. Lily Debussy shot herself and was taken to a nursing home severely wounded near the heart. The Paris world flamed with scandal. On all sides Debussy was accused of having crudely sold himself to a rich woman. Most of his friends deserted him.

It is difficult to reconstruct the episode without being influenced by the views of one party or another. Emma Bardac, *née* Moyse, was a Jewess, the wife of a prominent financier and the mistress of Gabriel Fauré. She was a woman of the world, a brilliant talker and a delightful singer. Debussy had become intimate with her shortly after his marriage with Rosalie Texier and had considered abandoning his wife for her many times before the final rupture. What decided him is not clear. He told Robert Godet that the sound of Lily's voice 'made his blood run cold.' On the other hand, we know nothing of his love for Mme Bardac. The life she offered was certainly alluring, and it has been argued that Debussy, always susceptible to the luxuries of life (and in particular to fine cooking), foresaw, principally, freedom from material worries. As Lily bluntly said of her successor: 'Elle l'a pris par la gueule.' But we know as yet too little of the inner history of the affair to form any judgment of Debussy's action. So far as the material side of the question is concerned his new alliance involved him in endless complications.

In the autumn of 1905 a girl was born. She was named Claude-Emma. Debussy and Mme Bardac both petitioned for divorce and were married some time later.

On 19th September 1904 Debussy sent the following letter to Messager:

My life during the last few months has been strange and bizarre, much more so than I could have wished. It is not easy to give you particulars, it would be rather embarrassing. I would rather wait and tell you over some of that excellent whisky of the old days. I have been working . . . but not as I should have liked. . . . Perhaps I was over-anxious or perhaps I was aiming too high. Whatever the cause, I have had many a fall, and have hurt myself so much that I have felt utterly exhausted for hours afterwards. There are numerous reasons for this of which I will tell you some day . . . if I have the courage, for it is all very sad. There are times when one spends one's days mourning for the past, and I have been mourning the Claude Debussy who worked so joyfully at *Pelléas,* for, between ourselves, I have not been able to recapture him, and that is one of my many sorrows.[1]

Two years later he told his friend Paul-Jean Toulet that the troubles of this period came 'probably to finish me.'

[1] Translation by Maire and Grace O'Brien.

DEBUSSY AND HIS SECOND WIFE, EMMA BARDAC

CHAPTER IX

THE YEARS OF 'DEBUSSYISM'—1904–1913

AT the time of his separation from Lily, Debussy was engaged on some incidental music to *King Lear,* which was about to be produced at the Odéon by Antoine, the great producer of the Théâtre Libre. In January 1904 Debussy promised to have several short pieces ready by October. But at the time of the rehearsals they were far from complete, and *Lear* was given with the music of one Edmond Missa. Of these troubled months we have an illuminating document in a letter of 14th April 1905 to a new friend, the critic Louis Laloy.

You should know how people have deserted me! It is enough to make one sick of every one called a man. I shan't tell you of all that I have gone through. It's ugly and tragic and ironically reminds one of a novel a concierge might read. Morally I have suffered terribly. Have I some forgotten debt to pay to life? I don't know; but often I've had to smile so that no one should see that I was going to cry. So, my dear friend, be assured of my joy on seeing you again. I shall try to bring up the old Claude Debussy you knew. If he is rather care-ridden don't mind, for his affection for you is unshaken.

His new alliance did not begin under very auspicious circumstances. A series of lawsuits started which continued until the end of his life, and indeed long after. In the summer of 1905 he came to England. On 28th August, from the Grand Hotel at Eastbourne, he wrote to Laloy:

It would have been unpardonable to leave Paris without seeing you if my departure had not been a flight. I fled from all that tedious fuss. I fled from myself, who was finally only allowed to think by permission of the usher. I've been here a month. It's a little English seaside place, silly as these places sometimes are. I shall have to go because there are too many draughts and too much music—but I don't quite know where. . . . I am trying somehow to get back to myself. I have written a certain amount of music, as I have not done for quite a time.

After the birth of his daughter in October, Debussy and his family moved into a little house at the end of the Avenue du Bois de Boulogne (now the Avenue Foch), where he lived for the rest of his life. Laloy speaks of the arrival of Claude-Emma, alias Chouchou, as 'the fulfilment of one of his most cherished hopes.' Four years later, on the score of the piano pieces, *Children's Corner,* there appeared the dedication: 'To my dear little Chouchou, with her father's affectionate apologies for what follows.' But one is not to assume that she was an infant prodigy. 'Chouchou' only took piano lessons (from 'a lady in black who looks like a drawing by Odilon Redon') at the age of nine. She died in 1919.[1]

On 15th October *La Mer,* finished at Eastbourne, was conducted by Chevillard at the Concerts Lamoureux. 'The work was awaited in Paris with an impatience that was not kindly disposed,' writes M. Laloy. 'Prudish indignation had not yet been appeased, and on all sides people were ready to make the artist pay dearly for the wrongs that were imputed to the man.' A fierce controversy broke out in the press. A number of critics took advantage of the fact that the work marked a new phase in Debussy's development to maintain an attitude that was definitely hostile. Pierre Lalo, in *Le Temps,* concluded his derogatory report with the words: 'I neither hear, nor see, nor feel the sea.' And Gaston Carraud wrote in *La Liberté:* 'It is certainly genuine Debussy—that is to say, the most individual, the most precious, and the most

[1] Lily Debussy died in 1932 and Emma Debussy in 1934.

subtle expression of our art—but it almost suggests the possibility that some day we may have an Americanized Debussy.'
On the other side the chief praise came from Louis Laloy and
M. D. Calvocoressi. Debussy was again mercilessly held in
the limelight. Émile Vuillermoz whipped up an excited
controversy between the followers of Debussy and those of
Vincent d'Indy, the director of the Schola Cantorum and
champion of César Franck and the German Romantic composers. The very different art of Ravel was dragged into the
discussions and opposed to 'Debussyism' and 'd'Indyism.'[1]
In 1907 the performance of Paul Dukas's opera, *Ariane et
Barbe-Bleue,* on a libretto of Maeterlinck, provided a fresh
opportunity to attack *Pelléas.*

All this bickering created in Debussy nothing but a feeling
of disgust. His admirers, who made a cult of 'Debussyism'
as previously they had of 'Wagnerism,' regarded him as their
chef d'école, a function he never wished to perform and for which
he was singularly unsuited. In 1908, on the occasion of the
twenty-fifth anniversary of the death of Wagner, he declared
to a journalist, Maurice Leclercq: 'There are no more schools
of music. The main business of musicians to-day is to avoid
any kind of outside influence.' A climax to the controversies
came when the interview in which this statement was made
was published against Debussy's wishes, and a questionnaire
sent to a number of noted people in France and abroad by the
Revue du temps présent. 'Is Debussy the leader of a school?'
the questionnaire said. 'Should he form a school? Is he an
original personality or an accidental phenomenon?'—and so
forth. The replies, together with the interview with Maurice

---

[1] Sometime in the nineties Edmond Bailly predicted to René
Peter: 'You will see, one day they will speak of the Debussyists
and the d'Indyists as once they spoke of the Gluckists and the
Piccinnists.' Debussy, on being informed of this, said simply:
'I only hope no one will ever speak of "d'Indyists."'

Leclercq, were published in a little book called *Le Cas Debussy* by C. Francis Caillard and José de Bérys. It will be sufficient to quote the sarcastic reply of Romain Rolland, signed 'Jean-Christophe':

> I don't like all your modern French music very much and I am not mad about your M. Debussy. But what I can't understand is that, being so poor in artists, you have to quarrel about the greatest one you have.
>
> As for the question of whether he is the leader of a school, and what this school will be worth, one can simply say that every great artist has a school and that all schools are evil. It might then be better if there were no great artists?

Debussy's own feelings on the matter are to be found in a letter of March 1908 to Durand:

> I find these times particularly ungracious in that a lot of noise is made about things of no importance. We have no right to poke fun at American 'bluff' whilst we cultivate this sort of artistic 'bluff' which we shall have to pay for one of these days—and very unpleasant it will be for our French vanity.

Five years later, in a conversation recorded by Mr. Calvo-coressi, 'he declared that, wishing to concentrate upon his own work, he had made it a rule to hear as little music as possible.' Of the evils of premature discussion of young composers he said:

> I consider it almost a crime. The former policy of allowing artists to mature in peace was far sounder. It is wicked to unsettle them by making them the subjects of debates that are, generally, as shallow as they are prejudiced. Hardly does a composer appear when people start devoting essays to him and weighing his music down with ambitious definitions. They do far greater harm than even the fiercest detractors could do.

After *La Mer* the next important work was the series of *Images*, of which there are in all three sets. The two piano

sets are of 1905 and 1907. The orchestral set, first conceived
for two pianos, was begun in 1906 and finished six years
later. It consists of *Ibéria* and *Rondes de printemps* (written
between 1906 and 1909) and *Gigues* (written between 1909
and 1912). During these years Debussy travelled extensively,
conducting his works in foreign towns.

The first journey was to England. In 1907 one T. J.
Guéritte founded in England the *Société des concerts français*
and organized concerts in London, Newcastle, Sheffield and
Leeds. By the initiative of G. Jean-Aubry, to whom, with
his brother-in-law Guéritte, Debussy's early reputation in
England was largely due, the Quartet received its first English
performance at these concerts in December 1907. In February
of the following year Debussy was invited to conduct *L'Après-
midi d'un faune* (which was first played in England at a Ballad
Concert conducted by Sir Henry Wood in 1904) and *La Mer*
at Queen's Hall. Here are some very strange extracts from
the criticism that appeared in *The Times* of 3rd February:

As in all his maturer works, it is obvious that he renounces
melody as definitely as Alberich renounces love: whether the
ultimate object of that renunciation is the same we do not know as
yet. . . . For perfect enjoyment of this music there is no attitude
of mind more to be recommended than the passive, unintelligent
rumination of the typical amateur of the mid-Victorian era. As
long as actual sleep can be avoided, the hearer can derive great
pleasure from the strange sounds that enter his ears, if he will only
put away all idea of definite construction or logical development.
. . . M. Debussy is a master of colouring, and there may be some
good reason for his abandonment of that element of music which
has been considered as the most essential of all from the earliest ages
until now. . . . At all events the practical result of this music is
to make the musician hungry for music that is merely logical and
beautiful, and many regrets were expressed by those who were
obliged to leave the long concert before the Unfinished Symphony.

The following year he came again to London to conduct

the *Nocturnes* and was to have gone to Manchester and Edin-burgh. But he was prevented from doing so by a serious illness. In January of this year, 1909, he became afflicted with cancer. Scarcely more than a fortnight before his visit he was suffering to the extent of having to resort to morphine and cocaine. Of the concert at Queen's Hall he wrote to Durand:

Fêtes was encored and it only depended on me to get an encore for *L'Après-midi d'un faune*. But I was ready to drop—a very bad posture for conducting anything.

To-night I have to go to a reception organized by the Musicians' Club. What sort of a figure will I cut? I shall look like a man condemned to death. I can't get out of it, apparently because of the Entente Cordiale and other sentimental conceptions, most likely calculated to hasten the death of others.

On 21st May 1909 *Pelléas* was performed at Covent Garden. Debussy came to supervise the rehearsals, but did not attend the performance.

They demanded the composer for a quarter of an hour [he wrote to Durand], but he was peacefully reposing at his hotel suspecting no such glory. Cleofonte Campanini [the conductor] was twice recalled and telephoned me that the opera had an enormous *souccès*, such as had rarely been known in England. He came to see me the next morning to tell me about it in his Punchinello manner and embraced me as if I were some medal blessed by the Pope.

The Times spoke of it as the work which had provoked the most discussion in recent times—'excepting of course the works of Richard Strauss'—and praised 'a hand almost as certain as Wagner's own.' From this time on, Debussy gained great popularity in England, and English musicians began to take into serious account developments in France. The first book on Debussy was, in fact, by an Englishwoman, Mrs. Franz Liebich. It appeared in 1908.

In 1910 in Vienna and Budapest, in 1911 in Turin (where

he met Elgar [1] and Strauss) and in 1913 in Moscow and St. Petersburg, Debussy was invited to conduct his works. He undertook these tours primarily to meet financial exigencies, for conducting had little appeal for him. 'It's amusing,' he told Paul-Jean Toulet, 'while you seek out the colours with the end of the little stick; but after a time it's like an exhibition, and the greeting from the audience is not very different from the greeting a showman at a circus gets.' Nor was he an inspiring conductor. At Turin it became necessary for the Italian conductor, Vittorio Gui, to take over the rehearsals. 'At the concert,' Gui writes, 'Debussy conducted as well as he could, but without any feeling or control; and the audience remained unimpressed.' After the journey to Vienna he wrote to Durand: 'I am not the composer to take my wares abroad. You are required to have the heroism of a travelling salesman.'

In 1910 he conducted *Rondes de printemps* at the Concerts Durand in Paris. *Ibéria* had been given some days previously by Gabriel Pierné. The reception was again hostile and led to the same futile bickering among the critics. This was also the year of the first set of *Préludes* for piano and of the songs, *Le Promenoir des deux amants* and *Ballades de Villon*. Alluding to the lines of Villon:

> Ung temps viendra qui fera desséicher,
> Jaulnir, flestrir vostre espanie fleur,[2]

---

[1] There is unfortunately no record of Debussy's opinion of Elgar. Most likely he never heard his music. But he did know one English musician well whom he greatly admired: that was Sullivan. On 10th September 1909 Debussy wrote to T. J. Guéritte: 'You may be assured of my greatest sympathy with your plan to establish a Society for British Music in Paris, and you may certainly make use of my name in whatever way you please.' As far as I know this society never materialized.

[2] Shall come a time when your bloom will have gone:
And sear, and dry, your beauty's flow'r turn.
From the translation by Nita Cox.

he says in a letter to Durand: 'To-day I received the *Ballades*. They are perfect, although I should like the parchment to have been more yellow. But a time will come when it will have withered—and the music too. Anyhow, the edition is pretty.' The despair is sad. A week later, on 25th September, he writes: 'I am in a period of disquietude—rather like someone waiting for a train in a dark waiting-room. I have a desire to go no matter where and at the same time a fear of going away. I need a lot of patience to put up with myself.'

On 22nd May 1911 *Le Martyre de saint Sébastien,* a new dramatic work of Debussy's, was given at the Théâtre du Châtelet. The text was a miracle-play by Gabriele d'Annunzio. Whereas the composition of *Pelléas* was spread over ten years, *Le Martyre de saint Sébastien* was written in a few weeks, the work having been commissioned for immediate production by Ida Rubinstein, who played the part of the Saint. In the circumstances the score could only be hurriedly sketched out and most of the orchestration was entrusted to the conductor, André Caplet. Moreover, during the period of its composition Debussy was in a very bad state of health. The last bars were sent to Durand a month only before the performance, with the words: 'I admit that I'm not displeased with it. But, as I've told you several times, I'm at the end of my tether.'

The Archbishop of Paris censured the production— ostensibly for the presentation of a saint on the stage, but possibly also for the incursion of Debussy into the realm of quasi-sacred music. As a dramatic work it was a failure and as such it was never revived in France. From the following letter of July 1911 to Durand we can imagine Debussy's disheartenment:

Truth to tell, *Le Martyre de saint Sébastien* tired me out more than I imagined and the journey to Turin finished me. That is how we pay for things in this life. They used to say: 'Don't force your talent,' which simply means, Don't hurry. You are quite right, my dear friend, to like your country house so. Everything is so temporary in life that to live in the house in which you played as a child and grew up, must be very lovely and something I feel the lack of very sadly at my age. This doesn't sound very American nor very modern, but very sincere and very 'Vieille France.'

The following year Maud Allan commissioned him to write a short music-hall number, an Egyptian ballet to be called *Khamma*. The piano score was again hurriedly sketched out and the orchestration entrusted to Charles Koechlin. But this work was not completed until after Debussy's death. The same year (1912) the score of *Gigues* (the first part of the *Images* for orchestra) was finished by André Caplet and given at the Concerts Colonne in January 1913. Debussy then undertook to write a children's ballet, *Boîte à joujoux,* the scenario of which was by André Hellé. This again remained unfinished and was completed only some ten years later by Caplet. Debussy had apparently not the strength or the interest to complete these works himself.

The last of his stage works was the ballet, *Jeux,* the scenario and choreography of which were by Nijinsky. Debussy (like Stravinsky) had no respect for Nijinsky as a producer, and one can only assume that he consented to collaborate with him for material reasons. When, in 1912, Nijinsky produced for Diaghilev a ballet on the music of *L'Après-midi d'un faune,* Debussy scornfully wrote to Godet:

Nijinsky's perverse genius is entirely devoted to peculiar mathematical processes. The man adds up demisemiquavers with his feet and proves the result with his arms. Then, as if suddenly stricken with partial paralysis, he stands listening to the music with a most baleful eye. . . . It is ugly; Dalcrozian in fact.[1]

---

[1] Translation by Maire and Grace O'Brien. Those who are interested in the scandal that followed Nijinsky's choreography for *L'Après-midi* (Stravinsky maintains that it was Bakst who was really responsible for this choreography) will find a detailed account

Debussy

Jeux was performed by Diaghilev's Russian Ballet in 1913 in the same year as Stravinsky's *Le Sacre du printemps* and a year later than Ravel's *Daphnis et Chloé*. It was not one of Diaghilev's most successful productions. In the summer of 1913 appeared the songs, *Soupir, Placet futile* and *Éventail*, on the poems of Mallarmé. Writing to Durand of playing them over to a friend, Debussy says: 'We were sorry—the songs and I—that you didn't hear them. Moments such as these are lovely—but God knows how rare!'

What was at heart the cause of this unhappy state of mind? There is no doubt that after *La Mer*, just when one would have expected Debussy to enter into full possession of his powers, his works show a pitiful decline. The old idealism had gone. At the age of thirty he threw to the winds a collaboration with Catulle Mendès, in *Rodrigue et Chimène*, that would have solved all his material worries; at the age of fifty he burdened himself with commissions from people for whom he had little or no artistic respect. In the words of Ernest Newman, the works of the last years 'showed many signs of something like a collapse.' Some deep-seated trouble has to be accounted for.

Two causes have been suggested by those who recognize this decline: one, that he was largely incapacitated by illness, and the other, that he was unable to stand the glare of publicity. Both are reasonable. Debussy's friends have all maintained that he suffered physically more than he showed. In the letters to Durand references to the inroads made by

---

in *Nijinsky,* by Romola Nijinsky (London, 1933). One result was that Rodin, Nijinsky's champion, was maintained for the rest of his life in the Hôtel Biron, which after his death became the Musée Rodin. Mme Nijinsky rather naïvely says that Debussy 'was delighted with the sensation that *Faune* created,' and that he was 'enthusiastic at the idea of collaborating with Nijinsky on a new composition.'

his cancer are frequent. As for the second explanation, if there is any need to give further evidence of this great esoteric's revulsion from publicity a remark may be quoted which, in the literature on Debussy, is famous. 'I say, Claude,' said René Peter the last time they met, 'the Debussyists are getting on my nerves.' 'They're killing me!' Debussy replied.

These are important things to consider in the character of a man who was not what is conventionally called strong-minded. But they do not explain everything. When Debussy told his friend Toulet that the troubles following his flight from Lily 'came probably to finish me,' and when, in 1910, he told Durand 'I have a desire to go no matter where and at the same time a fear of going away,' we may be allowed to suspect a cause of his unhappiness in the relationship with his second wife. If, some day, the correspondence with Lily at the time of his divorce and the dossiers of his numerous lawsuits are made public it may be possible to investigate this strange and pitiful period in the life of a great artist. Some idea of the inner nature of his life during the later years, however, may be had from a work of fiction. In 1908 Henry Bataille published a play called *La Femme nue,* the plot of which is based on the story of Debussy's divorce. It is a work of fiction, yet the situations tally so well with what one would conceive of the affair from the few hints that have been given out, that I will quote a few lines. This is how Pierre Bernier (a painter impersonating Debussy) describes his feelings for the Princesse de Chabran (impersonating Mme Bardac):

Don't think it's your luxury that befuddles me. It's the harmony of the setting. From a painter's point of view, just look at the quality of your linen, not too white, nor too much colour, against the mat colour of your skin. It's unbelievable. There's inspiration! One must be a Narcissus and know oneself as you do to care for everything like this. Love in such surroundings must be a bit of heaven. The harmony is complete. All the senses are transported. . . .

Note the shallow immediateness of these sentiments. Paul Dukas has said that Debussy was particularly sensitive to the decorative side of his love affairs. But there must have come a time when he perhaps noticed the lack of some deeper emotions. Between Pierre Bernier and the Princesse de Chabran there is only a desire for immediate gratification, and, on her part, selfishness and snobbery. One of her passages contains a strange comparison:

I don't know that I haven't failed in life. What are you laughing at? You're mistaken. You don't understand me. I was really made for art. I should have realized some great dream, with my millions, like Ludwig II—only more tastefully. But you wouldn't have been big enough. You were a little *bourgeois*. What did you marry that woman for? She isn't worthy of you.

When finally Bernier resolves to leave his wife, Loulou (i.e. Lily) warns her successor: 'Ah, he wasn't always the *chic* gentleman that you know.' Debussy a '*chic* gentleman'? One has only to note the bloated, dull look he had in middle age to realize that he did not long remain one.

At the end of his fifty-first year he was ill and worried; and the growing disillusionment of these later years turned to despondency. Morally, the four years of the war came to demolish him.

CHAPTER X

THE WAR—1914–1918

THE war broke out in the first days of August 1914. Mallarmé had been dead sixteen years; Verlaine had died a drunkard and a vagabond; Rimbaud, before his death, had become a business man; Huysmans had retreated to the Trappists. Romain Rolland's John-Christopher could hear 'in the distance the rumbling of cannon, coming to batter down that worn-out civilization, that perishing little Greece.' That perishing little Greece! It was gone long ago for Debussy.

On 8th August 1914 he sent this note to Durand:

My DEAR JACQUES,

Your letter has reassured me and I am really glad to have got your news.

You know that I have no *sang-froid* and certainly nothing of the army spirit. I've never had a rifle in my hands. My recollections of 1870 and the anxiety of my wife, whose son and son-in-law are in the army, prevent me from becoming very enthusiastic.

All this makes my life intense and troubled. I am just a poor little atom crushed in this terrible cataclysm. What I am doing seems so wretchedly small. I've got to the state of envying Satie who, as a corporal, is really going to defend Paris.

And so, my dear Jacques, if you have any work that you can give me, do not forget me. Forgive me for counting on you, but you are really all I have.

Your devoted,
C. D.

In the next letter, of 18th August, there is more determination. My age and fitness allow me at most to guard a fence,' he writes, 'but if, to assure victory, they are absolutely in need of another face to be bashed in, I'll offer mine without question.'

Then began a period of unproductiveness. 'It is almost impossible to work,' he writes. 'To tell the truth one hardly dares to, for the asides of the war are more distressing than one imagines.' During the first year of the war he edited the *Valses* and the *Polonaises* of Chopin which Durand's brought out to replace the German editions, and published the *Six Épigraphes antiques* for piano duet. (According to a discovery of Léon Vallas these were originally sketches for certain further *Chansons de Bilitis*, written about 1900.) The only new work written between the summers of 1914 and 1915 was the *Berceuse héroïque* composed for *King Albert's Book* and inscribed to the King of the Belgians and his soldiers.

The summer of 1915 was spent at Pourville, near Dieppe. In June he was seized with a sudden determination to work and produced, in rapid succession, the *Douze Études* for piano; the pieces for two pianos entitled *En blanc et noir*, inspired by the greys of Velasquez; and two Sonatas, one for cello and piano and the other for flute, viola and harp. At the beginning of October he wrote to Durand:

I am enjoying these last days of liberty. I think of Paris as a sort of prison where one has not even the right to think and where even the walls have ears. . . . I am writing down all the music that comes into my head—like a madman, and rather sadly too. Now the curtains have gone from the windows and when I see a trunk it makes me feel as sad as a cat. . . .

Earlier he had written: 'I want to work, not so much for myself, but to give proof, however small it may be, that even if there were thirty million Boches French thought will not be destroyed.'

On the title-page of the Sonatas, under the composer's name appeared the words, *musicien français*. Were they not then superfluous? One's regret is that they were not ascribed to the

98

Debussy who valiantly strove for the independence of French
music in the early nineties.

On his return to Paris his cancer took a turn for the worse.
At the very end of 1915 one further composition was written,
the charming song, *Noël des enfants qui n'ont plus de maisons,*
the words of which were suggested to Debussy by the horrible
devastations in France and Belgium. Then an operation
became necessary. From this time on he was a sick man.
He became thinner and gradually lost strength. The following
summer was spent at Le Moulleau-Arcachon and the summer
of 1917 at Saint-Jean-de-Luz. His unhappy state of mind
during these years may best be judged from the following
extracts from his letters to Durand:

Paris, *8th June* 1916.

The sick man again thanks you for your friendly inquiries. As
the days go by I must admit that I am losing patience. I have been
tried too long. I wonder whether this illness isn't incurable? I
might as well be told at once. 'Alors! Oh! Alors!' as poor
Golaud cries.

Life has become too hard, and Claude Debussy, writing no more
music, has no longer any reason to exist. I have no hobbies. They
never taught me anything but music. That wouldn't matter if I
wrote a great deal; but to tap on an empty head is disrespectful.

Le Moulleau-Arcachon,

16th October 1916.

Le Moulleau has not been able to help me and I shall not bring
back any masterpieces. I might have a few sketches to be used
later. I have never found hotel life so unpleasant. Even the walls
are hostile—not to speak of this life in a numbered box.

Yesterday I had a visit from X. He made me sorry for a moment
that I had ever written a sonata and made me doubtful of my own
writing. Well, no doubt there are bad musicians everywhere.
But this incident very much disturbed me. It means a great deal,
and I shall no longer be surprised at the lack of understanding my

poor music meets with. . . . It was frightening. Why wasn't I taught to polish eye-glasses, like Spinoza? I should never have expected to earn my living by music.

SAINT-JEAN-DE-LUZ,
22nd July 1917.

Up till now I've been horribly tired. My last illness has left me with an aversion to doing anything. There are mornings when dressing is like one of the twelve labours of Hercules and I don't know what I expect—a revolution or an earthquake—so that I shan't have to go on. But without being unduly pessimistic, mine is a hard life. I have to fight against illness and against myself I feel a nuisance to every one.

The piano and violin Sonata was completed in the early spring of 1917. It was his last work. During the previous winter a big choral work, *Ode à la France,* was sketched out on a libretto by Laloy, but was left incomplete. 'Do not be grieved,' he wrote to Godet in most beautiful terms of mingled despair and pity, 'if I no longer write to you of my plans There is no reason to weep if music forsakes me. I cannot help it. And I have never forced any one to love me.'

On 5th May 1917 he appeared on a concert platform in Paris for the last time. With Gaston Poulet he played the piano and violin Sonata. André Suarès, who saw him at a concert a few weeks before, was struck by his absent expression and extreme lassitude.

His complexion was the colour of melted wax or of ashes [Suarès writes]. In his eyes there was no feverish flame, but the dull reflections of silent pools. There was not even bitterness in his gloomy smile. . . . His fat, plump hand, like the hand of a priest, hung from his arm, his arm from his shoulder and his head from his body. . . . As he sat down, his eyes, under their flickering lids, moved slowly round, like those of people who would see without being seen, who steal a glance at something they seem only half to see.

At the beginning of 1918 he was confined to his house.

His features became hollowed out [writes Louis Laloy] and his look grew dull. He had first to stay in his room, then in bed. 'Always in bed, in bed!' he used to say despairingly. At the Opéra they were rehearsing *Castor et Pollux,* given on 21st March in the afternoon, for in the evening there was the fear of raids. One of his last regrets was not to be able to go. 'Remember me to Monsieur Castor,' he said feebly, trying to smile as I went off.

The bombardment of Paris by long-range weapon started on Saturday, 23rd March. During those last days he heard the dreadful sound of the shells exploding in the streets. By this time he was too weak to be carried down to the cellar. He died on Monday, 25th March, at ten o'clock in the evening.

The funeral took place on the following Thursday.

I can see as in a bad dream [Laloy writes] the coffin near the piano and the musicians in their soldiers' uniforms. . . . The door kept on opening and closing and there was no more room for the flowers. The Minister of Education took his place at the head of the procession. Side by side, in front of me, the two conductors of our great philharmonic societies, Camille Chevillard and Gabriel Pierné, walked in silence. All those concerts in which they had taken care of his music were over. The sky was overcast. There was a rumbling in the distance. Was it a storm or the explosion of a shell? Along the wide avenues there was nothing to be seen but military trucks. The people on the pavements pressed ahead hurriedly. But there was still a bustle in the populous uphill streets of Montmartre. The children made way and stood in a line in the gutter and stared at us. The shopkeepers questioned each other at their doors and glanced at the streamers on the wreaths. 'Il paraît que c'était un musicien,' they said.

By the time the procession reached the cemetery of Père-Lachaise, half of the fifty-odd people who had started out from the Avenue du Bois de Boulogne had made off on the way. Only one oration was made, for the grave times, it was held, made such orations superfluous. Some time later the body was removed to the cemetery at Passy.

CHAPTER XI

THE ABANDONED OPERAS—1902-1918

AFTER the production of *Pelléas* Debussy contemplated or began no fewer than five other operas. They were: *Comme il vous plaira* (*As You Like It*), which was first suggested to him at the Villa Medici and which he kept at the back of his mind till the end of his life; two stage works on tales by Edgar Allan Poe, *Le Diable dans le beffroi* (*The Devil in the Belfry*) and *La Chute de la maison Usher* (*The Fall of the House of Usher*), the librettos of which Debussy adapted himself; a *Tristan*; and an *Orpheus*. None of these materialized.

Debussy's *Tristan* was to be based on *La Légende de Tristan* by Joseph Bédier. The project dates from 1907. In a letter to Durand of 23rd August Debussy enclosed this little note:

One of the 363 themes of the ROMAN DE TRISTAN

A month later, on 25th September, he wrote: 'On Monday Mourey [1] passed the day with me. We worked and discussed and I think we have got hold of something good. You will excuse my not having come to see you on account of *Tristan*.'

[1] Gabriel Mourey, who was to have arranged Bédier's *Tristan*.

This is all that is known of this attempt, 'whose episodical character,' writes Vallas, 'would have been related to the tales of chivalry' and 'diametrically opposed' to the Germanic conception of Wagner.

The text of *Orphée-roi* was specially written by Victor Ségalen. It would have been as different from Gluck's *Orfeo* as the *Tristan* from Wagner's. When *Iphigénie en Aulide* was performed at the Opéra in 1903 Debussy wrote in the paper *Gil Blas,* an 'Open Letter to M. le Chevalier C. W. Gluck,' condemning Gluck in favour of Rameau and maintaining that it was Gluck who propagated 'the germs of the Wagnerian formulae.' Judging from a conversation with Ségalen, he seemed to have little more regard for *Orfeo.* 'Gluck's *Orfeo* is only the sentimental side of the legend,' he said. 'Orpheus was not a man, nor any human being, living or dead. Orpheus is the Desire to hear and to be heard. Orpheus is the symbol of Power in the world of sound.' (Can one not see in those words, tinged as they may be by a certain prevalent chauvinism, the composer who conceived music as an expression of 'the naked flesh of emotion'?[1]) Victor Ségalen's *Orphée-roi* was published in 1921, but no music by Debussy is known to exist. According to Vallas, the work was to have been mainly choral.

The first mention of *Comme il vous plaira* is in a letter from Bichain, of the summer of 1902, addressed to the poet, Paul-Jean Toulet:

I would like to have news of *Comme il vous plaira.* I'm continually thinking of it and would like to think of it with you in my mind. I am working very hard at doing nothing. . . .

By October Toulet had submitted certain sketches.

Now let us talk of good Monsieur William [Debussy wrote eagerly]. The second plan you sent me suits me in every way.

---

[1] From a letter to Robert Godet.

Don't you think we might heighten the interest of the first scene by
the introduction of a choir off-stage which would comment on the
various incidents of Orlando's wrestle? They would have exclama-
tions to sing such as 'He's down! No, he's not! Ah! He's
no coward!' But, all joking apart, I think that musically it will
be quite original. And I would like to have some of the songs
sung by a group of people. The duke is rich enough to have the
Chanteurs de Saint-Gervais [a well-known choral society] and
their conductor come to the Forest of Arden. We must find some
pretty ceremonial for the betrothal and have it all end happily.
Whenever you can replace the exact word by its lyrical counterpart
don't hesitate. That doesn't mean that the tone in which the two
scenes are written doesn't please me. Quite the contrary. I suggest
it because of your fear of being too rhythmical. . . .

I have an idea which I offer to you for what it is worth. Couldn't
we use the scene between Charles the wrestler and Oliver (Shakespeare scene i) as an introduction?

Send me everything you can before you leave. I'm convinced
we've got hold of something really admirable.

Four days later he again wrote enthusiastically of the betrothal
scene, in which 'wonderfully clothed people would appear to
clearly marked rhythms and would announce the entry of
Orlando's Rosalind—all this intermingled with chants in the
ancient style, that is to say, describing the action.' But all
these plans came to nothing. Toulet left for Tongking in
Indo-China and the project was abandoned.

Fifteen years later, in 1917, Gémier having produced *The
Merchant of Venice* at the Odéon, Debussy suggested an *As
You Like It*. But it was again Toulet who failed him. 'I
distrust Gémier,' Toulet wrote to Mme Debussy. 'I rather
think that, like Antoine, he is afflicted with "chexpyrite"
and wants a severely literal translation.' Debussy implored
him to see the play from Gémier's viewpoint.

Like poor Mélisande [he wrote], 'je ne fais pas ce que je veux,'
which is indeed the greatest punishment. You imagine Gémier

to be too much of a disciple of Shakespeare. If only you knew the translation of *The Merchant of Venice* you would be reassured. All Gémier wants is to use his gifts as a producer and to make his crowds move about. *As You Like It* will not be of much use to him for this. But he'll find some means of doing what he wants, you may be sure. If necessary he'll make the theatre attendants act or have the people in the stalls go and change places with the people in the balcony. But without any pointless jokes, I believe you could do *As You Like It*.

From a letter to Durand of November 1917 it appears that Toulet and Gémier came to some agreement. But, again, nothing is known of any music by Debussy. In a private collection there exists Toulet's manuscript version in which Debussy has underlined every word that seemed to him too direct and which was to be replaced by its 'lyrical equivalent.'

During that same summer of 1902 came the first ideas for *Le Diable dans le beffroi*. To Messager Debussy wrote:

There's something to be got from this tale in which reality and fantasy are so happily combined. The devil is much more ironic and cruel than the traditional sort of red clown. I want to destroy the idea of the devil as the spirit of evil. He is rather the spirit of contradiction.

In 1903 the libretto was 'practically finished.'

As for the people who are so kind as to think that I'll never get beyond *Pelléas* [he comments], they can't see further than their noses. They evidently don't know that if that were the case I should immediately begin growing pine-apples. For the worst thing one can do is to reproduce what one has already done. Most likely these same people will find it scandalous that I should abandon the shadowy Mélisande for the irony of the devil.

What could reveal better the saturnine recluse on the one hand, shy and highly introspective, and on the other the cynic labouring under a screen of bristling irony, than the choice, first of *Pelléas et Mélisande* and then of *The Devil in the Belfry*?

The theory that a composer reveals himself in his choice of a libretto is nowhere so strikingly illustrated as here. In the letters to Durand *Le Diable* is referred to in 1906 and again, and for the last time, in 1911. It appears that the devil was only to have whistled, while the music of the crowd, unlike that in the *Meistersinger* or in *Boris,* was to have been very fluid. (In a letter to Godet Debussy speaks of the music he has written as a 'sly cheating of the ear.')

La Chute de la maison Usher was begun in 1908 and had not been discarded when the composer died. Here are the references in the letters to Durand.

June 1908.

These last days I have been working hard on *La Chute de la maison Usher.* . . . There are moments when I lose the feeling of things around me and if the sister of Roderick Usher were to come into my house I shouldn't be very surprised.

July 1909.

I have almost finished a long monologue of poor Roderick. It almost makes the stones weep. The mustiness is charmingly rendered by contrasting the low notes of the oboe with harmonics of the violin. . . . Don't speak of this to any one; I think a great deal of it.

July 1910.

I spend my existence in the House of Usher. . . . and leave it with my nerves as taut as the strings of a violin.

July 1911.

I am afraid the charms of Houlgate may not be sufficient to let me forget the Usher family.

September 1912.

Although very tired [*Jeux* was just completed] I have gone back to my old work. I like it well enough to get new strength from it. At least that is what I am hoping.

In 1916 he completely recast the libretto and the following

year sent it to Durand. This curious note to Godet must be of 1917 from Saint-Jean-de-Luz:

This house has a curious resemblance to the House of Usher. Although I haven't the mind troubles of Roderick, nor his passion for the last thought of C. M. von Weber,[1] we are alike in our super-sensitiveness. . . . On this point I could tell you things that would make your beard fall off, which would be most unpleasant—not for your beard but for me, who don't like attracting attention.

The history of these unfinished works brings us to consider several points. There is no actual record of music having been written for *Comme il vous plaira,* nor for *Orphée-roi.* Possibly he never got as far as writing the music. But what has become of the music for the two works of Poe which, between them, occupied him during the whole of his later life? In a footnote to a letter referring to the music for *Lear,* Durand says: 'If the rest of this incidental music was written the composer must either have destroyed it or used it in other works.' Could he similarly have utilized the chorus of *Le Diable dans le beffroi* in *Le Martyre de saint Sébastien* or *Jeux*? It is unlikely—although in the practice of incorporating sketches for one work in the body of another Debussy would not have lacked precedents. (Berlioz, for all his adherence to a pro-gramme 'as the spoken text of an opera, inspiring the character and expression of the music,' thought nothing of using for the *idée fixe* of his *Symphonie fantastique* a theme borrowed from a discarded cantata written for the *Prix de Rome.* And that was the theme symbolizing Harriet Smithson!)

We know that an unpublished scene of *La Chute de la maison Usher* is in a private collection. But is this all that was written of this work during nine years? Speaking of the later unfinished works in a letter to René Peter, Albert Carré

[1] Allusion to this passage in *The Fall of the House of Usher*: 'Among other things I hold painfully in mind a certain singular perversion and amplification of the wild air of the last waltz of von Weber.'

says: 'I am sure that the bitter memories Debussy had of the dress rehearsal of *Pelléas et Melisande* were in some way account-able for the lack of courage he subsequently showed and the doubts that obsessed him.'[1] The experience of *Pelléas* may have increased his natural diffidence, but it does not account for it. It was in Debussy's nature to dwell on, and to think round, an idea, but less often to carry an idea to an end. From the two years at Rome, *Diane au bois* started the long list of un-finished or discarded works, and it is perhaps only as he would have wished that his last two big works should remain un-finished and unknown. Certainly he lacked no assurance that they would be performed, for in 1908 he sold the rights of production to Gatti-Casazza, of the Metropolitan Opera of New York. It was only with difficulty that Debussy was persuaded to sign an agreement, for there existed then barely more than the sketch of the librettos. As Gatti-Casazza left, Debussy made it quite clear that he felt under no obligation. 'Do not forget,' he said, 'that I am a lazy composer and that I sometimes require weeks to decide on one harmonious chord in preference to another. Remember also that you are the one who insisted on making this agreement and that probably you will not receive anything!'

'Define one's aims? Finish works?' we hear M. Croche, the imaginary interlocutor of Debussy's journalistic essays, sardonically querying. 'These are questions of childish vanity. . . .'

---

[1] In this letter Carré mentions that Debussy thought of writing a *Don Juan*.

DEBUSSY (*right*), AND LOUIS LALOY FLYING A KITE

WORK

CHAPTER XII

THE SONGS

'THOSE who had the greatest influence on Debussy,' Paul Dukas once said, 'were not the musicians but the poets.' The truth of this is illustrated in the songs. Indeed, Debussy is above all the poets' musician.

The earliest of the known songs are *Nuit d'étoiles* (1876), *Beau Soir* and *Fleur des blés* (both 1878). Léon Vallas is inclined to question these dates, and, if they were correct, we should have to note an extraordinary facility in one who had hardly begun the study of harmony. A facility, but no individual musical feeling. The dominant spirit is Massenet at his most mawkish. In the first there is an unmistakable allusion to 'Mon cœur s'ouvre à ta voix,' the well-known aria from Saint-Saëns's *Samson et Dalila*.[1] *Beau Soir* is the best of the three, and for those who can appreciate the old-fashioned sentimentality of Paul Bourget's poem—'At sunset when the river-banks are rose-coloured and a warm breeze runs over the cornfields . . .'—the setting is charming. The melodic line is delicately shaped and one can see in the accompaniment the beginnings of that fluid, transparent texture that later becomes so characteristic. Debussy published this song only a year before beginning *Pelléas*.

The next songs are those written at the time of his association with Mme von Meck, or shortly after, when he was in Guiraud's composition class at the Conservatoire. They are still very derivative. One can get some idea of *La Belle au bois dormant*

[1] The fact that this work was only published in Paris in 1877 brings further doubt to the question of dates.

III

from the picture on the cover. It is a drawing of a full-busted lady with a brooch in the shape of a lyre. She is against a dense wood and birds are flying in the distance. Like the music, the words for which are by E. Vincent Hypsa, the poet of the Montmartre cabaret, *Le Chat noir,* it reflects the popular artistic taste of the day. In this song Debussy uses the popular round, *Nous n'irons plus au bois,* which he introduces some twenty years later into *Jardins sous la pluie* and again towards the end of his life in *Rondes de printemps.* In another song of this period, *Paysage sentimental,* one can discern the influence of Borodin. It is noticeable in this passage:

But this early Russian influence was without any far-reaching effect on the vocal music. In other early songs there are passages reminiscent of some warm lyrical air by Massenet or Gounod which are far more characteristic.

Of this same period (1880–3) are *Pantomime, Fantoches* and *Mandoline.* These are the first of the series of songs on texts from Verlaine's *Fêtes galantes,*[1] a set of poems which describe with delicate satire the eighteenth-century scenes in the pictures of Watteau and Fragonard. Debussy's settings are little gems in a tart style not unlike the music of Ravel, or even the lighter fantastic music of Berlioz. In spite of the difference of scene, *Mandoline* reminds one of the serenade of Mephistopheles in Berlioz's *Damnation de Faust.* Not that Debussy was consciously affected by this work. But one notices in the two pieces the same pointedness in the melodic line, the same stringent harmony, the same lightness of touch. One can imagine, for instance, that Berlioz would have highly approved of such a passage as this:

Sous les ra-mu-res chan-teu

---

[1] Only *Fantoches,* however, appears in one of the two sets of Debussy's songs of this title. It was published in 1903 and dedicated then to a Mme Lucien Fontaine, though it was written originally for Mme Vasnier. *Mandoline* was published separately and *Pantomime* appeared in a supplement to *La Revue musicale* for May 1926.

Then there is another quality which establishes a lineage between Berlioz and Debussy, namely, their common disregard for that type of thematic development which Mozart perfected and which reaches its apogee in Beethoven. When we come to consider the piano and chamber music we shall see that Debussy's themes never really grow. At first sight the opening line of *Fantoches*:

seems to contain a number of dissimilar elements and one may wonder what kind of a medley to expect. But somehow, as with Berlioz, an impulse carries the thing through and there is no lack of unity.

Fantoches and *Mandoline* are the most popular songs which Debussy wrote while still at the Conservatoire. One other early Verlaine song, *Chevaux de bois,* deserves to be placed with them. This realistic illustration of a roundabout, with its whirling arpeggios, unusual modulations and ironic touches of sweet-and-sourness, is not very far from Moussorgsky. But at the Villa Medici Debussy decided to have done with this early manner. Was he perhaps thinking of these first Verlaine songs when he wrote to Émile Baron that 'the public has had enough of cavatinas and *pantalonnades*'? He told Vasnier that the songs he wrote at the Villa Medici were 'like the song of Marlborough.' He regarded them as failures and they have disappeared.

Vallas has fixed the date of the *Cinq Poèmes de Baudelaire* as 1887–9. This was roughly the time, it will be remembered, of the journeys to Bayreuth. And, indeed, the reader who follows the songs in chronological order and comes upon the high-flown declaiming in *Le Balcon,* the first of the group, sees immediately that Debussy has here entered upon a radically new phase. The phrases are longer and meatier. The accompaniment is so laden that it might be an arrangement of an orchestral score. And the form depends principally on the use of a recurring motive—a *Leitmotiv*! Yet *Le Balcon* is by no means a blind imitation of Wagner. If any one wishes to see the transition from Wagner to Debussy he can do no better than study this song. How unmistakably Wagnerian this *Leitmotiv* is:

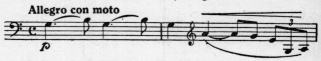

And how unmistakably Debussyan this treatment of it:

Then there are patches of quiet intimacy—an intimacy that Wagner never knew. Such a passage as that quoted on page 118, for instance, which might well pass unnoticed in some corner of the Wagnerian panorama, opens a lovely glimpse into the future Debussy. *La Mort des amants,* written a short time previously, has the same luxurious texture, though the highly imaginative poem:

> Un soir fait de rose et de bleu mystique,
> Nous échangerons un éclair unique,

lends itself less to a characteristically Wagnerian treatment. The music has some of the feeling of a Pre-Raphaelite painting. *Harmonie du soir,* concentrated and passionate, has still a good deal of Wagner, and so has *Recueillement,* the opening bars of which recall strikingly the horns of *Tristan.* The most beautiful of the set is *Le Jet d'eau.* What is remarkable here is the way in which the arpeggios, which suggest 'a sheaf of water,' are worked into the accompaniment of the intensely erotic lines which follow. The music is of a still and lovely sweetness; the texture is clearer, the sentiment finer. In this important

Debussy

La nuit s'é - pais - sis - sait ain - si qu'u - ne cloi - son

sempre dolcissimo

118

group of songs *Le Jet d'eau* marks the end of the Wagnerian domination and, compared to *Le Balcon*, shows the distance travelled in that Paris world of Wagnerism in the course of the years 1888 and 1889.

Still, a Wagnerian treatment suits these poems from Baude-laire's *Fleurs du mal* very well. It is proper, one feels, that Baudelaire and Debussy should have come together through the agency of Wagner; and there is reason to think that Debussy might have thought as much himself, for a con-temporary group of songs on poems of Verlaine shows no influence of Wagner at all. The Baudelaire songs are all crimson and purple; these Verlaine songs, commonly known as the *Ariettes oubliées*,[1] have the soft shades of a water-colour. Here, in *C'est l'extase*, to take the first in the set, is a manner that even those who are little acquainted with Debussy's music will immediately recognize:

---

[1] Published under this title in 1903. Three of the poems are from Verlaine's *Romances sans paroles*; the remaining three are from his *Paysages belges* and *Aquarelles*. The six songs were published separately in 1888.

It is the Debussy of the chords of the ninth. In this case it is
one chord of the ninth which, by subtle harmonic devices,
is spread over eight bars. Here is nothing complicated,
nothing rhetorical. The whole song is founded on a bit
of harmony.

> C'est l'extase langoureuse,
> C'est la fatigue amoureuse.

How well those lines suit Debussy! As he said of his
improvisations at the Conservatoire, this song is a 'feast
for the ear.' *Il pleure dans mon cœur* (one of the numerous
poems of the Symbolists called *Spleen,* but not to be mistaken
for the other *Spleen* of this group) is written to words that
are very much of the day before yesterday. Verlaine was a
lovely, a great poet, but the lines:

> For a heart full of pain
> Faintly patters the rain,[1]

would bring a smile from a sentimental schoolgirl. However,
the song is charming, as no one will deny. It is the first of
what may be called Debussy's 'water-pieces,' a genre much

[1] From the translation by M. D. Calvocoressi.

favoured by French musicians of before the war, who were very apt to find inspiration in rain, lakes, ponds and running water.[1] So striking a peculiarity of modern music did these 'water-pieces' seem to one critic that he announced a lecture on *La Musique aquatique*. And then . . . Well, as the lecturer began to speak—he was an old man and obliged to hold his paper very near—he was annoyed by clicking and popping sounds. He decided to make a complaint and put down his paper. As he looked down from his dais he saw that each member of his high-spirited audience had put up his umbrella.

The song that catches most surely the strange perfume of Verlaine's poetry is the one called *Green*. What quiet warmth there is in the play of 4–8 against 6–8 time—nothing that was not done a hundred times before, but never with such sweet effect as this:

---

[1] There is a charming note of Mallarmé to Debussy in which, excusing a delay, he says: 'I didn't put aside *Le Faune,* which of course you came to get; but suddenly, yesterday, as I saw the water flowing, I thought of it. Why?'

à vos pieds re-po - sé - e

And what of those warmly stressed low notes at the end while
the piano rounds off with a cadence, slyly sentimental in the
manner of some air from an *opéra-comique*? (*see page* 123):
We are here far from the robust, strident Wagner. This
song has the quality of a water-colour which painters say
'sings.'

Between the *Ariettes oubliées* of 1888 and the *Chansons de
Bilitis* of 1897 comes the definitive version of the first set of
Fêtes galantes, of which we have already considered *Fantoches*
(here hardly changed), and of which the most popular number
is *Clair de lune.* This is completely different from the original
version (published by *La Revue musicale*), which was little
more than a pastiche of Massenet, nor has it anything to do
with the *Clair de lune* in the *Suite bergamasque* for piano. In
this song the composer seems almost to have forgotten the
touch of irony that Verlaine intended to bring to this eighteenth-century portrait of lovers in the moonlight. Debussy
seems to take at its face value the sentimental scene that Verlaine
was half laughing at. No matter! In later years he would
certainly never have missed such an opportunity. There is
no lack of irony in the second set of *Fêtes galantes* which
appeared twelve years later. Here one notices, for the first

time, a use of counterpoint. The scene of the youthful lovers
(*Les Ingénus*) is woven out of clear-cut dance figures; a dancing
faun (*Le Faune*) is represented by flute-like runs against a *basso
ostinato*, and the resigned colloquy of disillusioned lovers
(*Colloque sentimental*) chiefly by means of a type of recitative
used in *Pelléas*. The characterization in these songs is perhaps keener, but it is also harder and less human. The
last of the eighteen songs on poems of Verlaine, they are

actually in a style we shall see better in other works of this period.[1]

What are we now to make of the four *Proses lyriques* of the years 1892–3, for which Debussy wrote the texts himself? No one would imagine that these prose-poems were by one who had steeped himself in Baudelaire and Verlaine. How did Debussy come to write these trite words? Here is a literal translation of the beginning of the second song, *De grève (Of the Shore)*:

Twilight falls on the sea,
Thin white silk.
The waves prattle like silly women, like little girls with their rustling dresses,
Irisated green silk!
The clouds, grave travellers, are debating the coming storm.
Really it is too heavy a background for this English water-colour.

De soir, where at least one would expect some respect for 'atmosphere,' is mostly about Sunday excursion trains: 'On Sunday the trains go fast, devoured by insatiable tunnels, and the good signals exchange by means of their single eyes most mechanical impressions.' What a curious commentary on Debussy the sensualist! But it may afford his admirers some satisfaction to know that the music is almost as bad as the texts. They are clumsy songs, there is a good deal of pointless repetition, and the over-wrought piano accompaniment might be an arrangement of some hack orchestration. Small wonder that Debussy, who was able, as few composers

---

[1] Among the numerous projects at the end of his life Debussy considered an adaptation of his settings of the *Fêtes galantes* to a ballet. What a pity this idea never materialized! One can imagine such a ballet making a very suitable pendant to Schumann's *Carnaval*. Some enterprising choreographer might still consider it.

have been able, to evoke so precisely in music the feeling of a poem, found little inspiration in these texts. What is surprising is that they are contemporary with *L'Après-midi d'un faune* and the beginning of *Pelléas*.

The songs which are really worthy companions of *Pelléas* are the three *Chansons de Bilitis*. These are perhaps Debussy's most perfect songs. Bilitis, it will be remembered, was Pierre Louÿs's imaginary hedonist in ancient Greece. I will quote a passage from the third song, *Le Tombeau des Naïades*:

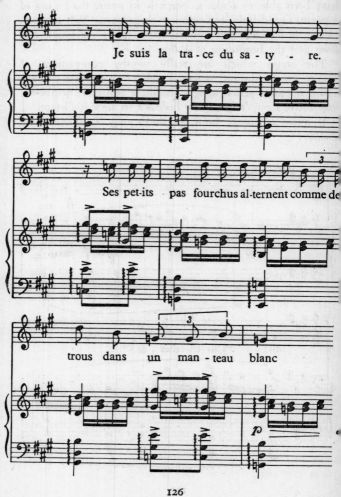

Je suis la tra - ce du sa - ty - re.

Ses pet-its pas fourchus al-ternent comme de

trous dans un man - teau blanc

Surely the Dionysiac music of the Greeks must have sounded like this. This beautiful chant makes its way from one end of the song to the other like a dancer slowly crossing a stage. Sometimes it halts a long time on a repeated note, the ensuing inflections then deriving an intense expressiveness. Against it, the accompaniment tells of Bilitis's slow tramping in the snow to the tomb of the Naiads. One is reminded of another journey told in music, *Der Erlkönig,* where the accompaniment illustrates the narrative in the same way. But whereas Schubert turned his tale into a miniature drama, Debussy, seeking here the decorative rather than the emotional side of his texts, gave his the reality of a frieze.

A translation of *La Chevelure* has been given in a previous chapter. One may wonder how any setting of a dream of love can be called decorative. But it is the right word. For this is not a real live dream with passionate suspensions, but a reconstructed dream told in clear harmony and archaic-sounding recitative. In the opening bars of *La Flûte de Pan* we have the much-heard-of whole-tone scale:

Lent et sans rigueur de rythme

Contrary to a current opinion, Debussy uses this scale sparingly. It is used here in contrast to a three-note figure, strikingly suggestive, according to where it appears on the piano, of the bright and dark timbres of the flute. Bilitis is sitting on her lover's knees learning to play. 'He plays after me, but so softly that I scarcely hear him.' The workmanship of the piano part at this point is exquisite. Then, when it is late, begins 'the chant of the green frogs.' A brittle arrangement of dissonances leads to a sombre low-lying chant to be sung 'almost without voice.' Very softly the original scale-figure reaches a high A and a modal cadence brings the apparition to a close. Apparitions these songs truly are: friezes of scenes from ancient Greece. How variedly Debussy adapts his means to the requirements of each poet!

After *Pelléas*—we have constantly to take this work as a landmark—the songs are fewer and also less known. At the time of Debussy's death the *Noël des enfants qui n'ont plus de maisons,* the last song he wrote, was very popular. Written as a Christmas carol for the children of the devastated areas, it has a tune which is easy to remember and words in the patriotic vein of the war years. It is now almost forgotten. Nor does one often see the three songs of 1913 on poems of Mallarmé on a programme. From a study of the score, they seem to be rather fragmentary, lacking any sustained melody, or any sequence of ideas that can be readily grasped. To set to music Mallarmé's later poetry, which intends to be so much music itself, was audacious, not to say superfluous. Debussy's settings would probably sound best if they were not allowed to usurp the attention due to the poetry. One can imagine that the *scherzando* for the poem about the fan (*L'Éventail*) and the slow, minuet-like accompaniment for the porcelain princess (*Placet futile*) would sound admirable if played in another room while the singer declaimed her charged and abstruse lines in a manner not very different from Schönberg's *Sprechsingen.*

These songs, written twenty years after *L'Après-midi d'un faune,* mark the end of Debussy's connection with the Symbolists. He was now more interested in medieval and classical poetry; and, indeed, the finest of the later songs are the settings of songs of Charles, Duke of Orléans, and of François Villon. One can hardly rank with these the three songs on extracts from Tristan Lhermite's ode, *Le Promenoir des deux amants.* Tristan

Lhermite was a mediocre poet of the seventeenth century. Can one imagine the classical scenes of the age of Louis XIV, with their grottoes, fountains and nymphs, described by Debussy? These songs, which some hold to mark the beginning of a new phase, are artificial and laboured. They are perhaps all that could have been done with a text that makes play with artificiality; one wonders only how Debussy came to be attracted to such a text.

The settings of Charles d'Orléans consist of two *Rondels* and three unaccompanied choruses. It is ironical that the composer who never ceased voicing contempt for the stiffnesses of form should have been so inspired by the poet for whom a scholastic rigidity of form was almost everything. What appealed, however, was again the pictorial aspect of the poetry, the sombre grace of the *jongleurs* and minstrels at Charles's fifteenth-century court at the Château de Blois. To this remote world, remote enough to bear kinship with the world of *Pelléas et Mélisande,* which was of no time at all, Debussy finally turned. 'I tell thee, dead is sweet pleasure,' sings the minstrel in the second *Rondel (Pour ce que plaisance est morte)*; and there follows this long, dignified arabesque to announce that he will go into mourning:

noir ;

This music, imbued with the spirit of the early contrapuntists that so many of Debussy's followers have tried to recapture, is deeply penetrating and human.

But the best examples of his last years are the songs on the poems of Villon. Villon was all that his contemporary, the Duke of Orléans, was not. He too used the rigid forms of the *rondel* and the *ballade,* but he had fire and passion. He was something of a Don Juan, a robber and a murderer. Debussy set three of the *Ballades*: to the women of Paris, a gay, rollicking song full of obvious humour; the famous prayer to the Virgin Mary, in which an extraordinarily subtle use is made of modal counterpoint; and the ballad from Villon to his love. Is it strange that this last love song should be relentlessly grim? Gone are the voluptuous settings of Verlaine and the potent music for Baudelaire. This is a song of the disillusions of love—'A cank'rous love eating as rust eats iron'; of 'Love like a thief that steals on one unseen'; of the hopeless despair of the debauchee: 'Where shall I turn? Where my dishonour hide?' The piano has a slow, halting rhythm and the voice a long, broad recitative. As a climax come these piercing accents of anguish:

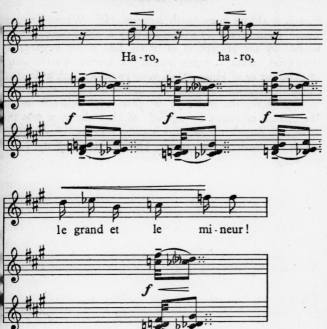

Ha - ro,   ha - ro,

le grand et   le   mi - neur !

It is one of the few passages marked *forte* in the whole of this
extraordinary collection.

Considered chronologically, the songs show Debussy's music
to be much more varied than it is generally supposed to be.
The Baudelaire songs are different from the Verlaine songs;
the Verlaine songs are different from the *Chansons de Bilitis*;
and these again are different from the *Ballades de Villon*. In
the best of them the characterization is so careful that it would
be possible to recognize the poet, if not the poem, without
hearing the words; while at the same time the Debussyan

flavour is always immediately recognizable. Where does this music come from? To suggest that a composer's style is formed by the absorption of poetry into music is generally superficial. Such a theory would not account for the songs of Schubert or of Hugo Wolf, who could let forth a flood of music that carried off one or two poems in a day; nor would it account for the music of Wagner, who believed in the 'fertilzation of poetry by music.' With Debussy it was the other way round: the musical impulse was nourished, not so much on music as on poetry. He was above all the poets' musician.

CHAPTER XIII

THE PIANO WORKS

In the past Debussy's reputation in this country rested mainly on his piano works. One can perhaps see why. They are more numerous than the orchestral works, more readily appreciated than the songs and certainly easier to perform. Pianists delight in Debussy. Then, in the days before the radio, there was a natural tendency for a composer to become best known by his piano works. It was not always to his advantage. Debussy, in fact, suffered somewhat like Liszt in this respect. Also, like Liszt, he was himself an extraordinary pianist, though, of course, of a very different type.

To see Debussy's piano works in their proper light one should consider their dates; and for this purpose it is convenient to think of his output as divided into three periods: (1) From about 1880 to 1892, i.e. from the last years at the Conservatoire to the beginning of *Pelléas*; (2) from 1892 till about 1904, the period of his best works; and (3) from 1904 to 1918, a period of decline. We note first of all that the piano works in the first two periods are relatively few. Apart from the insignificant *Danse bohémienne* and five small pieces that appeared in 1890, but which seem to be of an earlier date, there is nothing until the two *Arabesques* of 1888. The *Petite Suite* and the *Fantaisie* (published posthumously) are of 1889. The original form of the *Suite bergamasque* is also of this year, but it was withheld from publication and only appeared in a revised form in 1905. The next work is the suite, *Pour le piano,* written in 1896. Then there is nothing at all until the *Estampes* of 1903. In all, then, five works (discounting the small pieces) in fifteen years. It will be remembered that by 1903 Debussy had written most of his songs. Consider now the works of the last period: *L'Isle joyeuse* (1904), *Images* (first series) (1905), *Children's Corner* (1906–8), *Images* (second series) (1907), *Préludes* (1910–13), *Boîte à joujoux* (1913), *Six Épigraphes antiques* (1914), the *Études* and *En blanc et noir* (both 1915). The greater part were written in the later, declining years.

But this is not the only observation to be made since these dates were carefully established by Léon Vallas. We see now that until the age of forty Debussy produced little of note for the piano and almost nothing to indicate his later, very individual style of piano writing. The early piano works are disappointing and indeed perplexing. Can one believe that the *Petite Suite* was contemporary with the *Poèmes de Baudelaire,* or *Pour le piano* with the *Chansons de Bilitis*? While the songs show him to be entering into full possession of his powers, the contemporary piano pieces, which are absolute music, are little more than student's work. It seems that Debussy needed at all times some extra-musical—poetic or pictorial—stimulus.

These early piano works are, however, worth dwelling on for a moment to see, by their very faults, the nature of his musical mind. When Tchaikovsky said that in Debussy's *Danse bohémienne* 'not a single thought is developed to the end, the form is bungled, and there is no unity,' he put his finger on what would appear to be a fundamental weakness. Debussy would not have regarded it as a weakness, for the reason that the classical unity Tchaikovsky had in mind was precisely what he revolted against. The question in form for Debussy was not 'Where does this go?' nor even 'What comes next?' but 'How long can this last?' His is music not of sentiments but of sensations.

He was thus incapable of seeing the perspective of form. In the *Arabesques,* for instance, the phrases are neatly pieced together, but wherever one would expect a theme to take root it withers. Occasionally we do see an attempt at conventional development; and then such a trite progression as this, from the *Mazurka,* is typical:

He seems never to have thought of a modulation as a pivot. In the later works, where harmony is more and more released from tonality, modulations, as such, are hardly perceptible. In his early days he had an aversion to modulations, which led to his rupture with César Franck at the Conservatoire. 'Modulate, modulate,' the old organist used to exhort his pupil, who was improvising at the piano. 'But I am quite happy in this key,' said Debussy resentfully. 'Why do you want me to modulate?' And he left in a huff. It may be said in parenthesis that César Franck realized the strength of a modulation no more than Debussy.

From all of which one can see that his revolt against classical form was something more than a conscious revolt. Remark the naïvety of the structure of the *Ballade* (originally entitled *Ballade slave*). A phrase of obvious Russian extraction is repeated with slight variations. Suddenly a short intermediary section is opened up by a phrase two bars long. The rest consists of figurations of both of these phrases and a return to the first denuded of ornaments. The mosaic-like effect is pretty, but like so much Russian music, the piece might stop where it does or go on much longer.

The Russian influence is much more noticeable in the piano works than in the songs. 'The Russian,' says Gerald Abraham, 'seems usually to be over-concerned with the thrill of the present moment in sound'; and the same might be said of Debussy. The *Danse* (originally entitled *Tarentelle styrienne*[1]) shows the kind of piano writing that suggests an orchestra—here the orchestra of Rimsky-Korsakov. Who would imagine that this passage was written by Debussy?

[1] Was this title suggested, perhaps, by Erik Satie's *Tyrolienne turque,* or discarded because of it? The *Danse* was written about the time Debussy first met Satie.

Incidentally, it is this work that Ravel, whose kinship with Rimsky-Korsakov has often been noted, chose, of all Debussy's works, to orchestrate.

We may pass over the other early piano pieces until we come to the three published under the title *Pour le piano*. Of these the *Toccata* was written for Debussy's piano pupil, Nicolas Coronio, and seems to be little more than an exercise. One cannot say much more of the *Prélude*. But in the *Sarabande* is seen for the first time a type of writing with which all who have played Debussy are familiar (*see page* 137).

This reproduction of a chord on different degrees of the scale is known as 'Impressionism.' Is not Debussy commonly referred to as the Impressionist musician? It has been shown that the songs were to a large extent suggested by the poetry of the Symbolists; the best of the piano music, and, as we shall see later, certain of the orchestral works, have an affinity of feeling with the painting of the Impressionists, notably with Renoir and Claude Monet.[1]

We come suddenly upon Debussy's characteristic and highly individual style of piano writing, of which the above example is only a slight foretaste, in the *Estampes*. These three 'prints' of the Orient, Spain and the Île de France are all based on popular music. *Pagodes* makes use of the five-note scale that Ravel used so effectively in his *Ma mère l'Oie* and which was borrowed from, or at any rate suggested by, the music of the Javanese and Cambodian dancers heard at the Paris World Exhibition. It appears first simply and nonchalantly:

---

[1] One should beware of far-fetched explanations of musical Impressionism in which an influence is sought from an actual painting technique. The main concern of the Impressionist painters was the play of light upon form for which, it almost goes without saying, there can be no analogy in music, since musical form is not in space but in time.

délicatement et presque sans nuances

and then worked into this delicate fabric:

La Soirée dans Grenade is one of the most beautiful of the numerous Spanish pieces written by French musicians ever since Bizet's *Carmen* and Chabrier's *España* turned their eyes across the Pyrenees. On the authority of Manuel de Falla it is 'characteristically Spanish down to its smallest details.' How much it was inspired by the *Habanera* of Ravel (which first appeared as a piano piece in 1898 before it was incorporated in his *Rapsodie espagnole*) is a moot point, though it is of little importance. The forms of the two works are quite different. Here Debussy's form consists of nothing more than a play of colour derived from the contrast of registers. This, for instance, from the opening:

is followed by:

and immediately by:

This kaleidoscopic arrangement of patterns and bits of themes is what is offered in place of conventional development. Finally, *Jardins sous la pluie* is a toccata based on two French folksongs. As a rule Debussy was not very successful with pieces in quick *tempo*. The main exceptions are the scherzo from the Quartet, *Fêtes* from the *Nocturnes* and this delicate little patter. It was a great artist who could suggest a spray of rain by a semiquaver figure marked 'net et vif' on a piano which, as we shall see presently, he conceived to be 'without hammers.' Played in the right way, but only on this condition, for it demands a very specialized touch, it is Debussy's masterpiece among the piano works.

To appreciate the elements of this new writing we should see what kind of a pianist Debussy was himself. From the accounts of contemporaries one gathers that his playing was extremely subdued. On at least one occasion he was accused of maintaining a continuous *pianissimo* to the extent of being inaudible. Note that the above quotations never once break out even into a *mezzo-forte*. 'He was an original virtuoso,' writes Vallas, 'remarkable for the delicacy and mellowness of his touch. He made one forget that the piano has hammers —an effect which he used to request his interpreters to aim at— and he achieved particularly characteristic effects by the use of both pedals.' A piano without hammers! One can as well imagine a violin without a bow. The truth is that Debussy had no conception of the piano as a percussion instrument. If it was to serve his elusive music at all it would have to assume the characteristics of that recently discovered instrument that seems to draw music from the circumambient air.[1] Some such conception seems to have been in his mind when he gave Louis Laloy certain indications for the use of his interpreters. 'The pianist,' Laloy wrote, 'must renounce his claim to bring out the melody. He will, of course, find for himself the necessary slight contrast; but too much will bring him to romantic affectation.' There was apparently the danger of mistaking Debussy for Liszt, for we read further: 'He must not attach undue importance to the runs, for these should surround the main melodic lines, suggesting the harmony in the characteristic manner of the piano [*sic*] and give life to the background.' Finally, 'the most important quality to seek is unity of tone.' In short, nothing should be allowed to protrude, to destroy the illusion that the piano is not a piano.

The later piano works, then, are the result of a compromise. Unless they are played with the proper lightness of touch and delicacy of tone the illusion is lost. All those effects marked 'laissez vibrer,' 'doux et estompé,' 'le plus doux du monde,' the glissando-like runs, the tinges of harmony against a continuous design like dots of colour in a wash, the contrast of registers, the Impressionist reproduction of chords, opened up a new world of piano technique. This technique of illusion was Debussy's own creation.

Yet, as a matter of fact, it owed certain effects to another master of piano writing with whom Debussy's name is often associated: Maurice Ravel. Let it be said that Ravel was much more at home in composing for the piano than Debussy. He had nothing to overcome in the nature of the instrument,

[1] Le Martenot.

which, in fact, suited him much better than the orchestra. Whereas Debussy's *Images,* to take one of his typical later works, is only just in a state of consciousness, the piano music of Ravel, taking a good deal from Liszt, is clear and scintillating. There is no mistaking the two styles, yet with the knowledge that Ravel's *Jeux d'eau* was written in 1901, it is possible to see how Debussy adapted certain processes in this work to his own use in the *Estampes*.[1]

Nor is this the only instance of an influence from the younger master. We have noted a connection between *La Soirée dans Grenade* and Ravel's *Habanera.* The influence of *Jeux d'eau,* which is perhaps the most original of modern French piano works, is even more noticeable in *L'Isle joyeuse.* This illustration of Watteau's *Embarquement pour Cythère* is the most ambitious work Debussy wrote for the piano after the early *Fantaisie.* It is brisk and lively but it is peculiarly hard-set. Debussy did not hide the fact that it was virtuoso writing, though it was the kind of virtuosity which Ravel was better able to turn into something truly musical.

We come now to the main piano works of the later years, in all, counting each number of the various groups, over sixty pieces. Taking a general view of them, they seem rather mixed. They are all written with perfect taste, a quality which Debussy never lacked, though it does not compensate for a lack of genuine feeling. The better examples seem to be near the date of the *Estampes,* while towards the last years there is a tendency to reproduce effects mechanically.

A lovely piece is *Reflets dans l'eau,* the first of the *Images.* The subject cries out for an Impressionist treatment and we have at the beginning these floating chords:

---

[1] See the article by Henri Gil-Marchex, *La Technique de piano,* in *La Revue musicale,* April 1925, special number devoted to Ravel.

Andantino molto *(tempo rubato)*

followed shortly by these delicate touches of colour:

The *Hommage à Rameau* has one beautiful line which may be extracted from its context and quoted like a line of poetry:

though it has nothing particularly reminiscent of Rameau, unless a certain gravity which unfortunately turns to heaviness.

In the second set *Et la lune descend sur le temple qui fut*—the curious title, reminiscent of Chinese poetry, was given by Louis Laloy after the work was written—has many subtle touches, and one should mention the last number, *Poissons d'or,* a piece of rich fantasy which is a favourite with pianists. There is here, however, a certain rigidity in the harmony which was quite absent from the other pieces and which reminds one less of Debussy than of Reger. The following quotation is typical:

Debussy

dim. molto

The six little pieces that make up *Children's Corner* are deservedly popular. They are perhaps not so penetrating as the children's music of Schumann or Moussorgsky, though as pictures of childish innocence they are more subtle. At times they have some of the old charm that came from Massenet. Consider, for instance, this passage from the *Doll's Serenade*:

They are sensitive pieces, very dainty and very artistic. *The Snow is Dancing* is a beautiful piece of filigree work. And they have a touch of humour—in *Jimbo's Lullaby*, for instance (Jimbo was an elephant doll of Chouchou's)—which is very dear. Sometimes it is not so subtle. In the *Golliwog's Cake-Walk*, which makes use of a tune which Debussy heard played by the Grenadier Guards in London, there is this caustic reference to the prelude to *Tristan*:

Yet when he heard *Tristan* some five years later, according to a friend, 'he literally shook with emotion.' What a complex!

Then there are the *Préludes*. The writing in these twenty-four little pieces is very varied, as indeed are their subjects, which are: Greek dancers (*Danseuses de Delphes*); music-hall types (*General Lavine-eccentric* and *Minstrels*); characters from Shakespeare (*Danse de Puck*) and Dickens (*Hommage à S. Pickwick, Esq., P.P.M.P.C.*—foreigners are always amused at the English habit of putting letters after names); poems of Baudelaire (*Les sons et les parfums tournent dans l'air du soir*) and Leconte de Lisle (*La Fille aux cheveux de lin*); a Breton legend (*La Cathédrale engloutie*); a picture post card (*La Puerta del Vino*); and a number of atmospheric landscapes and seascapes. Often, I imagine, the composition must have been started by coming upon a phrase too good not to make into a piece, a suitable subject being found afterwards. They are like pages from an artist's sketch-book, some catching the life of some movement or form, some no more than promising and some that should have been scrapped. Seldom is anything much thought out, though the best of them leave no impression of sketchiness. *Voiles,* with its neatly-contrasted thirds and fourths and its slow succession of runs delicately topped by staccato notes, is a model of economy in writing. *Le Vent dans la plaine* wisps along at a breakneck speed with a lilt that another composer would have been tempted to develop into an effective cadence. Debussy, instead, hangs on to three common chords, C major, D flat and D, and then sends the piece into thin air with a B flat marked 'laissez vibrer.' *La Cathédrale engloutie* has enjoyed great popularity, but rather on account, one feels, of its obvious picturesqueness than because of its intrinsic musical worth. An intimate and sensitive piece is *La Fille aux cheveux de lin.* Here is hardly any sequence of ideas that one can perceive, yet, inexplicably, it is entirely satisfying. One notices that the best examples are in the first of the two books. In the second one might mention *Les Fées sont d'exquises danseuses* and *General Lavine-eccentric,* a kind of musical Toulouse-Lautrec, but the others are mostly lacking in spontaneity. In *Brouillards* and *Canope* there are signs that Debussy was becoming a prey to his own 'formulas.'

This was his final and most ironic tragedy. After the *Préludes* the piano works written during those terrible last years have little value. The *Six Épigraphes antiques* were adaptations of long-discarded sketches; the *Douze Études* were intended primarily as technical exercises; the *Berceuse héroïque,* dedicated to King Albert, and at least one of the three pieces for piano duet entitled *En blanc et noir,* were topical war pieces. Few of these are played nowadays: they are too dull. And dull music is the last thing one can accept from a composer who sets out purely to delight. Musically, Debussy died at the beginning of the war.

CHAPTER XIV

THE CHAMBER WORKS

IN the last chapter it was argued that Debussy was most successful when following some literary or pictorial idea. The
songs show him to be the poet's musician; the best of the
piano pieces, the painter's musician. With his abhorrence
for professionalism, he did more than any other composer to
bring music out of its own isolated world into a wider world
where art, literature and music interacted on each other freely.[1]
Is it, then, surprising that, with one exception, his examples of
absolute music are failures? But that one exception is a
masterpiece: it is the string Quartet.

The question that will immediately be asked is: 'How was
Debussy to overcome his natural inability to use the sonata
form, some type of which is, after all, needed in a large-scale
quartet?' Characteristically, he depends, throughout each of
the four movements principally, and in one movement entirely,
on the subtle transformations of a single motive. Let us see

[1] I am reminded here of a letter from Moussorgsky to Stassov.
'Tell me,' he asks, 'why, when I listen to the conversation of young
artists, painters or sculptors, I can follow their thoughts and understand their opinions and aims, and I seldom hear them mention
technique, save in certain cases of absolute necessity? On the other
hand, when I find myself among musicians I rarely hear them utter
a living idea; one would think they were still at school; they know
nothing of anything but technique and shop-talk. Is the art of
music so young that it has to be studied in this puerile way?' (Translation by Gerald Abraham, *Studies in Russian Music.*) This would
express Debussy's feelings exactly.

what happens. The first movement opens with this motive
in the Phrygian mode:

In the exposition there are two episodes (not counter-themes)
which come and go with the minimum of effect on the general
structure. In fact, they are never heard again. The main
motive appears with prismatic changes of harmony, but
melodically it is scarcely developed at all. This is about all
that happens to it.

The second subject:

appears only at the very end of the exposition.

The development section—for Debussy does attempt here some kind of ternary form—consists of a series of minute variations pieced together into a mosaic. They are mainly on the second subject. Here it is on the first violin:

here on the cello:

and here again on the first violin with a different figuration in the accompaniment:

with a change of key:

all of which is in the thirty-four bars of the first part of the development section leading to the high light of the whole movement, a rushing figure in triplets derived from the accompaniment of the second violin in the quotations above. One comes to the final section not, as in Beethoven, to see a deeper significance in the subject-matter, but to be enthralled a little longer by still further variations, designs and shifting harmonies. The movement ends with a short codetta based on the first half of the main motive.

The second movement is one of the most piquant pieces of string writing in the whole range of chamber music. The main motive of the first movement is now in 6–8 time, in G major and given to the viola:

bove this the first violin, *pizzicato,* makes these pert gestures:

Debussy

The whole of the first section consists of this drumming repetition of the theme on the viola while the other strings work around it a texture of flying *pizzicati*. The harmony is extremely simple. An intermediary passage consists of an enlargement of the same theme given to the first violin against a throbbing semiquaver accompaniment on the second violin and viola, while the cello maintains a *pizzicato* bass. Coming immediately after the excited play of counterpoint in the first section, the beginning of this luscious passage must be quoted as one of Debussy's supreme master-strokes (*see page* 159). No other theme is used in this movement.

The third movement is in *Lied* form. Among many beautiful transformations of the original theme, I will quote this, which reminds one of the contemporary score of *L'Après-midi d'un faune* (*see pages* 161–2).

But, after this, the little triplet figure loses its fertility. The last movement is laboured. It attempts the grandiose, and whenever Debussy makes this fatal mistake he falls into commonplace.

Debussy wrote this Quartet at the age of thirty-one. How different it is from Beethoven's F major Quartet (Op. 18, No. 1), written at the age of thirty! That philosophic unity, that dignity, that drama which Beethoven perceived meant nothing to Debussy. In their essence his qualities are ephemeral. As Beethoven's spacious structure is dependent on the growth of ideas, Debussy's mosaic-like form is made to convey a series of sensations. I am reminded of what César Franck said of the earlier Debussy: 'It is music on needle points.' One might say that the Quartet is music of the nerves. It is music that delights as no other—while it lasts.

With the Quartet of Ravel, the Debussy Quartet is rightly considered one of the two greatest quartets written by Frenchmen. But as an example of absolute music it was a success that was never repeated. In an earlier chapter we have seen

that Debussy contemplated writing another quartet shortly afterwards, in which he was going to 'bring more dignity to the form.' According to Vallas, a Belgian newspaper announced that the third movement had been finished. At about the same time he was thinking of another chamber work. From a letter to Durand we learn that in June 1894 he was writing, or had in mind to write, a Sonata for violin and piano. But these must be added to the long list of works unfinished or discarded for mysterious reasons. The next chamber work, written some ten years later, is a *Rapsodie* for saxophone, commissioned by a Mrs. Elisa Hall. What is interesting about this is the story of its composition. It is told by Vallas:

He had undertaken the disagreeable task of composing a work to order . . . for Mrs. Elisa Hall, president of the Boston Orchestral Club. For the sake of her health this lady had devoted herself to an instrument which had not yet achieved the popularity it has since acquired, thanks to the triumph of jazz. Wishing, regardless of cost, to build up a special repertoire for herself, she had given various French composers orders for important compositions. Debussy was very dilatory in the matter; he was almost incapable of composing to order, and, besides, he knew very little about the technique of this solo instrument. On 8th June [1903] he wrote to Messager: 'The Americans are proverbially tenacious. The saxophone lady landed in Paris at 58 Rue Cardinet, eight ot ten days ago, and is inquiring about her piece. Of course I assured her that, with the exception of Rameses II, it is the only subject that occupies my thoughts. All the same, I have had to set to work on it. So here I am, searching desperately for novel combinations calculated to show off this aquatic instrument. . . . I have been working as hard as in the good old days of *Pelléas*. . . .'[1]

The following year Mrs. Hall played a work of Vincent d'Indy. Debussy 'thought it ridiculous to see a lady in a pink frock

[1] Translation by Maire and Grace O'Brien.

playing on such an ungainly instrument; and he was not at all anxious that his work should provide a similar spectacle.' The composition was finally presented to the courageous lady in an unfinished state, and only completed in 1919 by Roger-Ducasse. It is a stillborn work and hardly ever performed.

Of the year 1910 there are two works for clarinet, the piano accompaniments of which were subsequently orchestrated. The first is another *Rapsodie,* intended as a competition piece for students at the Conservatoire, where Debussy adjudicated at the wind instrument examinations; the other, *Petite Pièce,* was a sight-reading test. They are both exquisitely written for the instrument, though, again, they bear the stamp of works which were commissioned.

Then there is nothing, if we except the delicate little flute piece, *Syrinx* (originally entitled *Flûte de Pan* and intended as a piece of incidental music to Gabriel Mourey's drama, *Psyché*), until the three Sonatas of 1915–17. The style of these, which Vallas describes as 'neo-classical,' 'was partly induced,' he says, 'by his national tendencies, and partly, perhaps, by the instinctive need which had prompted him shortly before the war to return to the processes he had formerly condemned.' Some see in these works an affinity with Couperin. It is not easily discernible. Surely, if Debussy was attracted to the French clavecinists of the eighteenth century, it was for patriotic rather than for aesthetic reasons. Can one imagine anything more dissimilar than the metallic 'tin-tin du clavecin' and the veiled, suggestive art of Debussy?

Far from having anything to do with Couperin, the cello Sonata, the first of the group, consists of three short movements suggested by Italian comedy. It was to have been called *Pierrot fâché avec la lune.* The first movement has obvious signs of having been written in a great hurry. Bits of themes from earlier works are pushed in for the sake of padding. The cello theme on the second stave of page 2 is taken from *Le*

Tombeau des Naïades and the passage for piano at figure 2 on page 3 from *La Cathédrale engloutie.* The humour of the second movement is rather pitiful. Even Vallas, who considers the first two of these Sonatas as the 'supreme musical expression of the doctrines Debussy preached as a critic and illustrated as a composer for over thirty years,' admits its 'pathetic banter.' The cello writing, in imitation of a mandoline, is little more than studied buffoonery. The finale, where the themes seem to be based on folksongs, sadly fails in an attempt to recapture the verve of the old song, *Fantoches.* The best thing in the whole work is a passage of twelve bars marked *con morbidezza.* It seems to be the only genuine utterance.

The second Sonata, for flute, viola and harp, is at least more dignified. Again it was a work written in a great hurry, not because ideas came quickly—Debussy was certainly never fortunate in this way—but rather, one feels, because he was anxious in those last desperate years to achieve something, whatever it was, lest his illness should draw him into a state of complete inactivity, which, in fact, it finally did. Still, he could always fall back on an unfailing sense of taste; he wrote nothing that was ugly. The combination of instruments for which this work is written afforded an opportunity of producing something very tasteful and elegant, but nothing more.

Finally we come to the piano and violin Sonata. Here are passages reminiscent of Stravinsky, of Spanish folksong, allusions to his own *Ibéria* and *La Flûte de Pan,* artificial repetitions and padding—a jumble, it seems, of everything that came into the composer's head. In the words of Vallas, who remains to the last Debussy's staunchest admirer, 'the whole work betrays fatigue and effort. There is an impotent vehemence about it. It suggests a fight for life, a struggle against death. . . .' And with this we may leave this unhappy period of Debussy's life for the last time.

CHAPTER XV

THE ORCHESTRAL WORKS

SOME ten years before Debussy wrote his *Prélude* to *L'Après-midi d'un faune,* he had begun a stage work on a subject which dealt with the same theme as Mallarmé's poem. This was *Diane au bois,* the comedy of Théodore de Banville. Curiously enough, it was Banville who urged Mallarmé to write *L'Après-midi* and actually supplied him with the theme from his own work. It is perhaps no mere coincidence that Debussy set to music both of these works, though what connection there may be between them we do not know. *Diane au bois* has disappeared. Of the music to *L'Après-midi* we know only the prelude, though, as we have seen in a previous chapter, Debussy planned, and actually announced for performance, a *Prélude, interlude et paraphrase finale.* Mallarmé conceived his poem as a monologue to be spoken by an actor on a stage, and it may be that Debussy originally had such a presentation in mind.

The first thing to say about Mallarmé's poem is that it is extremely obscure. Even to students of the period it is only intelligible after patient searching. Two translations, however, have been made into English for which every one should be very grateful. One is by Mr. A. I. Ellis in his *Stéphane Mallarmé in English Verse*, and the other by Mr. Alexander Cohen, published in *Musical Opinion* for September 1935. Of the two, Mr. Cohen's makes the meaning clearer, which would recommend it in one way, though not in the Mallarméan view, where clarity is not exactly a virtue. Mr. Ellis's translation is less definite (that is a virtue!) and reproduces remarkably the clotted richness of the language. In the following résumé the quotations are from this version.

A faun awakens from a dream. He has seen two nymphs, one with 'Eyes cold as tearful spring,' the other like 'Breath in the fire of noon.' He meditates awhile, playing the flute. He remembers cutting the reeds that his lips now caress and bathing in the fountains of the Naiads. But now he is alone,

> Standing as once, alone in light's full stream
> A lily, innocent as none of you.

Suddenly his passion is aroused by the 'bite of love's mysteries.' He would live for rapturous pleasure alone.

> And when I've drain'd the grape of living light
> By fancy's shift Regret is driven to flight
> Smiling I lift the void skin heaven to
> And breathing swell its lustrous side wherethro'
> I gaze till eve, with passion's wine aglow.

He returns to memories of the nymphs playing amongst the reeds. In the fever of his imagination, he grasps two Naiads:

> I seize them, severing not, and swiftly hie
> To rose-bed that the wanton shadows fly—
> Its perfume all outpouréd to the skies—
> Rosy our frolic be as day that dies.

But they are frightened by his burning kisses and they struggle away. One succeeds; and the illusion vanishes. Still his passion is unappeased. As twilight falls over the forests he pursues a vision of Venus on Etna's summit. That means chastisement.

> Ah, no!
> My body slumber-weigh'd, my soul voice-numb
> At last to midday's silent pride succumb.

And he stretches himself out on the sand to sleep.

What does Mallarmé wish to convey in this highly symbolical language? The core of the poem is in these lines, which the faun says in praise of animal voluptuousness:

> Passion, thou know'st at purple's ripening
> The granate bursts for bees' fierce murmuring;
> Our blood, ere caught to be encaptured fain
> Flows too for vibrant swarming of love's pain.

As one critic has said: 'It is the violent love of an adolescent exploited in poetry by a sad, disappointed man.'[1] It is certainly violent. He might have taken as a motto, this critic suggests, the words of Prospero: 'We are such stuff as dreams are made on.' And, indeed, one can hardly think of a finer motto for the music. Mallarmé spoke of the music as an 'illustration . . . which would present no dissonance with my text. Rather does it go much further into the nostalgia and light with subtlety, malaise and richness.' Those words are well chosen, but he omitted to mention one important difference. Whereas the poem is clotted and obscure, the music is lucidity itself. Those who do not know this work of Debussy might imagine something extremely Wagnerian. With *L'Après-midi d'un faune* we come suddenly upon the wonder of Debussy's orchestra, as different from the orchestra of Wagner as a running brook from a waterfall. It remains to-day one of the subtlest examples of orchestral writing in existence.

One should not seek any line-for-line connection between the text and the music. Nor should one attempt to analyse

[1] Albert Thibaudet, *La Poésie de Mallarmé*.

a score which is so purely instinctive. When the faun's
flute:

is met by this voluptuous ascent on the horns:

Debussy

when this inertia:

...ddenly breaks into a moment's flight:

...hen this fabric of light and colour:

Debussy

passes finally into this intense languor (*see page* 174), I am reminded, in trying to give some idea of the underlying emotion, of Shelley's lines:

> And what is that most brief and bright delight
> Which rushes through the touch and through the sight,
> And stands before the spirit's inmost throne,
> A naked Seraph?

And Shelley answers: 'None hath ever known.' But perhaps it was a naked Seraph? Or at least a dream of one?

As *L'Après-midi* is the blossom of a poem, so the *Nocturnes* must be thought of in connection with certain paintings. It has often been said that the title was suggested by the 'Nocturnes' of Whistler, though Debussy himself never mentioned this. He described this work in these words:

The title *Nocturnes* is to be interpreted here in a general and, more particularly, in a decorative sense. Therefore it is not meant to

designate the usual form of the nocturne, but rather all the various impressions and the special effects of light that the word suggests. *Nuages* renders the immutable aspect of the sky and the slow, solemn motion of the clouds, fading away in grey tones lightly tinged with white. *Fêtes* gives us the vibrating atmosphere with sudden flashes of light. There is also the episode of the procession (a dazzling fantastic vision) which passes through the festive scene and becomes merged in it. But the background remains persistently the same; the festival, with its blending of music and luminous dust, participating in the cosmic rhythm. *Sirènes* depicts the sea and its countless rhythms and presently, amongst the waves silvered by the moonlight, is heard the mysterious song of the Sirens as they laugh and pass on.[1]

We have seen that, in its original form, for violin and orchestra, Debussy compared this work to 'a study in grey in painting.' The comparison suits the first movement, *Nuages,* admirably. The main theme, heard first on the clarinets and bassoons:

is given, over a long passage, to the strings subdivided into ten, twelve and sometimes fourteen parts. Vallas says that 'every note' of this theme is taken from a song of Moussorgsky, 'The noisy day has sped its flight,' from the cycle called *Sunless.* It is difficult to believe that it was taken from Moussorgsky, but even if it was, the context gives it an entirely different meaning. The scoring has never the slightest trace

[1] Translation by Maire and Grace O'Brien.

of heaviness or strain. Particularly lovely is the passage where, after all the woodwind have been playing in unison against *tenuto* notes on the strings—a deliberately colourless episode—the first violins return to the design of the initial theme in crotchets against a *pizzicato* accompaniment in quavers, while the sharp timbre of the cor anglais marks out this short fragment of a theme, said to have been suggested by the hooting of the passenger steamers that used to pass up and down the Seine:

Flutes and horns, violin and viola solos, discreetly enter and pass through the score like wisps of clouds across the sky. At the end, the 'immutable aspect of the sky' is portrayed by a fragment of the opening theme on one half of the cellos, while the other half has a slow chromatic figure, *tremolando*. Very slowly, the flute makes a last graceful appearance, the horns cast a faint glow of warmth, and the piece ends with the softest *pizzicati* against a drum roll. It is like a picture of Claude Monet.

'Nocturnes'

Fêtes is the perfect musical counterpart of some southern landscape by Renoir. It would almost seem that Debussy had Renoir in mind when he spoke, in the notice quoted above, of 'the vibrating, dancing rhythm of the atmosphere with sudden flashes of light.' The scene of this movement is some popular rejoicing in a wood. The orchestration is now bright and luminous. Trumpets, trombones and cymbals are added. In a *tempo* marked 'animated and very rhythmic' the woodwind let forth this joyous theme (*see page* 177): There follows some imaginary dance. A languorous theme on the oboe is heard against a throbbing accompaniment and is presently intertwined with another on the clarinet. A moment of excitement occurs when a way seems to be cleared: drums, harps and *pizzicato* basses have a martial rhythm. And then three muted trumpets announce a procession of soldiers (*see page* 177): Was there ever a lovelier fanfare? I remember sitting behind the trumpets at a rehearsal of this work by a famous German orchestra. As the players put down their instruments, the first trumpet leaned over to his colleagues and whispered admiringly into their ears: 'Echt französisch.' What a touching compliment to Debussy!

The band seems to approach and a nearer vision is created by combining the first dance theme, heard now on the strings, punctuated by the woodwind, while the band motive persists on the brass. But they are gone as the fanciful visions are piled one on another. Presently, as the excitement dies down, we seem to sense the approach of dusk and the couples dancing, smiling in the hot, perfumed air:

In the distance the band can be heard again. Fragments of their theme are tossed from the horns to the flutes. Over a low A on the tuba a new theme is interlaced by the woodwind. It brings just the right sentimental touch, and the visions disappear with the softest exit of the lower strings.

The third movement, *Sirènes,* introduces a female choir. The voices are regarded as instruments. Sometimes they are required to burst out suddenly like horns, but generally they are given a long melodic line around which the orchestra weaves its lacy patterns. The form here is more spacious than in the other movements. The texture is airy, the work flows. If *Fêtes* reminds one of Renoir, *Sirènes* is the equivalent of a water-colour by Turner, a painter whom Debussy greatly admired. It is seldom played nowadays and is generally omitted from a performance of the *Nocturnes.* One can perhaps see why. Delightful as it is in itself, it is not altogether successful as the third panel of this triptych. Its lower vitality is hardly what one expects or wants after the glowing *Fêtes,* especially as there is already the subdued *Nuages.*

It is comparatively easy to suggest the type of artistic thought of *L'Après-midi* and the *Nocturnes,* neither of which, it may have been noticed, has any easily recognizable affinity with other music. But it is more difficult to tell the reader about *La Mer,* the three symphonic sketches written between 1903 and 1905. One can begin, perhaps, by saying what they are not. They have none of that inner glow, that quality which

Charles Koechlin has aptly described as 'une force aimante,' of the orchestral works we have just considered. Nor are they, as the title might suggest, the work of a poetic Pantheist. That, certainly, Debussy never was. In none of the numerous landscapes and seascapes from the earliest songs, *Beau soir* and *Paysage sentimental,* to *Voiles* and *Brouillards* of the *Préludes* does one ever feel, in his attitude to nature, anything comparable to the contemplativeness of, say, the English Lake Poets. Nature's appeal for Debussy would seem to consist in the possibility of transferring the almost tactile quality of things in nature—gardens under rain, sailing-boats in a port, mists rising over a heath—into the world of personal sensations. This is the essential difference between Debussy and Delius, as it is between Verlaine and Wordsworth or Renoir and the painters of the Barbizon school. This may help us to appreciate *Fêtes* or *Jardins sous la pluie,* but it does not bring us any nearer *La Mer,* which is not in the least like his other big seascapes, *Sirènes* and the sea music in *Pelléas.*

In a careful study of Debussy's styles, Ladislas Fábián maintains that *La Mer* foreshadows the formal Sonatas written during the war. This is no doubt true if we consider that in *La Mer* respect is shown for the first time for classical proportions of form, and if we therefore regard it as the beginning of a new style deliberately repudiating the semi-conscious dreaminess of the former works. But I am not sure that we should. I am rather inclined to seek its origin in certain earlier works and to regard it as a product on a large scale of that decorativeness—there is no more precise word—which was already obvious in the *Chansons de Bilitis* and the second set of *Fêtes galantes*. It is significant, though it is only a small point, that the cover of *La Mer* should consist of a reproduction of a wave by the Japanese, Hokusai, the decorative artist *par excellence*.

This is not to say that one cannot easily recognize, in this score, certain realistic effects—the crash of waves against the rocks, the spray lit up by a gleam of sunlight, the gurgling backwash—but these are 'motives' worked into a play of patterns. The themes are strikingly contrasted. Sometimes they are set against a piece of intricate orchestral filigree work, such as the first theme of the first sketch, *De l'aube à midi sur la mer* (*see pages* 180–1). And sometimes they are of bold, determined contours such as this counter-theme heard on the cellos in four parts:

In the last movement, *Dialogue du vent et de la mer,* the long passage of arpeggios on the upper strings, against which the bassoons and basses mark out a dramatic theme punctuated by sharp interjections from the horns, is one of the most notable effects in modern orchestration. The scoring is brilliant yet terse. Throughout, the intricate texture is knit with perfect artistry. The numerous themes merge or collide as the occasion demands, fresh horizons are opened up by a sudden transference of the material in hand to a new group of instruments, the woodwind chatter, the violins whirl, the horns swell out. A climax comes when an arabesque-like figure breaks into a tremendous utterance from the brass (*see page* 184). That from Debussy! One is impressed by the strength and energy of the work. These are not words that can often be used in this book. It seems that in *La Mer* a latent force that for years had been lying dormant is brought to a head.

After *La Mer* Debussy wrote only two more works for orchestra: the five *Images,* which have no connection with the *Images* for piano, and the ballet, *Jeux,* produced by Diaghilev. The 'Egyptian ballet,' *Khamma,* commissioned by Maud Allan, can hardly be counted as a third, for it was merely sketched out by Debussy and orchestrated by Charles Koechlin. Debussy himself had no love for it and referred to it in a letter to Durand as 'that queer ballet with its trumpet calls, which suggest a riot, or an outbreak of fire, and give one the shivers.' It was given only at a concert in 1924 and achieved little or no success.

Debussy

184

In the last works for orchestra the vitality of *La Mer* turns to harshness. In one way the *Images* may be classed with the *Estampes* for piano, for each of the five movements is based on folksongs. But the technique and the general feeling of the two works have little in common. In a letter to Durand, Debussy says of the *Images*: 'I am trying to do something "different"—something that might be called reality, but what the fools call "Impressionism," a term that is utterly misapplied, especially by the critics who don't hesitate to apply it to Turner, the greatest creator of mystery in art.' There is nothing of Turner in the *Images*. In the first movement a deliberately academic use is made of that favourite folksong of Debussy's, *Nous n'irons plus au bois,* which he had used so spontaneously in *Jardins sous la pluie.* The augmentations and diminutions of portions of this song and the cyclical form in which the work is cast is accompanied by a taste for sharp dissonances and a feeling for orchestral colour that reminds one of the Stravinsky of *Petrouchka* and *Le Rossignol.* Stravinsky is again a name that comes to mind in the second movement, *Ibéria.* One is reminded too of the vivid *Iberia* of Albeniz which Debussy knew and greatly admired. On the whole it is rather blatant; one would have expected something subtler from the composer of *La Soirée dans Grenade.* The movement is in three sections bearing separate titles. The ending of *Par les rues et par les chemins* is a sensitive piece of writing and there are several beautiful pages in *Parfums de la nuit*; but these are exceptions. *Au matin d'un jour de fête* has the realism of a picture post card. As one critic said when it was first performed, it is 'just one more rhapsody "tras los montes," neither better nor worse, and certainly not better constructed, than the ones we have been listening to for the last twelve years.' The last movement, *Gigues* (originally entitled *Gigues tristes*), was finished by André Caplet, who has spoken of it as 'the portrait of a soul in pain.' It is a grim work, with caustic outbursts of violence and angular, marionette-like rhythms, through which there flows a long, plaintive melody, ironically given to the *oboe d'amore*.

It would be unfair to judge *Jeux* without having seen the ballet. Nijinsky's scenario is about tennis-players who lose their ball and play hide-and-seek. They sulk and quarrel; and then embrace, when they are disturbed by another ball thrown by a mischievous hand. That is all. Nijinsky saw in this scenario the possibility of presenting 'a plastic vindication of the man of 1913.' From a study of the score, one can see that there is delicacy, but a studied delicacy. The music moves, but without any impulse behind it. It was abandoned by Diaghilev, revived for a short time by the Swedish Ballet, and given only once at a concert.

Debussy's works for orchestra alone would scarcely fill two concerts. But this handful of works contains the most precious examples of orchestral colour from a generation that was rich in superb orchestrators. No amount of fine scoring can obscure a paucity of ideas, says the teacher of composition. To which Debussy would probably have replied that no worth-while musical idea could be conceived (for him) apart from its instrumental setting. Debussy was a composer who had a feeling for the orchestra in his blood. The effects of colour he achieved in *L'Après-midi*, the *Nocturnes* and, as we shall see shortly, in *Pelléas*, effects that seem to have a bloom on them—these are among the loveliest things in music.

CHAPTER XVI

THE CHORAL AND DRAMATIC WORKS

'No self-respecting teacher of composition would stoop to teach symphony,' once said Ambroise Thomas, director of the Conservatoire during Debussy's student days. That remark was no doubt made by the elderly composer in some special circumstance, for even in his own day there were several self-respecting teachers who taught 'symphony.' But it brings home a point that people in this country are apt to overlook: throughout the nineteenth century composers in France were expected to be first and foremost composers of dramatic music. The *Prix de Rome* is a prize awarded to this day for ability to write a dramatic work. Many French composers of the past, it is true, were prevented from developing their gifts for drama by the conservatism of the Opéra and the Opéra-Comique; and it is rather ironical that, given this dramatic bias, these two state-supported opera houses should have persistently frowned at and discouraged any sign of a progressive spirit in the whole line of composers from Berlioz to Debussy. Hence the fact that Berlioz's programme music is often drama that seems to have got into the concert hall by mistake. Is it not so? Look at *Lélio,* with its drop curtain. There can be little doubt that if Berlioz had been successful with his first opera, *Les Francs Juges,* he would have become a dramatic composer of the first order. As it was, he was able to turn his whole energies to the stage only in the last years of his life; and then the struggle against public indifference

was too much for him. 'Mais vous voyez, ils viennent,' said
a friend, pointing to the people flocking to one of his last
appearances at the Opéra. 'Oui, ils viennent; mais moi, je
m'en vais.'

What has this to do with Debussy? It has much to do with
him. In his last year at the Conservatoire Debussy asked
Gounod to recommend an early stage work he had written
to the director of the Opéra. We do not know which work
this was, possibly something he had written in preparation
for the *Concours de Rome*. 'I shall ask,' Gounod said, 'but
I can answer for nothing—or rather I can answer for a refusal.'
Very likely Debussy's early work was quite immature and
Gounod's words were justified. But at the same time his
reply shows that very hostility of the Opéra from which
Berlioz suffered and which seemed to be arming itself against
Debussy. In the chapter on the abandoned operas it was seen
that Debussy had always some idea for a stage work at the
back of his mind. *Diane au bois, Rodrigue et Chimène, Pelléas
et Mélisande, Le Diable dans le beffroi, La Chute de la maison Usher*
—of these only one materialized.

There were, of course, several reasons for this. Still, Debussy,
like Berlioz, showed very early that he had the makings of a
great dramatic composer. Gounod was the first to realize
this when he heard *L'Enfant prodigue,* the lyrical scene that
won the *Prix de Rome*. Taking the young boy aside after
the performance before the severe judges of the Académie, he
whispered in his ear: 'Toi, tu as du génie.' One may wonder,
perhaps, what signs of genius are revealed in this short Massenet-
like score—for it is full of Massenet. A more important point
to observe is that it is genuinely dramatic. It would have been
very easy to dwell on Lia's sentimental effusions and the
Prodigal Son's destitution. That is what Debussy did not
do; he went straight to the heart of the story and gave the
work remarkable dramatic unity. This was no ordinary feat

UNPUBLISHED SKETCHES FOR 'LA CHUTE DE LA MAISON USHER'
The inscription at the top is in the handwriting of Emma Debussy

in face of the ensnaring sentimentality of the libretto by Édouard
Guinand. Debussy wrote as dignified a setting as one could
conceive. Some twenty years later he revised certain numbers
and in 1919 the work was given as a one-act drama at the
Théâtre Lyrique de Vaudeville. Some time later it was
given in the same form in London. It did not achieve much
success, but the fact that this dramatic work, written at the
age of twenty-two, outlived its composer is itself interesting,
for Debussy was not a composer who developed early.

The date of *La Damoiselle élue* is 1887–8. As already
mentioned, the text of this 'poème lyrique' was taken from
Gabriel Sarrazin's translation of Rossetti's *Blessed Damozel*.
People to-day have not generally a very high opinion of this
poem. It was originally published in a Pre-Raphaelite paper
called *The Germ,* and tells of a girl in Paradise who had a
vision of terrestrial love—the kind of subject that the Pre-
Raphaelites were continually harping on. She is a rather
backboneless creature, this angelic Damozel. Leaning out
'from the gold bar of Heaven':

> Her eyes were deeper than the depth
> Of waters stilled at even;
> She had three lilies in her hand,
> And the stars in her hair were seven.

The trouble with much of Rossetti's poetry is that it is not
sufficiently ripe and voluptuous to compensate for its lack of
vigour.

> Her hair that lay along her back
> Was yellow like ripe corn.

And

> Her voice was like the voice the stars
> Had when they sang together.

Compare that with Verlaine's portraits of women. Her lover,
when he arrives in Paradise, 'shall fear, haply, and be dumb':

Then will I lay my cheek
To his, and tell about our love,
Not once abashed or weak:
And the dear Mother will approve
My pride, and let me speak.

It may seem impertinent to summarize a poem by giving
a few quotations, but there is little more to the argument,
which is really too slight for the length of the poem. Sarrazin,
in his not very literal translation, cut most of the parenthetic
passages and Debussy cut again from Sarrazin's version, with
the result that the poem that has been set to music is exactly
half the length of the original. Debussy's text contains twelve
verses, Rossetti's poem twenty-four. For euphonic purposes
Debussy also altered a number of words and substituted the
name Blanchelys for Gertrude, one of Mary's 'five hand-
maidens, whose names are five sweet symphonies.' This was
to rhyme with the name of another handmaiden, Rosalys.

The work is scored for two soprano solos (the Damozel and
a narrator), female chorus and orchestra. On the whole the
musical setting is much more acceptable than the poem. It
might easily have been something terribly sentimental. Just
think what Massenet would have done! There are touches
of Massenet here and there, but fortunately Debussy was
almost at the end of his Massenet stage. The work that was
in his mind was *Parsifal*, which he had just heard at Bayreuth.
Debussy's mature opinion of *Parsifal* will be given in a moment
and we shall see then that he had not much appreciation of
the character of Parsifal himself. But in those formative years
following his return from Rome he no doubt thought of this
work as the least overwhelming, symphonically, of Wagner's
operas, and he seems to have seen some resemblance between
the characters of Parsifal and the Blessed Damozel. At any
rate each of the four motives which appear in the prelude and
are treated as *Leitmotive* in the short score have a flavour of the

Parsifal motives in Wagner's opera. It is interesting to note that *La Damoiselle élue* was of all Debussy's works the one that met with the unqualified praise of the 'bande à Franck.' Franck himself admired it; Ernest Chausson said it was a masterpiece; and Vincent d'Indy spoke of it in 'terms that would bring a blush to the lilies that lie asleep between the fingers of the Blessed Damozel.'[1] *La Damoiselle élue* then, is the nearest Debussy ever came to César Franck. It was no accident that it was by the intermediation of Rossetti.

At the other end of his life is *Le Martyre de saint Sébastien*. This is not, as it is often imagined to be, an opera or a cantata, but incidental music to the mystery play by Gabriele d'Annunzio. Incidental music of a special kind, it is true, rather like the music in the medieval mystery and nativity plays that were enacted in churches. As in these old plays, music is called in for the high lights of the drama. It brings into relief the lament of the twin brothers, Marc and Marcellien, before the miracle, the weeping of the women of Byblos at the death of their Adonis, and Sebastian's ecstatic dance on the burning coals. There is a prelude to each of the five acts and there are numerous orchestral and choral interludes. The whole score is often played at a concert, occupying about half the programme. During the war Debussy did contemplate adapting the play for an opera, but that was another opera that was never written. The rights of dramatic production are in the hands of Ida Rubinstein, who commissioned both the play and the music.

In 1920 Émile Vuillermoz wrote: '*Le Martyre de saint Sébastien* is a masterpiece that has not yet been understood. Debussy wrote his *Parsifal* that day.' Aha! Well, the comparison is tempting: both subjects deal with aspects of the Christian faith and both were written in the latter years of the composer's life. Are they examples of a sublimation in

[1] From a letter from Debussy to Ernest Chausson.

religion of that bitter disillusionment that must eventually befall the out-and-out sensualist? *Parsifal* perhaps, but not *Le Martyre,* neither d'Annunzio's nor Debussy's. Is it not highly significant that the character Debussy admired in *Parsifal* was Klingsor? 'He was an ex-Knight of the Grail,' he jocularly wrote, 'turned out of the Holy Place for his original ideas on chastity.' And he goes on:

This crafty magician is not only the one human character, but the one moral character in the drama—a drama in which the young Parsifal is the guileless hero of the most false ideas on religion and morals. In this Christian drama no one wishes to sacrifice himself; yet sacrifice is one of the most beautiful of Christian virtues. If Parsifal finds his magic spear, it is thanks to that old Kundry who is the real sacrificed one of the drama. She is the victim both of Klingsor's diabolical intrigues and of the guileless but evil thoughts (*la sainte mauvaise humeur*) of the Knight of the Grail. The general feeling is certainly religious, but why do children's voices sometimes have that suspicious hoarseness? (Just think of the childish candour that Palestrina would have expressed.)

All this has only to do with the poet in Wagner, whom one usually admires, and nothing to do with the decorative side of *Parsifal,* which is always supremely beautiful. The orchestral writing has a unique, incalculable beauty and it is noble and powerful.

And he concludes: '*Parsifal* is one of the most beautiful monuments raised to the imperturbable glory of music.'[1] Again, then, it was the decorativeness of the work that he admired—that feeling for abstract design in music that may or may not underline some philosophical or psychological idea, but which itself is intensely expressive—of what no one need ask. Note too that what he admired in Bach was not the religious fervour, but what he called Bach's 'arabesques.'

[1] *Gil Blas,* 6th April 1903. *Parsifal et la Société des Grandes Auditions de France.*

Clearly, what he admired in both Bach and Wagner was their inherent sensuousness.

I mentioned the decorative element in Debussy's music when speaking of *La Mer*. The incidental music to *Le Martyre* has much in common with *La Mer*: it is powerful in the same way, the themes are sharply defined, there is a good deal of counterpoint and hardly any of that soft luscious writing that gives one the feeling, Debussy's detractors might say, of a musical Turkish bath. But the orchestration is quite different: it is highly coloured. And the choral writing is very vigorous and austere. Whether it was exactly the music that d'Annunzio expected we do not know. D'Annunzio loved Debussy's music passionately. In the published play he included in the preface a long poem in praise of 'Claude de France,' and at certain points in the margin noted: *Magister Claudius sonum dedit*. But what he loved particularly were his songs on the poems of Charles d'Orléans and François Villon, and it may well be that he expected *Le Martyre* to be in this vein. If he did he must have been disappointed, for there is nothing in *Le Martyre* so subtle or so pure as those magnificent songs. After the first performance in 1911 Pierre Lalo wrote in *Le Temps*:

Debussy has been led to modify the character and form of his musical ideas, of his music itself, even of his orchestra; he has given them greater breadth and expansiveness, more assurance, almost more form; the idiom is more definite, less restrained and subtle. . . . This is excellent music, but it is foreign to M. Debussy's real nature; it forms an incident, a parenthesis, in his work and in his artistic development.[1]

That opinion holds to-day.

And now we must hurry to Debussy's great masterpiece, *Pelléas et Mélisande*.

Maeterlinck's drama preaches the fatalistic philosophy that

---

[1] Translation by Maire and Grace O'Brien.

man's incapacity to escape from the mysterious forces which determine the course of life is the tragedy of his existence. In his pessimistic view there is only one certain reality—death. Death hovers over all Maeterlinck's plays, liberating his creatures from their world of dreams. Character, then, and qualities of the mind are not what we have to look for. Maeterlinck's *Pelléas* has nothing to appeal to the psychologist; but it has some beautiful poetry.

The action passes in the imaginary kingdom of Allemonde in a remote and undetermined past. Mélisande is weeping by a well in the forest. Golaud, grandson of Arkel, the king, has lost his way and approaches her. He is a giant compared to her frail young self and she forbids him to touch her. All have done her a wrong; she has fled from far. She will not, cannot tell him any more. Golaud discovers her name and, on condition that he does not touch her, persuades her to come with him. 'But where will you go?' she asks. 'How can I tell, for I too am astray.'[1] Those words, as the two go out, set the mysterious tone of the play.

In the following scene Arkel is informed of their marriage. He does not view it with much approval, but consents to it as a manifestation of fate. Fate, too, compels Pelléas, Golaud's half-brother, to postpone his departure to a friend's deathbed. Some days later, when Mélisande is in the dark gardens that surround Arkel's castle, in which she has come to live with Golaud, Geneviève, her mother-in-law, shows her the light from the sea. Pelléas enters. Then the boat which brought Mélisande leaves the port, and together Pelléas and Mélisande return to the castle.

The second act presents a string of symbolic events. With Pelléas, by a well in the park, Mélisande is playing with her wedding-ring and drops it into the water. 'I threw it up too

[1] This and the following extracts are taken from the excellent translation of the libretto by Henry G. Chapman.

high in the rays of the sun,' she says. In the next scene we learn that, at the moment it fell, Golaud was thrown from his horse, which suddenly, at the stroke of twelve, 'ran like a blind fool straight into a tree trunk.' 'No doubt I fell,' he tells his young wife, 'the horse, I take it, fell upon me; but it seemed as though the woods themselves lay on my body. I felt sure that my heart had been torn in two.' Mélisande tends him and for no apparent reason bursts into tears. 'What has happened to you?' Golaud inquires. 'Has someone done you wrong? . . . Is it the king? Is it my mother? Is it Pelléas?' 'No, no, it is not Pelléas. It is no one. Oh! I know you can't understand me.' Golaud takes hold of her hands and sees that she has not her ring. She must go and find it at once. 'Ask Pelléas if he will not go with you.' She has not told Golaud that the ring had dropped into the well—the clear and deep well that 'could heal the eyes of the sightless.' She goes with Pelléas to find it in a grotto 'full of very dark blue shadows,' knowing perfectly well that it is not there. Frightened by the sight of three paupers revealed by a flood of light from the moon, she runs away, dragging Pelléas after her.

In the first scene of Act III Mélisande is combing her long hair at a window of one of the castle towers. Pelléas passes and greets her cheerfully. As she leans out to let him have her hand, her hair suddenly falls down by the side of the tower, enveloping Pelléas down to his knees. There follows a sensuously poetic passage rather like *La Chevelure* from Pierre Louÿs's *Chansons de Bilitis*. 'They are here in my hands,' Pelléas sings, 'in my mouth too I hold them. . . . Can you not hear my kisses all along your hair?' Doves come out of the tower and fly about them in the darkness. But Golaud enters, perturbed. 'Stop playing like this out here in the dark. You 're children, both of you'; and he dismisses them with a nervous laugh.

The drama deepens. In the castle vaults Golaud symbolically shows Pelléas the stagnating water from which there rises a stench of death and a chasm of which he sees the 'very bottom.' When they come out on to the terrace Golaud warns his brother that this childish play with Mélisande must stop. He has become fiercely jealous and his anxiety drives him, in the next scene, to question his little son (by his first wife), Yniold. One evening in the woods they seat themselves under Mélisande's window and Yniold says that his mother and Pelléas quarrel 'about the door' and 'about the light,' and that once they kissed when it rained. Golaud can get little out of the child beyond these frightening replies, but when suddenly the window is lighted he hoists him up to spy. Pelléas is there, but still he learns only that they are close to each other and looking at the lamplight.

Arkel's affection for Mélisande is very beautiful. 'An old man feels the need now and then just to touch with his lips the brow of a maid or the cheek of a child, to keep on trusting in the freshness of life and drive away for a moment the menaces of death.' But it is she who is threatened by death. 'Thou hast the strange mien and errant look,' he tells her, 'of a creature ever waiting for some dreadful doom, in the sun, in a garden. . . .' Golaud breaks into this touching scene to announce that Pelléas is leaving that night. Mélisande had already been told of the decision and had arranged to meet Pelléas for the last time; but she says nothing. As she approaches Golaud to wipe some blood off his forehead, he angrily casts her aside. 'Do you see those great eyes?' he says to Arkel. 'I know them well, those eyes, I have seen them at work. Keep them shut! Keep them shut! or I'll close them for many a day.' He catches hold of her feverish hands and becomes hysterical: 'Get you away! 'Tis your flesh that disgusts me!' Then, seizing her by the hair, he drags her on her knees, calling on Absalom and laughing like an old man.

Arkel runs up, Golaud affects a sudden calm, and the scene ends with Arkel's fine line:

> If I were God I should have pity on the hearts of men.

The next scene is again one of those interpolations which rather too naïvely symbolize the fatality of the drama. By the well in the park Yniold tries in vain to lift a rock to regain his golden ball. Then he hears the bleating of sheep, crowding now to the right, now to the left. Suddenly they are quiet. 'Why don't they talk any more?' he asks the shepherd. 'Because they are not on their way to the stable.' The only excuse for this interpolation is that it separates the last dramatic scene from the next, in which Pelléas and Mélisande meet for the last time and confess their love. As the doors of the castle are bolted against them and their fate seems decided, Golaud appears 'at the end of their shadows.' As he draws his sword they embrace desperately, and he falls upon them. Pelléas is killed and Mélisande flees through the wood.

The last act is in one scene only. Mélisande, who has given birth to a child, is on her deathbed, surrounded by Arkel, Golaud and a physician. Golaud begs her forgiveness. 'Yes, yes, I have forgiven you. But what is there to be forgiven?' she asks in all innocence. Still Golaud is harassed by doubts and implores her to tell him the truth about her love for Pelléas. 'Did you love with a love that's forbid?' he stammers out. He will never know. Mélisande is shown her child, the serving women line the walls in silence and fall on their knees as she dies.

Such is the libretto of Debussy's opera. It is by no means the whole of Maeterlinck's play, nor does the text as it stands always conform to the original. Four whole scenes and a number of passages are cut and certain lines have been altered. Now the scenes that are cut (Act I, scene i; Act II, scene iv; Act III, scene i, and Act V, scene i of the play) are for the most part highly symbolical, like the scene of Yniold and the sheep in Act IV of the opera which, too, is generally cut at performances, presumably at Debussy's wish. The general opinion to-day is that these scenes merely hold up the action of the play by their too obvious insistence on the fatalism of the work. It is easy to see now why Maeterlinck was so displeased with Debussy's adaptation which, he said, was 'strange and almost hostile' to him.[1] That was probably an exaggeration. But, unlike the play, the libretto may be read without being greatly disturbed by the obviousness of the symbolic scenes, the number of which, as we have seen, Debussy reduced to a minimum. In the opera their obviousness disappears entirely.

This is not to say that this fatalistic element is not apparent in the opera. I do not think that in composing the score it was uppermost in Debussy's mind, but it was always present. When Arkel says to Mélisande: 'At my age there has grown upon me the belief one can often rely on events themselves,' and follows this by: 'Thou wilt be the one to open us the door for such a new era as I foresee,' the theme typifying Mélisande is heard at the same time as a rising figure on the horns:

Et c'est toi, main · te · nant, qui vas ou·vrir la

cresc. molto

porte   à   l'è-re nou - vel - le que j'entre - vois

(Mélisande's theme)

a theme that recurs when Arkel approves Golaud's marriage with the words: 'It may be there never occurs any event that is useless':

Il n'ar-ri-ve peut- ê - tre   pas__ d'é-vè-ne-

ments i‧nu‧ti‧les

and, among many other examples, when, at Mélisande's death, Arkel, refusing to let Golaud speak to her alone, says to him: 'Ah! you do not know this being, the soul':

vous ne sa‧vez pas‧ ce que c'est que l'â‧me

It is the *Leitmotiv* of destiny.

Now let us turn to the great and special beauty of the score, which lies in the extremely subtle way the music brings into relief the meaning of the words. It has often been said that aesthetically Debussy and Maeterlinck were perfectly matched. But this is only half-stating the case. The prose of Maeter-

linck in *Pelléas* is poetic, but not intensely so. His lines are
never charged with the bottled-up passion of the lines of
Mallarmé. On the contrary, they are extremely simple, resort-
ing to imagery only for occasional high-lights. What Debussy
achieved in *Pelléas* is Maeterlinck intensified, as *L'Après-midi*
is Mallarmé clarified. The very simplicity of the lines allowed
him—almost compelled him, unless he were to write something platitudinous in the style of Erik Satie—to create a richer
and a greater drama.

Yet the music never stifles the lines. In his excellent
analysis[1] Maurice Emmanuel quotes a prophecy of Jean-
Jacques Rousseau that a French musician would one day
realize the 'recitative appropriate to the simplicity and clarity
of our language.' This recitative, Rousseau said, 'should
proceed by very small intervals. The voice should neither
rise nor descend very much. There should be few sustained
notes; no sudden bursts and still less any shrieking; nothing
that resembles song; and little inequality in the duration or
the value of the notes.' This would be an exact description
of the recitative in *Pelléas*; and it is of the utmost beauty.
Here is an example from the letter that Geneviève reads to
Arkel announcing Golaud's marriage. The words are simply:
'I know neither her age nor who she is, nor where she belongs
and I do not dare to ask her yet.' This is rendered:

Je ne sais ni son â-ge,   ni qui elle est,   ni d'où el-le

[1] *Pelléas et Mélisande. Étude historique et critique.* (Paris, n.d.)

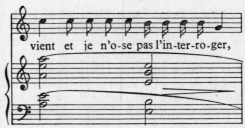

vient et je n'o-se pas l'in-ter-ro-ger,

Very similar in feeling is a line of Yniold in the scene with his father:

Oui, oui, toujours, petit père ; quand vous n'êtes pas là.

and Mélisande's meeting with Golaud when, in the last act, he asks her forgiveness:

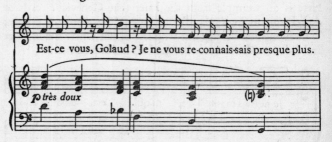

Est-ce vous, Golaud ? Je ne vous re-connais-sais presque plus.

p très doux

I have purposely put these passages together as the loveliest things in the whole score. Their beauty may not be immediately apparent, but gradually it creeps on one, as one might perceive the smile on some Gothic Virgin. Was not d'Annunzio thinking of such passages when he wrote in the preface to *Le Martyre de saint Sébastien*:

> Très douces gens, par lui, par lui,
> Vous entendrez chanter la Vierge,
> Qui est la couleur de l'aurore!

Pelléas provides the ideal answer to those who complain of the artificialities of opera, of its stylized recitatives and the high-flown arias overwhelming or obscuring the meaning of the words. No composer, unless it be Mozart, has ever made music accentuate speech more carefully, nor indeed more variedly. In the first scene of the opera, when Golaud suggests recovering Mélisande's crown which has fallen into the water, he has a line in which one can recognize the inflections of the spoken voice:

Mélisande will not hear of it. 'Leave it alone! If you do take it out I shall throw myself down there.' And she has an impassioned phrase spread over a whole octave: she breaks into song: [1]

Je n'en veux plus !   Si vous la re‑ti‑rez,

je me jette à sa pla‑ce !

[1] For a detailed analysis of this fusion of dramatic recitative and song that is a special characteristic of the vocal writing in *Pelléas* see M. Emmanuel's study. It is most interesting to note that this was the ideal of Mozart who, in 1778, wrote to his father about Benda's duologues *Medea* and *Ariadne auf Naxos*: 'You probably know that there is no singing, but declamation; sometimes, indeed,

Then look at the passage where Pelléas comforts Mélisande for the loss of her ring. 'It is naught, perhaps the ring will be recovered. If not, no doubt we can find you another.' What affection is implied in the setting! What is so poignant is the way in which a largish interval follows a series of repeated notes—as in the *Chansons de Bilitis*:

Ce n'est rien, nous la re-trou-ve-rons peut-ê-tre! Ou bien nous

words are spoken while the music is playing, and then the effect is most magnificent.' And he gives his opinion that 'most recitative should be treated in opera in this way; and only occasionally when the words are suitable for musical expression, should there be singing in the recitative.'

Un peu retenu

en re - trou - ve - rons une au - tre

And as Mélisande refuses, there is no mistaking her assent to Pélleas's advances. (Her lines are, of course, symbolical of this.)

a tempo

Non, non, nous ne la re-trou-ve-rons

mf

Un peu retenu

plus, nous n'en trou-ve-rons pas d'au-tres non plus.

dim.

Golaud's affection for Mélisande is quite different. It is something that he might be afraid of. 'You're very young, I fancy. How old may you be?' In the first scene this is about all he manages to say to her:

vous a - vez l'air très jeu - ne.

Quel âge a - vez - vous?

He seems afraid of his own affection; and indeed it only makes Mélisande recoil. To this question she makes the reply: 'I begin to feel so cold.' But how gracefully she recoils in the downward phrase (*quoted on page* 208). One could quote such subtly suggestive touches from almost every page. Golaud's doubts, superstitions, fury, repentance, Mélisande's whimsical moods, Pelléas's sudden streaks of passion, Arkel's 'pity for the hearts of men,' all this is treated simply and beautifully and in a way that makes one feel, as with the music of Mozart, that it could not possibly

Debussy

Je com - mence___ à a - voir froid

Librement

MÉLISANDE *(in a low voice)*

Je t'aime aus -

(Orchestra tacet)

PELLÉAS

Je t'ai - me

- si

Oh! qu'as - tu dit, Mé - li - san - de!

En retenant

Je ne l'ai pres - que pas en - ten - du!___

208

have been done in any other way. That is the test of the greatest art; one has to make no excuses. It is something to love—entirely. And above all it is simple. 'Take hold of Eloquence and wring her neck,' wrote Verlaine; that is what Debussy did. Compare, then, with the passion of Isolde, fiercely triumphant in her defiance of death, this simple confession of love from these creatures of fate (*see page* 208). There's feeling, there's passion, there's *reality*.

This would seem to be the antithesis of Wagner; but can one say that of *Pelléas* in every way? The writing for the voices brings out the finest shades of the words, but the drama is developed in the orchestra. This was the principle of Wagner, and there is no denying that *Pelléas* would never have been possible without *Tristan*. I like to think of Mélisande as the illegitimate daughter of Tristan and Isolde. Like them, she has a *Leitmotiv*, and so have each of the other characters. There is also a theme for destiny (already noted), the lost ring, death and pardon. Maurice Emmanuel, apologizing for such an 'outrage against Debussy's tastes,' gives a list of thirteen. It would be an outrage if one ticketed each theme off—'visiting cards' Debussy called the *Leitmotive* in the *Ring*—and said nothing more. But actually Debussy's *Leitmotive* are distinguishable as such only after careful searching and only by painfully extracting them from their flimsy context. See how discreetly, after Golaud's 'I cannot permit it, Méli-sande, so come, come, give me your hand' (Act I, scene i), Mélisande's theme enters on the double bass (*see page* 210). And then, as he warns her that 'the night will be so dark and so chilly,' the theme that opens the opera is heard on the violins (in minims) (*see page* 210).

This theme, says M. Emmanuel, 'represents nothing, nor anybody. It evokes only a far-off past.'

Throughout, the orchestration is a model of delicacy, transparency and discretion, and it is such that if the singers

MÉLISANDE

Oh! ne me tou-chez pas!

GOLAUD

Ne cri - ez - pas

Double Bass

Violins

La nuit se-ra très noire et très froi - de

enunciate clearly not a word is missed. Like a mirage of
the drama, it rises behind their lines, giving perspective to
the words of the moment. From a purely technical point of
view this was a wonderful feat. Romain Rolland has put
it well:

Rien de trop: that is the artist's motto. Instead of amalgamating
the instruments for mass effects, he throws into relief their indivi-
duality or delicately grafts one timbre on to another, without anything of their true nature being spoilt. Like the Impressionist
painters of those times, he paints with pure colours, with that delicate
sobriety that spurns all harshness and ugliness.

Again the Impressionists. When Émile Réty, the old
secretary of the Conservatoire who had turned away 'pale
with indignation' at Debussy's improvisations, heard *Pelléas,*
he exclaimed: 'C'est du Claude Monet.' Debussy was
flattered.

Standing back and looking at the main lines of the composition, one is struck by the dramatic inevitability in the
sequence of scenes. 'The composition of the work is such as to
make extracts utterly impossible.'[1] Yes: whatever complaints
might be made of the form of the instrumental works, Debussy
shows himself in *Pelléas* to be a musical dramatist of the first
order. Consider the various scenes between Pelléas and
Mélisande. There are in all six, so constructed that there is
not the slightest drag in the way the drama proceeds to its
goal—which, given the dreamy nature of the subject, there
might well have been. Of these six scenes, the three love
scenes stand in the middle of the canvas, making a progression
towards Golaud's mad killing of Pelléas, while the three
shorter ones—the meeting of Pelléas and Mélisande by the
sea, their frightened visit to the grotto, and their hurried

---

[1] From a letter to the Royal Philharmonic Society. See
Appendix E.

exchange of a few words in the castle before Golaud appears to drag Mélisande by her hair—offset the development of the love scenes like counter-themes in a movement of a symphony. The balance of the composition is supplied by the scenes between Golaud and Mélisande, growing in intensity in the opposite direction, as it were. The framework, it is true, is Maeterlinck's, but this does not detract from Debussy's achievement. In Yniold's spying scene and the scene in the vaults there is something Moussorgskian; in Golaud's fury and despair, contrasted with the magnificent serenity of Mélisande's death, there is something Shakespearian. One can hardly say any more.

CHAPTER XVII

THE LITERARY WORKS

THE literary works of Debussy it would be especially interesting to talk about are still in manuscript, and I have unfortunately not been able to consult them. These are the opera librettos adapted from the tales of Poe, of which we shall have some interesting details when Gabriel Mourey publishes his book on Debussy's methods of adapting texts for the stage. Until then it is only possible to point again to this lifelong hankering after the musical stage as one of Debussy's important characteristics as a composer. Apparently he considered himself a competent literary dramatist, for, over a period of eighteen months, about the year 1900, he gave lessons in writing for the stage to his young friend René Peter. Together they contemplated a fairy play entitled *Les Mille et une Nuits de n'importe où et d'ailleurs* and began a dramatic satire called *F.E.A.* (*Les Frères en art*). This, René Peter writes, 'is the story of an evil-minded painter who, at the height of his fame, managed, by the aid of a mutual assistance league (*Les F.E.A.*), in which he had complete authority, to stifle budding talents and to imperil the honour of his favourite pupil.' This play was accepted by a Paris theatre manager, but at the last moment Debussy seems to have thought it unworthy. 'I am just an old romantic,' he wrote to a friend of Peter's, 'who has chucked all desire for success out of the window.' Three acts of the play are still in manuscript. There is one other stage-work to be mentioned, a scenario for a ballet, *Masques et Bergamasques,* written at the request of Diaghilev. It is a conventional love-story from the Italian comedy which passes in eighteenth-century Venice. The music was never composed.

The main concern of this chapter, then, are Debussy's critical writings and his essays in musical journalism which are to be found in a number of Paris journals between the years 1901 and 1914. The bulk of these writings is in three series of articles: *La Revue blanche,* April to December 1901; *Gil Blas,* January to June 1903; and *La Revue S.I.M.* (the publication of the French section of the International Society of Music), November 1912 to March 1914. The complete critical writings have been listed and commented upon by Léon Vallas in his book, *Les Idées et les théories de Claude Debussy, musicien français,* to which the reader who wishes to investigate the subject more thoroughly may be referred.[1]

The title of this book was perhaps not very apt, for strictly speaking Debussy had no theories. In his first article in *La Revue blanche* of 1st April 1901 he makes this clear:

Having been asked to speak about music in this review, may I be allowed to explain what I intend to do? On these pages will be found sincere and honestly felt impressions rather than criticism; for this too often takes the form of brilliant variations on the theme of: 'You're wrong because you didn't do as I did,' or: 'You're talented and I'm not; that can't go on.' I will try to discover the forces that have brought works of art into being, which I think is more worth while than taking them to pieces like an old watch.

People hardly remember that as children they were never allowed to open the insides of their dolls. That would be a crime of lèse-mystery. Yet they still insist on sticking their aesthetic noses where they have no business. They no longer break their dolls; but they take them to pieces and kill the mystery in cold blood. Then they have something to talk about. Oh, yes—some may be excused

---

[1] The translations of Debussy's articles in this chapter are partly taken from the English translation of this book by Maire O'Brien, partly from *M. Croche the Dilettante-hater* and are partly my own.

on the grounds of ignorance, but others, more harmful, premeditate the crime. Well, mediocrity must be defended and those who undertake its defence may be sure of support.

I shall speak very little of works established by success or tradition. Once for all, Meyerbeer, Thalberg, Reyer are men of genius, and nothing more need be said.

On Sundays, when God is kind, I shall hear no music. Please accept my apologies. Lastly, remember the word 'impressions,' for I insist on keeping my emotion free from all parasitic aesthetics.

This harsh, wry sarcasm which grins in so much that Debussy wrote is curious, particularly as it is hardly noticeable in his music, at least not until the later works. The musician and the writer in Debussy were certainly very different people. It seems that he flung all his animosity, of which he had a great deal, into his prose or his conversation, or his letters, which often show the same harsh tone, so that he could preserve that inner glow of warmth for his music. One has to remember in reading his criticisms that, as Vallas notes, he was 'detested by reactionary artists who condemned, anathematized and excommunicated him'; and that he 'took little interest in these notes, which he never wrote except from sheer necessity in order to earn a little money.' Is his barbed tongue to be wondered at? This is how he begins an article on Nikisch:

On Sunday the overpowering glare of the sun seemed to make it unthinkable to listen to music. The Berlin Philharmonic Orchestra, conducted by Nikisch, took the opportunity of giving its first concert. I hope that God will forgive my having gone back on my resolutions and that others more fortunate paid homage to the grass generously spread by Him for the reception of sausage skins and the logical development of idylls.

To people to-day his style seems strained and self-conscious. It is precious. Preciosity was a characteristic of the Symbolist writers when they did not attain the stature of Mallarmé or Verlaine, or Jules Laforgue, a young writer of genius who

died at the age of twenty-eight and with whose style Debussy's
biting manner has often been compared, though it is difficult
for me to see any resemblance. In his prose Debussy seemed
to have little regard for the principle of 'economy of means.'
A style more replete with adjectives and images it would be
difficult to imagine. It reminds one that *La Revue blanche,*
for which the first articles were written, was almost contemporary with those *fin-de-siècle* reviews in London, the *Yellow
Book* and the *Savoy,* in which extravagance was the keynote.
In some ways Debussy's prose is like the drawings of Aubrey
Beardsley: it has that same baroque excess of energy that runs
into wild curlicues. What it certainly never reminds one of
is Debussy's music. Here is an example from a criticism of
some songs of Delius performed at the Société Nationale:

They are very sweet and innocent songs, music to rock the con-
valescents of the rich neighbourhoods. There is always a note
hanging over a chord like a water-lily in a lake, tired of being
watched by the moon, or like a little balloon blocked by the clouds.

Apparently Debussy thought this passage so good that two
years later he reproduced it exactly as it stands in a notice of
some songs of Grieg. He added then that another piece of
Grieg's music was like a 'pink sweet filled with snow.'

This brings us to an episode in Debussy's journalistic career
that left a rather unpleasant feeling. About 1900 Grieg
protested against the condemnation of Dreyfus by refusing to
come to France. Some years later, however, in 1903, he
accepted an engagement to play at the Concerts Colonne and
Debussy, who had instinctively taken sides with the nationalists,
seized the opportunity to pour abuse of a purely personal kind
on Grieg which, in a concert criticism, was out of place, to
say the least.

To begin with [he wrote] the number of Norwegians who usually
haunt the Concerts Colonne was tripled; we had never before been

privileged to see so much red hair or such extravagant hats—for the fashions in Christiania seem to me rather behind the times. Then the concert opened with a double turn: the performance of an overture called *Autumn* and the ejection of a crowd of Grieg's admirers, who, at the bidding of a police-constable, a slave to duty rather than to music, were sent to cool their enthusiasm on the banks of the Seine. . . .

At last I saw Grieg. From in front he looks like a genial photographer; from behind his way of doing his hair makes him look like the plants called sunflowers, dear to parrots and the gardens that decorate small country stations.

He then went on to say that Grieg was an exquisite musician when he interpreted the folk-music of his country, but 'apart from this he is no more than a clever musician, more concerned with effects than with genuine art.' Grieg was naturally very much offended, and in a letter to M. D. Calvocoressi made it clear how much he deplored Debussy's 'utter lack of comprehension of my art' and especially 'his venomous and contemptuous tone.' 'A genuine artist,' he added, 'ought to strive to maintain a high level in all things of the mind, and to respect the point of view of other artists' [1]—a feat of which such a subjective artist as Debussy was not always capable.

His quips, which sometimes suggest Erik Satie, were not everywhere appreciated. In an article entitled *Open-air Music*, written for *La Renaissance latine*, he proposes, among other things, that 'M. Gavioli, the famous maker of street organs, . . . should be induced to make his instruments worthy of playing the *Ring*. Did not Wagner declare again and again that he could be understood only in France? . . . The Opéra does not shrink from playing *Pagliacci*; shrink then no longer from making street organs worthy to perform the *Ring*.' Mr. Calvocoressi has explained why this article never appeared

[1] This letter is quoted in M. D. Calvocoressi's *Musicians' Gallery*.

in the journal for which it was written: 'The article was duly set in type, and lay waiting, when suddenly *La Renaissance latine* changed hands. The new proprietor and editor, coming across it, gave it a glance, exclaimed: "Mais c'est idiot!" and decreed, despite my expostulations, that it was not to be published.' It appeared in *La Revue blanche* of 1st June 1901.

And now, I think, we may turn to the more gratifying aspects of Debussy's journalism—of which there are many. He loved to watch at a concert. Often he would devote the whole of his notice to the performer's appearance ('le côté décoratif' again). In an account of the *Ballade* for piano and orchestra by Gabriel Fauré he says:

The *Ballade* is almost as lovely as Mme Hasselmans, the pianist. With a charming gesture she readjusted a shoulder-strap which slipped down at every lively passage. Somehow an association of ideas was established in my mind between the charm of the afore-mentioned gesture and the music of Fauré. It is a fact, however, that the play of the graceful, fleeting lines described by Fauré's music may be compared to the gesture of a beautiful woman without either suffering from the comparison.

Very charming. Debussy could be harsh and petulant; but beyond this exterior he was a very simple man and had that loving, ingenuous way of seeing beauty in tiny things. He tells that during a performance of the unfinished Symphony a flock of sparrows came to sit on the window-sill and that 'Nikisch had the grace not to demand their expulsion.' Such touches are those of a man who had a fine contempt for officialdom, grandiloquence and bombast. Virtuosity was, of course, anathema to him: 'The attraction of the virtuoso for the public is very much like that of the circus for the crowd. There is always a hope that something dangerous may happen: M. Ysaÿe may play the violin with M. Colonne on his shoulders; or M. Pugno may conclude his piece by lifting the piano with his teeth.' Not only virtuosity, but the whole machinery of the concert world, seemed to him suspect:

Music, nowadays, tends to become more and more an accompaniment for sentimental or tragic incidents, and plays the part of the showman at the door of a booth behind which is displayed the sinister form of 'Mr. Nobody.' True lovers of music seldom frequent fairs; they merely have a piano and feverishly play a few pages over and over again; as sure a means of intoxication as 'just, subtle and mighty opium,' and the least enervating way of spending happy hours.

Shortly before the war the growing popularity of the gramophone was beginning to afford that easy consumption of music which in recent years has been so much talked about. The following passage, written in *La Revue S.I.M.* on 15th May 1913, must be one of the first forebodings of the evils that mechanical music has worked:

At a time like ours, in which mechanical skill has attained unsuspected perfection, the most famous works may be heard as easily as one may drink a glass of beer, and it only costs ten centimes, like the automatic weighing machines. Should we not fear this domestication of sound, this magic that any one can bring from a disk at his will? Will it not bring to waste the mysterious force of an art which one might have thought indestructible? Why don't they understand that there is really no reason to have so many centuries of music behind us, to have thus profited by this magnificent intellectual heritage and to seek childishly to re-write history? Is not our duty, on the contrary, to find the symphonic music appropriate to our age, that which is demanded by progress, bravery and modern victories? The century of aeroplanes has a right to a music of its own.

In his numerous opinions of composers there is no attempt at objective criticism. He said what he liked or did not like, for any one who wanted to know, but he seldom became very enthusiastic. On the contrary, he was exceedingly scathing.

One has the feeling that he was always more interested in the music that he had not yet written than in the finished product of someone else. A composer is, after all, not a wine-taster.

The great value of these criticisms is that they taught, in an age when reverence was apt to be blind, that what counted most were 'honestly felt impressions.' He disliked the 'Pastoral' Symphony, and said so. Some songs of Schubert were like 'dried flowers . . . photographs that are dead indeed! The effect is repeated through endless verses and by the time the third is reached one begins to wonder if the time has not come to produce our own Paul Delmet.' Such things may be written to-day (though they are not likely to be), but in Debussy's day they were considered scandalous.

His preferences went to the very old and to the very new. Bach, he wrote, was 'a benevolent God, to whom musicians should offer a prayer before setting to work so that they may be preserved from mediocrity.' He admires in him 'that musical arabesque, or rather that principle of ornament, which is the basis of all forms of art' and which he sees too in Palestrina, Victoria and Orlandus Lassus. He esteemed Mozart very highly, though he seldom had occasion to write about him. He appreciated Beethoven's orchestra (curiously enough), the ninth Symphony, but not *Adelaide,* which 'the old master must have forgotten to burn.' In later years he called Beethoven 'le vieux sourd.' He was very critical of Gluck, to whose shade he wrote an open letter (published in *Gil Blas* on 23rd February 1903) on the occasion of the revival of *Iphigénie en Aulide.* In this curious letter he says: 'Between ourselves, your prosody was very bad; at least, you turn the French language into an accentuated language when it is, on the contrary, a language of fine shades.' That is interesting, but he objected to Gluck on other grounds. Elsewhere he says: 'Queen Marie Antoinette, who always remained an Austrian—a sentiment for which she was made to pay once

and for all—imposed Gluck on French taste. Thus our
beautiful traditions became warped, our desire for clarity
stifled, and, via Meyerbeer, we arrived quite logically at
Richard Wagner.' The composer he opposed to Gluck was
Rameau, who, he maintains, 'was infinitely more Greek.'

Of the romantic composers he placed Weber highest.
Berlioz 'is an exception—a monster. He is not a musician
at all. He creates the illusion of music by means borrowed
from literature and painting. Besides, there is, as far as I
can see, little that is French in him.' And further: 'His
passion is satisfied with leaves which literature has dried
between the pages of its books. . . . His genius found a
bitter pleasure in airing its longings in an artificial flower
shop.' He admired *L'Enfance du Christ,* the *Symphonie fantastique* and *Roméo et Juliette,* but not *Les Troyens.*

Of the more modern composers, Moussorgsky receives
special praise. Speaking of the set of songs called *The Nursery,*
he says that 'no one has given utterance to the best within us
in tones more gentle or profound: he is unique and will
remain so because his art is spontaneous and free from arid
formulas.' But the Russian vogue for folk-music brings
something sarcastic: 'The fashion for popular airs has spread
quickly throughout the musical world. From east to west
the tiniest villages have been ransacked and simple tunes,
plucked from the mouths of hoary peasants, find themselves,
to their consternation, trimmed with harmonic frills.' Of
Rimsky-Korsakov he admired *Antar,* but not *Scheberazade,*
which reminded him less of the Orient than of a bazaar.[1]
Borodin he does not have occasion to speak of at all. His
later opinion of Tchaikovsky I have not come across, but
Vallas notes that he disapproves of him, 'like all Frenchmen.'

The music of Massenet is 'vibrant with thrills, transports
and would-be embraces. The harmonies are like enlacing

[1] See the letter to Raoul Bardac on p. 275 (Appendix E).

arms, the melodies are the necks we kiss . . .' and so on.
He 'amply succeeded in what he set out to do, a fact which
caused some to believe that they were taking their revenge by
calling him—*sotto voce*—Paul Delmet's best pupil. That is
merely a joke in the worst possible taste.'[1] It is curious to
see his admiration for Richard Strauss, whose 'irresistible
domination it is not possible to withstand.' He is 'very nearly
a genius.' Debussy was, of course, not blind to Strauss's
vulgarity and begins a notice on *Tod und Verklärung*: 'In the
cookery book, under "Jugged Hare," will be seen this wise
recommendation: "Take a hare." Richard Strauss proceeds
otherwise. To write a symphonic poem he takes anything.'
Still he admits that 'he is one of the most assertive geniuses of
our time.'

On Wagner there is little to be added that would further
elucidate that sort of love-fear obsession with the composer to
whom Debussy owed more than any one. He speaks of the
Leitmotive in the *Ring,* which suggest 'a harmless lunatic who,
on presenting his visiting-card, would declaim his name in
song.' Yet this work 'is irresistible as the sea. . . . One does
not criticize a work of such magnitude as the *Ring*. . . . Its
too sumptuous greatness renders futile the legitimate desire to
grasp its proportions.' And he grandiloquently concludes:
'He can never quite die. He will eventually feel the cruel
hand with which time destroys the most beautiful things.
Some splendid ruins will, however, remain, in whose shade
our grandchildren will dream of the past greatness of a man
who, had he been but a little more human, would have been
great for all time.' He heard this performance of the *Ring* at
Covent Garden, and 'as a reward for good behaviour' spent
an evening at the Empire Music-Hall.

During the war Debussy made a selection of his articles

[1] It was, however, a joke made by Debussy himself. See the
letter to Pierre Louÿs on p. 70.

for publication in book form. Some were developed, others cut, and the first proofs of the twenty-five articles thus adapted were sent to G. Jean-Aubry in 1917. But the printing-presses were then in invaded territory and it was not possible to publish the book before 1921. Its title, *M. Croche antidilettante,* is the name of an imaginary interlocutor, an *alter ego* who is sketched in the first two essays.

M. Croche, whose 'features are best pictured by recalling those of Tom Lane, the jockey, and M. Thiers,' had an 'intolerable smile . . . especially evident when he talked of music.' Here is the explanation of the epithet following his name:

> I suddenly decided to ask him what his profession might be. He replied, in a voice which checked any attempt at comment: 'Dilettante-hater. Have you noticed the hostility of a concert-room audience? Have you studied their almost drugged expression of boredom, indifference and even stupidity? . . . I try to forget music because it obscures my perception of what I do not know or shall only know to-morrow.'

Those last words, the most striking in the book, are the kernel of Debussy's philosophy. 'Music is a sum total of scattered forces,' M. Croche goes on. 'You make an abstract ballad of them! I prefer the simple notes of an Egyptian shepherd's pipe. . . . To see the sun rise is more profitable than to hear the "Pastoral" Symphony. What is the use of your almost incomprehensible art?' This is a view often held by poets, but seldom by musicians. As a matter of fact, Debussy sketched the character of M. Croche after reading Paul Valéry's *Soirées avec M. Teste,* where a similarly wrinkled old man symbolizes a quest for the instinctive art. 'I haven't had any books for twenty years,' M. Teste says. 'I've burnt my papers too. . . . I can remember what I want. But the difficult thing is not that, but to *remember what I shall want to-morrow.'* These thoughts are almost identical with those of M. Croche; but M. Teste goes further. 'Je rature le vif,' he says (literally 'I cross out the living'), by which he means that he wishes to turn his back on the instinctive life and seek a higher spiritual world. That forms part of the philosophy of Valéry, as it does of the later Stravinsky, T. S. Eliot and *Parsifal*. But it was no more part of the philosophy of Debussy than of D. H. Lawrence.

CHAPTER XVIII

DEBUSSY'S INFLUENCE

In reply to an 'Inquiry on the German Influence,' instituted by the *Mercure de France* in 1903, Debussy wrote: 'Wagner, if I may express myself with some of the grandiloquence that suits him, was a beautiful sunset that was mistaken for a dawn.' That is true of Wagner, but it has proved even truer of Debussy himself.

The average musician, when asked if Debussy is a force in the growth of music to-day, will say 'No.' For the composer and the student of composition he is as remote as Mozart, if not more so. That 'little Greece,' as Romain Rolland called the world from which Debussy sprung, was shattered when the German guns fired at Liége; and it has not been seen again since.

Debussy having receded into history, then, it is only about now that an evaluation of his position has become possible. This difficult task has been attempted by a number of authors: by Cecil Gray in his *Survey of Contemporary Music*; by Hubert J. Foss in *Music in My Time*; by Constant Lambert in *Music Ho!* and, most thoroughly, in a valuable German study by Andreas Liess, *Claude Debussy. Das Werk im Zeitbild*. But it is still difficult to see the matter in true perspective, for although values in composition are changing much less rapidly than they were, they are still in a state of flux, and until the rumbles after the upheaval which Debussy caused are definitely behind us, one cannot hope to define his position as clearly as that of Monteverdi, Gluck or Wagner.

Taking a long view of twentieth-century music, we see Debussy as standing, first of all, for the collapse of the tonal system. This collapse was foreshadowed by Liszt, Dargomizh-sky, Moussorgsky, Dvořák, Grieg, and even by Beethoven; but it was Debussy who first formulated what amounted to a conscious revolt. We have evidence of this in one of those conversations with his master Ernest Guiraud which were noted down by Maurice Emmanuel and which it will be interesting to quote here in full. The date is 1889. Maurice Emmanuel explains that Guiraud was rather alarmed at the audacities of his pupil and asked him to justify himself.

'Is the octave not divisible into twenty-four semitones reduced by equal temperament to twelve at the keyboard?' replied the holder of the *Prix de Rome,* who had just escaped from the Villa Medici. 'With these one can make any scale one wishes. I no longer be-lieve in the omnipotence of your eternal *do, re, mi, fa, so, la, si, do.* It is not to be done away with, but there must be other scales, ranging from the six-tone scale [the whole-tone scale] to the scale of twenty-one semitones. [C to B naturals, C to B sharps, and C to B flats, which are of course reduced by equal temperament on keyboard instruments to twelve semitones.] Enharmony must be used freely, but we must distinguish between a G flat and an F sharp. Relative keys are nonsense! *Music is neither major nor minor.* Or rather it is both at the same time. Music may be revived by a continual interchange of major and minor thirds—by which the most remote modulations will immediately appear quite simple. When I mention the key of A, for instance, I imply no allegiance to one mode or another. *The mode is any mode which a musician thinks of at a given moment. It is inconstant.*

'With these twenty-four semitones of the octave one can thus construct ambiguous chords which may belong simultaneously to as many keys as one likes. There is even more reason to use in-complete chords and vague floating intervals. So that by *drowning the key* one can always arrive without difficulty *where one likes* and go out of and enter any door that one prefers. Thus our world of music becomes enlarged and also more subtle.'

Enlarged, yes; but more subtle? That depends on the artist. Debussy brought music to the unprecedented state in which, there no longer being any rules, technique was to be forged by each composer from music at large.[1] 'The musician of the twentieth century,' says H. C. Colles in the *Oxford History of Music,* 'postulates:

1. That a tune may be made on any series of notes, whether contained in the true (acoustic) scale, in the tempered scale of the keyboard (twelve semitones to the octave) or on a scale constructed *ad hoc*.
2. That two or more such tunes may be heard simultaneously, each one built on a different scale, and without conforming to any agreed standard of consonance.
3. That rhythm is capable of infinite variety, and need not be referred to any measurement by regularly recurring accents.'

In a final analysis, restrictions in the technique of composition are imposed only by the capabilities of instruments.

Anarchy ruled—or could rule. But the paradox in the situation was that, while Debussy opened the door to the wildest extravagance, his work itself is nothing so much as a model of sobriety and economy. As he once told Robert Godet, his aim was 'to say many things in a few words.' Like other figures at a critical period in the evolution of art, he faces two ways: towards the restrained and ordered sensuousness of Mozart and towards the barbaric sensuousness of Stravinsky. He was the last of the romantic composers and the initiator of the experimental era. But he was never an intellectual musician. His work remains one of the most

[1] That Debussy was conscious of being a revolutionary is seen from a letter of 2nd March 1896 to Pierre Louÿs about *Daphnis et Chloé,* in which he says: 'The anarchists of music are organizing meetings in my head and are stirring up my poor brain with their red flag of revolt.' And affecting a certain naïvety: 'I don't know what to do; so tell me when we can meet as soon as possible.'

superb challenges of instinct to intellect that music has ever known.

Strictly speaking, Debussy had no followers. He formed no school for the reason that he formulated no system, thereby astonishing a number of people in his day who were quick to interpret this as an indication of Debussy's lack of vitality. Two composers, Ernest Bloch, a Swiss Jew, and Charles Martin Loeffler, an Alsatian, both Americanized, were able to use Debussy's processes to advantage. But the idea of a school was as inimical to the romantic composers of the nineteenth century as it was necessary to the artisan composers of the eighteenth. It was indeed no more possible for Debussy to form a school than it was for Berlioz. The whole principle of the romantic composers' craving for freedom was that they should retain their right to say with Rousseau: 'I may be no better, but I am at least different.' And in truth, that music fertilized by poetry which Debussy perceived, not, as it were, on this side of poetry, but on the further, less conscious, side where, to adapt Walter Pater's famous dictum, 'all art recedes to the state of music,' perished as Debussy held it in his hands, like the nymphs that vanished from the sight of Mallarmé's Faun.

But if no one went further on the lines that he explored, he profoundly influenced almost all subsequent developments throughout Europe.

Debussy's most important influence was on Stravinsky. The two composers were intimate friends. One of the pieces of *En blanc et noir* is dedicated to Stravinsky, and together they played *Le Sacre du printemps* from the manuscript.[1] Stravinsky

[1] In *La Musique retrouvée* Louis Laloy writes: 'One bright afternoon in the spring of 1913 I was walking about in my garden with Debussy; we were expecting Stravinsky. As soon as he saw us the Russian musician ran with his arms outstretched to embrace the French master who, over his shoulder, gave me an amused but

was well acquainted with *L'Après-midi d'un faune* and perceived in Debussy ' "un certain ordre" which he did not find in Richard Strauss.' [1] Stravinsky was too forceful a personality to be lured into Debussy's world of dreams, but it was doubt-less Debussy who weaned him from his master, Rimsky-Korsakov, as Debussy himself had been weaned from Massenet by Rimsky-Korsakov, Borodin and Wagner. Debussyan elements in Stravinsky are noticeable in his *Le Faune et la bergère,* the *Scherzo fantastique, Le Rossignol* and in the two preludes of *Le Sacre.* There is a certain resemblance between *Petroushka* and Debussy's *Ibéria,* but what the con-nection may be here it is difficult to ascertain. It rather seems as if they were parallel developments in both composers, for although *Ibéria* was finished in 1908, it was not performed until 1910 when *Petroushka,* in its original form as a piano concerto, was well under way. On the other hand, Debussy's ballet, *Jeux,* undoubtedly owes something to *Le Sacre.*

France, curiously enough, was the first country to turn sharply away from Debussy. Paul Dukas, Florent Schmitt, Roger-Ducasse and Albert Roussel are each in varying ways indebted to him for shaking off the yoke of Wagner and for

---

compassionate look. He had brought an arrangement for four hands of his new work, *Le Sacre du printemps.* Debussy agreed to play the bass. Stravinsky asked if he could take his collar off. His sight was not improved by his glasses, and pointing his nose to the keyboard and sometimes humming a part that had been omitted from the arrangement, he led into a welter of sound the supple, agile hands of his friend. Debussy followed without a hitch and seemed to make light of the difficulty. When they had finished there was no question of embracing, nor even of compliments. We were dumbfounded, overwhelmed by this hurricane which had come from the depths of the ages and which had taken life by the roots.'

[1] André Schaeffner, *Stravinsky.* (Paris, 1931).

pointing the way to greater freedom; but they are not his followers. Some early compositions of Milhaud and Honegger show his influence, but in 1921 Jean Cocteau could write: 'A dreamer is always a bad poet,' and : '*Pelléas* is another example of music to be listened to with one's face in one's hands. All music to be listened to through the hands is suspect.' At about this time the group of composers known as *Les Six* realized that Debussy had refined his means of expression to a point which admitted of no further develop-ment and instinctively went back to a previous point in French musical history, Chabrier in his pre-Wagnerian phase and his successor Erik Satie. And there was another reason for this reaction. The democratization of music, which was hardly a problem in Debussy's day (although he did once have some sarcastic remarks to make about the Théâtre Populaire), became after the war a most acute problem. That craving for music which in France dates back to the Wagner craze of the eighties suddenly became so intense and so widespread that the esoteric composer was forced out of his hiding. Poulenc and Auric replied by writing cynical, freakish little pieces which were neither for the crowd nor for the initiated. They were an expression of what was known as *le snobisme,* for which Satie had provided an excellent precedent. As we now clearly see, this type of music has little more than a period value, although it is sociologically most interesting.[1]

In Italy Debussy was received as a welcome contrast to Puccini and counted for much in the formation of Pizzetti,

[1] To complete the picture, it should be said that none of the other musical forces in France contemporary with Debussy has proved any more fertile. Neither Gabriel Fauré, Maurice Ravel nor Vincent d'Indy has had any outstanding followers. The sad truth is that Paris, which in Debussy's day was the most vital musical centre in Europe, has fallen back to its relatively unimportant position of the middle of the nineteenth century.

Malipiero, Casella and Respighi, as also of Busoni. The Italians, like the Spaniards, hailed him as a Latin musician.[1] He had, however, no direct influence on the modern Spanish composers unless, following the example of Lalo, Chabrier, Bizet and Ravel, he taught them how to make the best of their own folk-music. In Germany Schönberg's atonality would have been impossible without Debussy. Strauss, however, remained impervious. One might say that, as Wagner turned into thin air in Debussy, in Schönberg he became inrooted and in Strauss he eventually turned to seed.

The young English musicians at the beginning of the century had to choose between Strauss and Debussy as between a gourmand and a gourmet, and on the whole they chose the latter. Writing in *La Revue S.I.M.* of March 1909, Jean-Aubry predicted that the winter of 1907-8 would mark the beginning of a salutary influence of French music in England. English people, he pointed out, were predisposed in favour of French music by their interest in recent French literature. Cyril Scott had translated Baudelaire, and in 1899 Arthur Symons published his famous book, *The Symbolist Movement in Literature*. There was another bond in the indebtedness of Claude Monet to Turner. Sir Henry Wood had given the first performance of *L'Après-midi d'un faune* in England in 1904, and four years later Jean-Aubry's brother-in-law, Mr. Tony J. Guéritte, a French engineer settled in England, organized a network of lectures and concerts for popularizing Debussy and other modern French composers all over the country. They were highly successful. In a paper on

---

[1] 'After the death of Debussy, Bossi, the director of the Santa Cecilia Academy in Rome, assuming that the director of the Paris Conservatoire was the most exalted representative of music in France, telegraphed to Gabriel Fauré that Italy owed its renaissance to Debussy, "for in the art of Debussy we have found its spiritual roots and flowers."'—VALLAS.

Debussy read to the Incorporated Society of Musicians in April 1908, A. E. Grimshaw said:

> To tell the plain truth, we children of the musical nursery were getting a little tired of our old toys; our enthusiasm had got a little run down, and it needed a tonic. Wagner and Brahms have long since been elected by a large majority to secure places in the Temple of the Immortals; somehow Tchaikovsky has ceased to thrill, and Richard Strauss's trick of saying nothing in particular in a compli-cated and impressive manner is getting tiresome. In a word, we wanted a new toy, and I think we have got one, in the person of the new French composer, that will keep us occupied for a long time to come.

This prognostic was correct. In 1908 Gustav Holst, John Ireland and Arnold Bax were all under thirty-five. Holst was the eldest and developed on lines of his own. But Ireland's use of the modes and Bax's 'Celtic atmosphere' were largely due to Debussy. The early pieces of Cyril Scott are very Debussyan.[1] Even stronger was Debussy's influence on Goossens, who in 1908 was only fifteen. The music of Vaughan Williams, who was then thirty-six, has certain features in common with Debussy, though these might have been the result of a collateral development. The same might be said of Delius, who was exactly Debussy's contemporary. In fact, the one prominent English composer of that period who owes nothing to Debussy is Elgar. 1908 was the date of the performance of his first Symphony.

To those musicians of Edwardian days, prepared to follow on the lines of Stanford and Parry, Debussy was an extra-ordinary revelation. In 1907 he wrote to Jean-Aubry: '. . . it has always seemed to me that English people have a merely

---

[1] But not his later works. Speaking of these in *My Years of Indiscretion,* Scott says: 'When I asked him [Debussy] if he saw any resemblance between my own music and his, the answer was unequivocally in the negative.'

"official" taste for music, the exigencies of which have, so far, been quite sufficiently met by Handel and Sullivan.' That was not far wrong. It was this 'official' attitude that Debussy's advent tended to destroy and it is no exaggeration to say that he thus changed the whole face of English music. In illustration of this I will quote at length from an article by Filson Young in the *Saturday Review* of 6th March 1909, which in view of its date is one of the finest pieces of Debussy criticism that have appeared in English. The writer begins:

It is most important that those who care for music as a living art should come to their critical bearings about Debussy. He is a discoverer; he has wandered into a new world of tonality and what for want of a better term we must call musical colour. . . . [His music] is remote from intellectual speculations, philosophic ideas, mental agonies or conflicts; it is founded on primitive matter, primitive sensation; it is an harmonic resultant or over-tone of these. One may extend the metaphor and say that all his music is written in harmonics, on the stopped and touched strings of emotion—hardly ever are the natural, open notes heard. And though the harmonics are very high and ethereal, the sensual, the material, the fundamental aspects of human nature are the pools from which these misty clouds are drawn, to float away and melt into the hot distance of desert skies. . . . For good or ill, he has deflected the compasses of all the younger school of navigators in the musical art, and his influence is bound to be great—greater, no doubt, than his individual achievement; and others will carry the possibilities of this new tonality farther than he will carry them, and so reap where he has sown. . . .

[This music] helps to make obsolete many forms which should have been obsolete long ago; forms in which the great composers of the past wrote great music, but in which no modern composer can write any but feeble music. It makes it a little more absurd for us to go on flogging those dead donkeys, the oratorio and cantata; it makes experiment respectable, and even fashionable, where yesterday it was deemed disgraceful. It helps in the real appreciation of the great composers of the past, and will help to send us back to

Bach for our fugues, Handel for our oratorios (if we really want oratorios), Schumann for our romance, Brahms for our musical philosophy; it will help us to discriminate between what was and what was not inspired in the works of the great, instead of accepting everything as pure gospel which bears the name of Mozart, Beethoven, Rameau, Bach, Palestrina. It will do this because, whatever its faults and failures, it appeals boldly on the single ground of beauty, and not of erudition, imitation or conservatism. It claims every licence, and stands or falls by its justification of that licence. . . .

Such was the position of Debussy. It is yet too early to say whether his influence was greater than his achievement. For the moment it looks as if he were that 'beautiful sunset that was mistaken for a dawn.' But a very beautiful sunset—while it lasts.

APPENDICES

APPENDIX A

CALENDAR

(Figures in brackets denote the age reached by the person mentioned during the year in question.)

Year	Age	Life	Contemporary Musicians
1862		Achille Claude Debussy born August 22, at Saint-Germain-en-Laye, near Paris, son of Manuel Achille Debussy (26), then a keeper of a china shop.	Delius born, Jan. 29; Halévy (63) dies, March 17. Albeniz aged 2; Alkan 49; Arensky 1; Auber 80; Balakirev 26; Balfe 54; Berlioz 59; Bizet 24; Boito 20; Borodin 38; Bossi 1; Brahms 29; Bréville 1; Bruckner 38; Bruneau 5; Chabrier 21; Charpentier 2; Chausson 7; Cornelius 38; Cui 27; Dargomizhsky 49; Delibes 26; Duparc 14; Dvořák 21; Elgar 5; Fauré 17; Franck 40; Gade 45; Goldmark 32; Gounod 44; Grieg 19; Heller 47; Humperdinck 8; d'Indy 11; Lalo 39; Leoncavallo 4; Liadov 7; Liszt 51; Loeffler 1; MacDowell 1; Mahler 2; Martucci 6;

Year	Age	Life	Contemporary Musicians
			Massenet 20; Mercadante 67; Meyerbeer 71; Moussorgsky 23; Offenbach 43; Parry 14; Pedrell 21; Ponchielli 28; Puccini 4; Raff 40; Rimsky-Korsakov 18; Rossini 70; Rubinstein 32; Saint-Saëns 27; Serov 42; Sgambati 19; Smetana 38; Stanford 10; Strauss (J. ii) 37; Sullivan 20; Taneiev 6; Tchaikovsky 22; Thomas (A.) 51; Verdi 49; Wagner 49; Wolf 2.
1863	1		Bordes born, May 12; Mascagni born, Dec. 7; Pierné born, Aug. 16.
1864	2		d'Albert born, April 10; Meyerbeer (73) dies, May 2; Ropartz born, June 15; Strauss (R.) born, June 11.
1865	3		Dukas born, Oct. 1; Glazounov born, July 29/Aug. 10; Sibelius born, Dec. 8.
1866	4		Busoni born, April 1; Satie born, March 17.
1867	5		Granados born, July 29
1868	6		Bantock born, Aug. 7; Rossini (76) dies, Nov. 13; Sinigaglia born, Aug. 14.
1869	7	Visit to Cannes, where he has his first piano lessons from an old Italian teacher, Cerutti.	Berlioz (66) dies, March 8; Dargomizhsky (56) dies, Jan.; Pfitzner born, May 5; Roussel born, April 5.

Year	Age	Life	Contemporary Musicians
1870	8	Meets Mme Mauté de Fleurville, a pupil of Chopin and Verlaine's mother-in-law. He studies the piano under her during the next three years.	Balfe (62) dies, Oct. 20; Mercadante (75) dies, Dec. 17; Novák born, Dec. 5; Schmitt (Florent) born, Sept. 28.
1871	9		Auber (89) dies, May 12; Serov (51) dies, Jan. 20/ Feb. 1.
1872	10		Scriabin born, Jan. 4 (N.S.); Vaughan Williams born, Oct. 12.
1873	11	Enters the Paris Conservatoire. Studies solfège under Lavignac (27) and piano under Marmontel (57).	Rachmaninov born, March 20/April 1; Reger born, March 19; Séverac born, July 20.
1874	12		Cornelius (50) dies, Oct. 26; Holst born, Sept. 21; Schönberg born, Sept. 13; Suk born, Jan. 4.
1875	13		Bizet (37) dies, June 3; Coleridge-Taylor born, Aug. 15; Montemezzi born, May 31; Ravel born, March 7; Roger-Ducasse born, April 18.
1876	14	Enters the harmony class of Émile Durand. Sets to music poems of Théodore de Banville (53).	Falla born, Nov. 23; Wolf-Ferrari born, Jan. 12.
1877	15	Wins second prize for piano playing and first for solfège.	Dohnányi born, July 27.
1878	16	Pays a short visit to London, where he hears Sullivan's (36) *H.M.S. Pinafore.*	Palmgren born, Feb. 16; Schreker born, March 23.

Year	Age	Life	Contemporary Musicians
1879	17	Fails to win the first prize at either of the annual piano examinations and his parents abandon their hopes of his becoming a virtuoso.	Bridge (Frank) born, Feb. 26; Caplet born, Nov. 27; Delage born, Nov. 13; Grovlez born, April 4; Ireland born, Aug. 13; Medtner born, Dec. 24; Respighi born, July 9; Scott (Cyril) born, Sept. 27.
1880	18	First prize in score-reading enables him to enter a composition class. At the very time that his career is decided he meets Tchaikovsky's (40) patroness, Nadezhda von Meck (50) and journeys with her, as a domestic musician and tutor to her children, to Switzerland and Italy. Tchaikovsky gives his opinion of D.'s early compositions. In Venice D. meets Wagner (67). On his return to Paris he enters the composition class of Ernest Guiraud (43).	Bloch born, July 24; Inghelbrecht born, Sept. 17; Offenbach (61) dies, Oct. 4; Pizzetti born, Sept. 20.
1881	19	Preparation for the *Grand Prix de Rome*. Mme Vasnier, the beautiful young wife of an architect, becomes his mistress. Visit to Mme von Meck in Moscow in the summer.	Bartók born, March 25; Miaskovsky born, April 8/20; Moussorgsky (42) dies, March 16/28.
1882	20	Becomes acquainted with the poetry of Verlaine (38)	Kodály born, Dec. 16; Malipiero born, March 18;

Year	Age	Life	Contemporary Musicians
		and Mallarmé (40) and dedicates the first of the *Fêtes galantes* (on poems of Verlaine) to Mme Vasnier.	Raff (60) dies, June 24–5; Stravinsky born, June 5/17; Turina born, Dec. 9; Vycpálek born.
1883	21	Gains second *Prix de Rome* with the cantata, *Le Gladiateur*.	Bax born, Nov. 6; Casella born, July 25; Szymanowski born; Wagner (70) dies, Feb. 13; Webern born, Dec. 3; Zandonai born, May 28.
1884	22	Begins a stage setting of Théodore de Banville's *Diane au bois,* gains the first *Prix de Rome* with the lyric scene, *L'Enfant prodigue,* and visits Moscow again.	van Dieren born, Dec. 27; Griffes born, Sept. 17; Smetana (60) dies, May 12.
1885	23	Leaves for the Villa Medici in Rome much against his will. Begins a choral work on Heine's drama, *Almanzor,* and continues to work on *Diane au bois,* but eventually abandons them both. He finds life at the Villa Medici distasteful but meets Liszt (74), Verdi (72), Leoncavallo (27) and Boito (43).	Berg born, Feb. 7; Wellesz born, Oct. 21.
1886	24	Flees to Paris. Returns after a few weeks and writes *Printemps,* his only 'envoi de Rome.'	Kaminski born, July 4; Liszt (75) dies, July 31; Ponchielli (52) dies, Jan. 16.
1887	25	Flees again from Rome, this time for good. Begins *La Damoiselle élue.* Meets poets of Mallarmé's (45)	Borodin (53) dies, Feb. 16/28; Toch born, Dec. 7.

Year	Age	Life	Contemporary Musicians
		circle and journeys to Vienna to see Brahms (54). Comes to London to get his compositions published, but is quite unsuccessful.	
1888	26	Visits Bayreuth to hear *Parsifal* and *Meistersinger*. Finishes *La Damoiselle élue* in Paris. Lives with a mistress named 'Gaby.'	Alkan (75) dies, March 29; Durey born; Heller (74) dies, Jan. 14.
1889	27	Second visit to Bayreuth to hear *Tristan*. On his return he becomes acquainted with the score of Moussorgsky's *Boris Godounov*, which he admires, but not uncritically. He is enthralled by the Javanese *gamelang* at the Exposition Universelle. Finishes the *Cinq Poèmes de Baudelaire*.	Shaporin born.
1890	28	Begins to write *Rodrigue et Chimène*, the libretto, by Catulle Mendès (49), based on Guillem de Castro's *Las Mocedades del Cid*.	Franck (68) dies, Nov. 8; Gade (73) dies, Dec. 21.
1891	29	Meets Erik Satie (25), who is a pianist in a Montmartre café, and forms a life-long friendship with him.	Bliss born, Aug. 2; Delibes (55) dies, Jan. 16; Migot born, Feb. 27; Prokofiev born, April 11/23; Roland-Manuel born, March 22.
1892	30	Sees Maeterlinck's (30) drama, *Pelléas et Mélisande*,	Honegger born, March 10; Jarnach born, July 26;

Year	Age	Life	Contemporary Musicians
		and immediately sets to writing some incidental music for it. Begins to write a *Prélude, Interlude et Paraphrase finale* for Mallarmé's (50) eclogue, *L'Après - midi d'un faune.* *Rodrigue et Chimène,* carried as far as the third act, abandoned.	Kilpinen born, Feb. 4; Lalo (69) dies, April 22; Milhaud born, Sept. 4; Tailleferre (Germaine) born, April 19.
1893	31	*La Damoiselle élue* and the Quartet performed at the Société Nationale, the first large works of D. to be heard. They meet with little success. He decides to write an opera on *Pelléas* and visits Maeterlinck (31) at Ghent. Enters into intimate friendship with Pierre Louÿs (23) and Ernest Chausson (38).	Goossens born, May 26; Gounod (75) dies, Oct. 18; Tchaikovsky (53) dies, Oct. 25/Nov. 6.
1894	32	The *Prélude à l'Après-midi d'un faune* performed at the Société Nationale, where it passes almost unnoticed. First version of the *Nocturnes* (for violin and orchestra, intended for performance by Ysaÿe (36)) begun.	Chabrier (53) dies, Sept. 13; Pijper born, Sept. 8; Rubinstein (64) dies, Nov. 8/20.
1895	33	First (? destroyed) version of *Pelléas* finished; second version begun immediately afterwards.	Castelnuovo-Tedesco born, April 13; Hindemith born, Nov. 16; Sowerby born, May 1.
1896	34	Begins a ballet, *Daphnis et Chloé,* on a scenario by	Bruckner (72) dies, Oct. 11; Sessions born, Dec.

Year	Age	Life	Contemporary Musicians
		Houston Stewart Chamberlain (41), the famous champion of Wagner, but quickly abandons it.	28; Thomas (A.) (85) dies, Feb. 12.
1897	35	Orchestrates Satie's (31) *Deux Gymnopédies* and sets three of Pierre Louÿs's (27) *Chansons de Bilitis*.	Brahms (64) dies, April 3; Korngold born, May 29.
1898	36	*Pelléas* progresses.	Rieti born, Jan. 28.
1899	37	Marries Rosalie Texier, a dressmaker, Oct. 19. Second version of the *Nocturnes* (for orchestra) finished.	Auric born; Chausson (44) dies, June 10; Poulenc born, Jan. 7; Strauss (J. ii) (74) dies, June 3.
1900	38	The *Nocturnes* conducted by Camille Chevillard (41) with great success.	Křenek born; Sullivan (58) dies, Nov. 22.
1901	39	*Pelléas* nearing completion. D. acts as music critic to *La Revue blanche*.	Verdi (88) dies, Jan. 27.
1902	40	The performance of *Pelléas*, April 30, at the Opéra-Comique creates a scandal. D. accepts the *Croix d'Honneur*. Writes the libretto of *Le Diable dans le beffroi*, an opera based on Poe's *Devil in the Belfry*, and plans to write another opera on Shakespeare's *As You Like It*.	Walton born, March 29.
1903	41	Acts as music critic to *Gil Blas*. Makes further plans for *Comme il vous plaira* (*As You Like It*) and writes the *Estampes*.	Wolf (43) dies, Feb. 22.

Appendix A—Calendar

Year	Age	Life	Contemporary Musicians
1904	42	D. abandons his wife for Emma Bardac. Lily attempts suicide. *La Mer* begun.	Dvořák (63) dies, May 1.
1905	43	Birth of Claude ‑ Emma (Chouchou). D. divorces his first wife and marries Mme Bardac. *La Mer* is finished and performed on Oct. 15.	Lambert born.
1906	44	Begins *Ibéria* (of the *Images*) for orchestra.	Arensky (45) dies, June 11; Cartan born, Dec. 1; Shostakovitch born.
1907	45	Finishes the *Images* for piano. Contemplates an opera on the legend of Tristan.	Grieg (64) dies, Sept. 4.
1908	46	Visits London and con‑ducts *L'Après‑midi* and *La Mer* at Queen's Hall, Feb. 1. Writes *Trois Chansons de Charles d'Orléans* for mixed voices. Begins an opera on Poe's *The Fall of the House of Usher* and sells the rights to the Metro‑politan Opera of New York.	MacDowell (47) dies, Jan. 24; Rimsky‑Korsakov (64) dies, June 21.
1909	47	Conducts the *Nocturnes* in London. Becomes afflicted with cancer. *Pelléas* performed at Covent Garden.	Albeniz (49) dies, June 16; Bordes (46) dies, Nov. 18; Martucci (53) dies, June 1.
1910	48	Conducts in Vienna and Budapest. *Préludes* for piano begun.	Balakirev (74) dies, May 30.

Year	*Age*	*Life*	*Contemporary Musicians*
1911	49	Conducts in Turin, where he meets Elgar (54) and Strauss (47). Writes *Le Martyre de saint Sébastien* on d'Annunzio's (48) drama in a few weeks. It is performed at the Théâtre du Châtelet with little success.	Mahler (51) dies, May 18.
1912	50	Nijinsky (22) produces for Diaghilev (40) a ballet on *L'Après-midi* which meets with no approval from D. He nevertheless consents to collaborate with Nijinsky in *Jeux*. Undertakes to write a music-hall number for Maud Allan, but leaves it unfinished.	Coleridge - Taylor (37) dies, Sept. 1; Massenet (70) dies, Aug. 13.
1913	51	*Jeux* produced with little success. Three songs to words by Mallarmé written. Second set of *Préludes* finished. Visit to Russia.	
1914	52	Composes the *Berceuse héroïque*, a war piece for King Albert's (39) Book.	Liadov (59) dies, Aug. 28; Sgambati (71) dies, Dec. 15.
1915	53	Composes numerous piano pieces—*En blanc et noir*, *Douze études*, the song, *Noël des enfants qui n'ont plus de maisons*, and two Sonatas published with the words 'musicien français' under the composer's name. His cancer deve-	Goldmark (85) dies, Jan. 2; Scriabin (44) dies, April 1/14; Taneiev (59) dies, June.

Year	Age	Life	Contemporary Musicians
		lops and he undergoes an operation. From now on he is a sick man.	
1916	54	Composes no music for a year. Recasts the libretto for *La Chute de la maison Usher*.	Granados (49) dies, March 24; Reger (43) dies, May 11.
1917	55	Plans again to write music for *As You Like It*. His last work, the piano and violin Sonata, completed in the spring.	
1918	56	Debussy dies in Paris, March 25, while the city is being bombarded by German guns.	Boito (76) dies, June 10; Cui (83) dies, March 14; Parry (70) dies, Oct. 7. d'Albert aged 54; Auric 19; Bantock 50; Bartók 37; Bax 35; Berg 33; Bliss 27; Bloch 38; Bossi 41; Bréville 57; Bridge (Frank) 39; Bruneau 61; Busoni 52; Cartan 12; Casella 35; Castelnuovo-Tedesco 23; Charpentier 58; Delius 56; van Dieren 34; Dohnányi 41; Dukas 53; Duparc 70; Durey 30; Falla 42; Fauré 73; Glazounov 53; Goossens 25; Griffes 34; Hindemith 23; Holst 44; Honegger 26; Humperdinck 64; d'Indy 67; Ireland 39; Jarnach 26; Kaminski 32; Kilpinen 26; Kodály 36; Korngold 21; Křenek 18; Lambert

Year	Age	Life	Contemporary Musicians
			13; Leoncavallo 60; Loeffler 57; Malipiero 36; Mascagni 55; Medtner 39; Miaskovsky 37; Milhaud 26; Montemezzi 43; Novák 48; Palmgren 40; Pedrell 77; Pfitzner 49; Pierné 55; Pijper 24; Pizzetti 38; Poulenc 19; Prokofiev 27; Puccini 60; Rachmaninov 45; Ravel 43; Respighi 39; Rieti 20; Roger ∕ Ducasse 43; Roland ∕ Manuel 27; Ropartz 54; Roussel 49; Saint∕Saëns 83; Satie 52; Schmitt (Florent) 48; Schönberg 44; Schreker 40; Scott (Cyril) 39; Sessions 22; Séverac 45; Shaporin 29; Shostako∕vitch 12; Sibelius 53; Sinigaglia 50; Sowerby 23; Stanford 66; Strauss (R.) 54; Stravinsky 36; Suk 44; Szymanowski 35; Toch 31; Turina 36; Vaughan Williams 46; Vycpálek 36; Walton 16; Webern 35; Wellesz 33; Wolf∕Ferrari 42; Zandonai 35.

APPENDIX B

CATALOGUE OF WORKS

THE dates of composition, except where works have been published in the last two or three years, or where I have discovered the existence of manuscripts, are based on those in the catalogue published in Léon Vallas's *Claude Debussy et son temps*. The names in brackets following the title are those of the authors of poems or librettos.

UNPUBLISHED WORKS

SONGS

Year

1880 *Caprice.*

1880–4 *Chanson espagnole* for two voices.
   Rondel chinois.
   Romance (Paul Bourget).[1]
   Aimons-nous (Théodore de Banville).
   La Fille aux cheveux de lin (Leconte de Lisle).[2]
   Eclogue (Leconte de Lisle) for soprano and tenor.

1908 *Berceuse* (René Peter) for the play, *La Tragédie de la mort.*

CHAMBER WORKS

1880 Trio in G major for piano, violin and cello.

1900 *Chansons de Bilitis.* Incidental music for the poems of
   Pierre Louÿs for 2 flutes, 2 harps and celesta.

---

[1] Not to be mistaken for the published *Romance* (Paul Bourget) of 1891.

[2] Dedicated to Mme Vasnier with the inscription: 'All that is any good in my mind is here; judge for yourself.' This song has no connection with the *Prélude* of the same title.

Choral, Dramatic and Literary Works

Year
1880–4   *Daniel* (Émile Cécile).   Cantata.

1883   *Le Gladiateur* (Émile Moreau).   Cantata.

1884   *Printemps* (Jules Barbier).   Chorus.

1891–2   *Rodrigue et Chimène* (Catulle Mendès).   Unfinished opera in three acts.

1900   *F.E.A.* (*Frères en art*).   Three scenes of a play, written with René Peter.

1903   *Le Diable dans le beffroi* (Poe-Debussy).   Orchestrated sketch for scene i.

1908–18   *La Chute de la maison Usher* (Poe-Debussy).   Libretto. Two versions.

Piano and Orchestral Works

1882   *Intermezzo* for orchestra based on a passage from Heine's *Intermezzo*.   Full score and piano duet arrangement.

1884   Two short pieces for piano written at Moscow.

PUBLISHED WORKS

Songs [1]

Dedicated to

1876 (?)   *Nuit d'étoiles* (Théodore de Banville).

1878 (?)   *Beau soir* (Paul Bourget).
          Fleur des blés (André Girod).   Mme E. Deguingand.

1880–3   *Mandoline* (Paul Verlaine).   Mme Vasnier.
          La Belle au bois dormant (Vincent Hypsa).
          Voici que le printemps (Paul Bourget).
          Paysage sentimental (Paul Bourget).

---

[1] The songs *Chanson d'un fou* (Alphonse Daudet) and *Ici-bas* (Sully Prudhomme), published under Debussy's name and attributed to the year 1882, are by Émile Pessard and the brothers Paul and Lucien Hillemacher respectively.

Appendix B—Catalogue of Works

Year	SONGS—*continued*	*Dedicated to*
1881	*Zéphyr* (Théodore de Banville).	
1882 (1)	*Rondeau* (Alfred de Musset).	Alexander von Meck.
1882–4	*Pantomime* (Paul Verlaine).	Mme Vasnier.
	Clair de lune (Paul Verlaine).[1]	Mme Vasnier.
	Pierrot (Théodore de Banville).	Mme Vasnier.
	Apparition (Stéphane Mallarmé).	Mme Vasnier.
1887–9	*Cinq Poèmes de Baudelaire.*	Étienne Dupin.
	Le Balcon.	
	Harmonie du soir.	
	Le Jet d'eau.[2]	
	Recueillement.	
	La Mort des amants.	
1888	*Ariettes oubliées* (Paul Verlaine).	Mary Garden.
	C'est l'extase . . .	
	Il pleure dans mon cœur . . .	
	L'ombre des arbres . . .	
	Chevaux de bois.	
	Green.	
	Spleen.	
1891	*Deux Romances* (Paul Bourget).	
	Romance.	
	Les Cloches.	
	Les Angélus (G. le Roy).	
	Dans le jardin (Paul Gravolet).	
	Trois Mélodies (Paul Verlaine).	
	La mer est plus belle . . .	Ernest Chausson.
	Le son du cor s'afflige . . .	Robert Godet.
	L'échelonnement des haies.	Robert Godet.
1892	*Fêtes galantes* (Paul Verlaine), first series.	
	En sourdine.	Mme Robert Godet.

[1] Not the *Clair de lune* (Paul Verlaine) of 1892.
[2] Piano accompaniment orchestrated by Debussy.

249

Debussy

Year	Songs—*continued*	Dedicated to
	Fantoches.	Mme Lucien Fontaine.
	Clair de lune.	Mme Arthur Fontaine.
1892–3	*Proses lyriques* (Claude Debussy).	
	De rêve.	V. Hocquet.
	De grève.	Raymond Bonheur.
	De fleurs.	Mme E. Chausson.
	De soir.	Henry Lerolle.
1897	*Chansons de Bilitis* (Pierre Louÿs).	Mme M. V. Peter.
	La Flûte de Pan.	
	La Chevelure.	
	Le Tombeau des Naïades.	
1904	*Fêtes galantes* (Paul Verlaine), second series.	Mme S. Bardac.[1]
	Les Ingénus.	
	Le Faune.	
	Colloque sentimental.	
	Trois Chansons de France.	Mme S. Bardac.
	Rondel: Le temps a laissié son manteau . . . (Charles d'Orléans).	
	La Grotte (Tristan Lhermite).[2]	
	Rondel: Pour ce que plaisance est morte . . . (Charles d'Orléans).	
1904–10	*Le Promenoir des deux amants* (Tristan Lhermite).	Emma Claude Debussy
	Auprès de cette grotte sombre . . .	
	Crois mon conseil . . .	
	Je tremble en voyant ton visage . . .	

[1] The dedication runs: 'Pour remercier, le mois de juin, 1904. A.l.p.M.' The initials stand for 'A la petite Mie' (To my little darling).

[2] This is the same song as *Auprès de cette grotte sombre*, the first of the next group.

Appendix B—Catalogue of Works

Year	SONGS—continued	Dedicated to
1910	*Trois Ballades de François Villon.* *Ballade de Villon à s'amye.* *Ballade que feit Villon à la requeste de* *sa mère pour prier Nostre-Dame.* *Ballade des femmes de Paris.*	
1913	*Trois Poèmes de Stéphane Mallarmé.* *Soupir.* *Placet futile.* *Éventail.*	Dr. Bonniot and to the memory of Stéphane Mallarmé.
1915	*Noël des enfants qui n'ont plus de maisons* (Claude Debussy). [1]	

PIANO WORKS [2]

(a) Piano Solo

Year		Dedicated to
1880	*Danse bohémienne.*	
1888	*Deux Arabesques.*	
1890	*Rêverie.* *Ballade.* *Danse.* *Valse romantique.* *Nocturne.*	Mlle Rose Depecker.
1890– 1905	*Suite bergamasque.* *Prélude.* *Menuet.* *Clair de lune.* *Passepied.*	
1891	*Mazurka.*	

---

[1] There also exists a version of this song for children's chorus.

[2] See also under Chamber Works and Works for Solo Instrument and Orchestra.

Year	Piano Works—*continued*	Dedicated to
1896–1901	*Pour le piano.*	
	Prélude.	Mlle M. W. de Romilly.
	Sarabande.	Mme E. Rouart.
	Toccata.	N. G. Coronio.
1903	*Estampes.*	Jacques-Émile Blanche.
	Pagodes.	
	Soirée dans Grenade.	
	Jardins sous la pluie.	
1903	*D'un cahier d'esquisses.*	
1904	*Masques.*	
	L'Isle joyeuse.	
1905	*Images,* first series.	
	Reflets dans l'eau.	
	Hommage à Rameau.	
	Mouvement.	
1907	*Images,* second series.	
	Cloches à travers les feuilles.	Alexandre Charpentier.
	Et la lune descend sur le temple qui fut.	Louis Laloy.
	Poissons d'or.	Ricardo Viñes.
1906–8	*Children's Corner.*	Claude-Emma Debussy (Chouchou).
	Doctor Gradus ad Parnassum.	
	Jimbo's Lullaby.	
	Serenade for the Doll.[1]	
	Snow is Dancing.	
	The Little Shepherd.	
	Golliwog's Cake-walk.	
1909	*Hommage à Haydn.*	
1910	*La plus que lente.*[2]	

---

[1] Should be, of course, *The Doll's Serenade.*

[2] Orchestrated by Debussy.

Year	PIANO WORKS—*continued*	Dedicated to

1910   *Douze Préludes*, first book.
             Danseuses de Delphes.
             Voiles.
             Le Vent dans la plaine.
             Les sons et les parfums tournent dans l'air du soir.
             Les Collines d'Anacapri.
             Des Pas sur la neige.
             Ce qu'a vu le vent d'ouest.
             La Fille aux cheveux de lin.
             La Sérénade interrompue.
             La Cathédrale engloutie.
             La Danse de Puck.
             Minstrels.

1910–13   *Douze Préludes*, second book.
             Brouillards.
             Feuilles mortes.
             La Puerta del Vino.
             Les Fées sont d'exquises danseuses.
             Bruyères.
             General Lavine-eccentric.
             La Terrasse des audiences au clair de lune.
             Ondine.
             Hommage à S. Pickwick, Esq., P.P.M.P.C.
             Canope.
             Les Tierces alternées.
             Feux d'artifice.

1913   *La Boîte à joujoux.* Children's ballet. Scenario by André Hellé.

1914   *Berceuse héroïque pour rendre hommage à S.M. le Roi Albert Ier de Belgique et à ses soldats.*

Year	Piano Works—*continued*	Dedicated to
1915	*Douze Études.*	The memory of Frédéric Chopin.

Book I:

Pour les cinq doigts.
Pour les tierces.
Pour les quartes.
Pour les sixtes.
Pour les octaves.
Pour les huit doigts.

Book II:

Pour les degrés chromatiques.
Pour les agréments.
Pour les notes répétées.
Pour les sonorités opposées.
Pour les arpèges.
Pour les accords.

(b) Piano Duet

1880	*Symphonie en si.* (One movement.)[1]	Mme von Meck.
1882 (?)	*Triomphe de Bacchus.* Orchestral interlude.	
1889	*Petite suite.*	
	En bateau.	
	Cortège.	
	Menuet.	
	Ballet.	
1891	*Marche écossaise sur un thème populaire.* (*The Earl of Ross March.*)[2]	

---

[1] This and the next work were intended to be orchestral works. The piano duet arrangements by Debussy are all that is known.

[2] Orchestrated by Debussy.

Year	PIANO WORKS—*continued*	Dedicated to
1914	*Six Épigraphes antiques.*[1]	

Pour invoquer Pan, dieu du vent
 d'été.
Pour un tombeau sans nom.
Pour que la nuit soit propice.
Pour la danseuse aux crotales.
Pour l'égyptienne.
Pour remercier la pluie au matin.

(c) Two Pianos

1901	*Lindaraja.*	
1915	*En blanc et noir.* (Three pieces.)	A. Koussevitsky, Lieutenant Jacques Charlot and Igor Stravinsky.

CHAMBER WORKS

1893	String Quartet	Ysaÿe Quartet (Ysaÿe, Crickboom, van Hout, Joseph Jacob).
1903–5	*Rapsodie* for saxophone and piano.[2]	Mrs. Elisa Hall.
1909–10	*Première Rapsodie* for clarinet and piano.[3]	P. Mimart.
1910	*Petite pièce* for clarinet and piano.[3]	
1912	*Syrinx* for unaccompanied flute.	Louis Fleury.

---

[1] There is also an arrangement of these pieces for piano solo.
[2] The piano accompaniment has been orchestrated by Roger-Ducasse.
[3] Orchestrated by Debussy.

Year	CHAMBER WORKS—*continued*	Dedicated to
1915	Sonata for cello and piano.	Emma Claude-Debussy.
	Sonata for flute, viola and harp.	Emma Claude-Debussy.
1916–17	Sonata for piano and violin.	Emma Claude-Debussy.

WORKS FOR SOLO INSTRUMENT AND ORCHESTRA

1889	*Fantaisie* for piano and orchestra.	René Chansarel.
1904	*Danse sacrée* and *Danse profane* for harp and strings.	Gustave Lyon.

ORCHESTRAL WORKS

1887	*Printemps*.[1]	The memory of Auguste Durand.
1892–4	*Prélude à l'Après-midi d'un faune.*	Raymond Bonheur.
1893–9	*Nocturnes.* *Nuages.* *Fêtes.* *Sirènes* (with female chorus).	Georges Hartmann.
1903–5	*La Mer.* Three symphonic sketches. *De l'aube à midi sur la mer.* *Jeux de vagues.* *Dialogue du vent et de la mer.*	Jacques Durand.
1904	Incidental music for *King Lear* (Shakespeare). *Fanfare.* *Sommeil de Lear*.[2]	

---

[1] Orchestration revised by Henri Büsser.
[2] There are a few rough notes in manuscript for six further pieces.

Year	ORCHESTRAL WORKS—*continued*	*Dedicated to*
1906–12	*Images.*	
	Gigues.[1]	
	Ibéria.	
	Rondes de Printemps.	Emma Claude Debussy.

UNACCOMPANIED CHORAL WORKS

1908	*Trois Chansons de Charles d'Orléans* for sopranos, contraltos, tenors and basses.
	Dieu! qu'il fait bon regarder!
	Quand j'ai ouy le tabourin . . .
	Yver, vous n'estes qu'un villain . . .

CHORAL AND DRAMATIC WORKS

1882	*Printemps* (Comte de Ségur). Chorus for female voices.[2]	
1883	*Invocation* (Lamartine). Chorus for male voices. Piano and vocal score only.	
1884	*L'Enfant prodigue* (Édouard Guinand). Cantata.	Ernest Guiraud.
1887–8	*La Damoiselle élue* (D. G. Rossetti–G. Sarrazin). Cantata for solo voices, chorus and orchestra.	Paul Dukas.

---

[1] The orchestration finished by André Caplet.

[2] The piano and vocal score, which is all that is available, has been made by Marius-François Gaillard.

CHORAL AND DRAMATIC WORKS—*continued*

Year		Dedicated to
1892–1902	*Pelléas et Mélisande* (Maurice Maeterlinck). Opera in five acts.	The memory of Georges Hartmann and to André Messager.
1911	*Le Martyre de saint Sébastien.* Incidental music to the mystery play by Gabriele d'Annunzio, for solo voices, chorus and orchestra.	
1912	*Jeux.* Ballet. Scenario and choreography by Nijinsky.	Mme Jacques Durand.
1912	*Khamma.* Ballet. Orchestrated by Charles Koechlin. Scenario by W. L. Courtney and Maud Allan.	
1916–17	*Ode à la France* (Louis Laloy). Cantata for solo, chorus and orchestra. Completed from sketches by Marius-François Gaillard.	

ARRANGEMENTS AND ORCHESTRATIONS

Gluck, C. W.	*Caprice* for piano on airs from the ballet of *Alceste*.
Raff, J.	*Humoresque en forme de valse.* Arrangement for piano solo.
Saint-Saëns, C.	Arrangement for piano solo of extracts from the opera *Étienne Marcel*.
	Introduction et Rondo capriccioso. Arrangement for two pianos.
	Second Symphony. Arrangement for two pianos.
Satie, Erik	Orchestration of *Deux Gymnopédies*.

ARRANGEMENTS AND ORCHESTRATIONS—*continued*

Schumann, R.   *Am Springbrunnen.* Arrangement for two pianos.
                Six Studies in canon form. Arrangement for
                two pianos.

Tchaikovsky, P. *The Swan Lake.* Arrangement of three dances
                for piano solo.

Wagner, R.   Overture to *The Flying Dutchman.* Arrangement
                for two pianos.

LITERARY WORKS

Articles in:

Comœdia   November 4, 1909.
                  January 31, December 17, 1910.
                  January 26, May 18, 1911.
                  February 1, 1914.[1]

Excelsior   March 9, 1911.

Le Figaro   May 8, 1908.
                  February 14, 1909.

Gil Blas   January 12 to June 28, 1903.

Mercure de France January 1903.

Musica   October 1902.
                  May 1903.
                  July 1906.
                  January 1908.
                  March 1911.

La Revue blanche April 1 to December 1, 1901.

La Revue bleue   March and April 1904.

La Revue S.I.M. November 1912 to May 15, 1913.
                   November 1913 to March 1914.

Monsieur Croche antidilettante. A selection of the above articles
    made by Debussy in 1917, but published posthumously.

Masques et Bergamasques. Scenario for a ballet written in 1910.

---

[1] These are all interviews.

APPENDIX C

Annunzio, Gabriele d' (*Gaetano Rapagnetto*) (born 1863), famous Italian poet, novelist, dramatist and patriot. Has always shown a great affection for France and wrote two of his plays, *Le Martyre de saint Sébastien* and *La Pisanella,* in French. In 1919, on behalf of Italy, he organized of his own will the military occupation of Fiume, which then belonged to Austria.

Bailly, Edmond (born 1878), French writer, owner of the Librairie de la Revue Indépendante, biographer of Maeterlinck (q.v.) and publisher of Debussy's *La Damoiselle élue.*

Banville, Théodore de (1823–91), French poet, follower of Victor Hugo, Alfred de Musset and Théophile Gautier, and at the same time a precursor of the Symbolists. Part of his comedy, *Diane au bois* (1864), and several of his poems were set to music by Debussy.

Bédier, Joseph (born 1864), distinguished scholar of French medieval literature, of which he holds the chair at the Collège de France. The author of the *Roman de Tristan et Yseult* (1900), which Debussy started to set to music and of which a fine English translation has been made by Hilaire Belloc.

Bonheur, Raymond, fellow-student of Debussy's at the Conservatoire and among his most intimate friends. *L'Après-midi d'un faune* is dedicated to him.

Bourget, Paul (1852–1935), poet and novelist who made his name as a writer on psychological, social and religious questions. Became a member of the Académie in 1894 and subsequently an ardent Royalist.

Bruneau, Alfred (1857–1934), French composer, pupil of Massenet and great friend of Zola, who wrote the librettos of his operas,

L'Ouragan and *Messidor*. One of the most prolific of modern French composers for the stage, though his works are little known outside of France.

Cabat, Louis (1812–93), French landscape painter. Director of the Villa Medici during the first year of Debussy's residence.

Caplet, André (1879–1925), French conductor and composer whose works were much influenced by Debussy. He completed the orchestration of several of Debussy's works and conducted chiefly in America.

Carré, Albert (born 1852), succeeded Carvalho as director of the Opéra-Comique, where he produced *Pelléas et Mélisande* in 1902. He subsequently became director of the Comédie-Française.

Chabrier, Emmanuel (1841–1894), French composer of light operas and symphonic music who had an important influence on French music *after* Debussy. Ravel, Poulenc, Auric and Milhaud all owe much to him. At the end of his life his original talent was unable, however, to stand up to the influence of Wagner.

Chamberlain, Houston Stewart (1855–1927), English music critic, educated in France, married Wagner's daughter and became a naturalized German. Great champion of Wagner and propagator of Pan-Germanist theories.

Chausson, Ernest (1855–99), pupil of César Franck, of whom he was a devout admirer. He wrote two operas, *La Légende de sainte Cécile* and *Le Roi Arthus,* and a number of symphonic and chamber works. He was killed in a bicycle accident.

Chevillard, Camille (1859–1923), conductor and composer, pupil of Chabrier (q.v.) and son-in-law of Charles Lamoureux (q.v.). He earned a reputation for conducting Russian music and became the conductor of the Concerts Lamoureux.

Colonne, Édouard (1838–1910), violinist and conductor, founder of the Concerts Colonne. He was the first to popularize Berlioz and was well known for his performances of Wagner, Tchaikovsky and Rimsky-Korsakov.

Doret, Gustave (born 1866), Swiss composer, studied the violin in Germany with Joachim and composition in Paris with Massenet.

Became conductor of the Société Nationale, where he gave the first performance of *L'Après-midi d'un faune*.

Dujardin, Édouard (born 1861), French writer. The founder of *La Revue wagnérienne*, *La Revue independante* and *La Revue des idées*. He introduced Mallarmé (q.v.) to the music of Wagner.

Dukas, Paul (1865–1935), French composer, pupil of Guiraud (q.v.) Wrote *L'Apprenti sorcier*, *La Péri* and *Ariane et Barbe-bleue*, an opera on a play of Maeterlinck (q.v.). He was professor of composition at the Conservatoire from 1927 until his death.

Fauré, Gabriel (1845–1924), after Debussy the greatest French composer at the end of the nineteenth century and the beginning of the twentieth. Well known for his chamber music and his songs. He was a pupil, disciple and life-long friend of Saint-Saëns, whom he equalled and even surpassed as a master of form. He might be called the French Brahms—with Debussy as his Wagner.

Ghil, René (1862–1925), French poet who evolved a number of strange theories by the application of which poetry was to become indistinguishable from music. He had an important influence on Mallarmé.

Godet, Robert, Swiss journalist, composer, translator of Houston Stewart Chamberlain (q.v.) and the author of a study of *Boris Godounov*. Debussy's life-long friend.

Guiraud, Ernest (1837–92), Debussy's teacher of composition at the Conservatoire. His operas include *Le Kobold*, *Mme Turlupin*, *Piccolino* and *La galante Aventure*.

Hébert, Ernest (1817–1908), French painter, pupil of David, friend of Gounod and director of the Villa Medici during the second year of Debussy's residence.

Huysmans, Joris Karl (1848–1907), French novelist who in his books, *A rebours* and *Là-bas*, was a keen observer of the artistic sensibility of his times. At the end of his life he became a Trappist.

Koechlin, Charles (born 1867), French composer and critic, pupil of Massenet and Fauré (q.v.).

Laforgue, Jules (1860–87), French writer who was engaged as a reader to the German Empress Augusta in Berlin. He married an English girl and died the next year of tuberculosis. His poetry is a strange mixture of sadness, irony and fantasy.

Laloy, Louis (born 1874), Debussy's intimate friend and his first biographer. Editor of the *Mercure musical*. In 1914 he became Secretary-General of the Opéra and in 1930 music critic of the *Revue des deux mondes*. He has written a valuable book on Chinese music.

Lamoureux, Charles (1834–99), French violinist and conductor. Founder of the Concerts Lamoureux, at which he made Wagner known to a wide public.

Lavignac, Albert (1846–1916), teacher of *solfège* and harmony and editor of the great *Encyclopédie de la musique et dictionnaire du Conservatoire*. Debussy's first master at the Conservatoire.

Leroux, Xavier (1863–1919), French composer, pupil of Massenet and Debussy's friend at Rome. Wrote numerous operas.

Louÿs, Pierre (1870–1925), French poet and novelist. One of Debussy's most intimate friends. 'A melancholy and voluptuous writer, he celebrated in a mystical way the beauty and the pleasures of the body. He was an artistic writer, supple, fluid and harmonious' (Larousse). His best-known novel is *Aphrodite*.

Maeterlinck, Maurice (born 1862), Belgian poet, author of the play, *Pelléas et Mélisande*. His first poems, *Serres chaudes*, were set to music by Chausson (q.v.), *Ariane et Barbe-bleue* served as the text for the opera by Dukas (q.v.), and Erik Satie (q.v.) attempted an opera on his *La Princesse Maleine*. If *Pelléas* had not been taken by Debussy, Maeterlinck would have authorized its use as an opera text by Puccini. Schönberg took the subject for a symphonic poem.

Mallarmé, Stéphane (1842–98), the most important of the French Symbolist poets. A teacher of English at a *lycée,* he became editor of *La Dernière Mode* and the translator of the poems of E. A. Poe. He wrote very little, but his work is extremely concentrated and clotted with imagery.

Marmontel, Antoine-François (1816–1898), French piano teacher, the author of several important works on piano playing and Debussy's master at the Conservatoire.

Mauté de Fleurville, Antoinette-Flore, née Chariat (died 1884), a pupil of Chopin and the mother of Mathilde, the young forsaken wife of Verlaine (q.v.). She was Debussy's piano teacher before he entered the Conservatoire.

Meck, Nadezhda Filaretovna von, née Fralovskaya (1831–94), patroness of Tchaikovsky. The daughter of a landowner, she married at seventeen a poor government engineer, Karl von Meck, who subsequently made a huge fortune which he bequeathed to her at his death in 1876. The same year she developed a passion for the personality of Tchaikovsky, or rather for the shadow of his personality, for she never met him, and carried on an intimate correspondence with him for sixteen years. In 1880 and 1881 she engaged Debussy as her domestic pianist.

Mendès, Catulle (1841–1909), French writer, married Judith, the daughter of Théophile Gautier, and wrote librettos for Pessard (q.v.), Chabrier (q.v.), Massenet and Debussy (*Rodrigue et Chimène*).

Messager, André (1853–1929), French composer and conductor, pupil of Saint-Saëns. Wrote a number of ballets for the Théâtre des Folies-Bergère, many light operas, conducted the *Ring* at the Paris Opéra and the first performance of *Pelléas* at the Opéra-Comique.

Monet, Claude (1840–1926), French Impressionist painter remarkable for his delicate monochromes.

Moréas, Jean, real name *Papadiamantopoulos* (1856–1910), French poet born at Athens. Editor of *Le Symboliste* and a prominent member of the so-called 'decadents.' In his later years he wrote some beautiful, lucid poetry.

Mourey, Gabriel (born 1865), French writer. Has written several volumes of verse and translated Poe and Swinburne. He adapted Joseph Bédier's (q.v.) *Tristan* for Debussy's projected opera.

Péladan, Joseph (1858–1918), French writer. An eccentric personality who assumed the title of *Sar* and grouped together certain French painters under the title 'Salon de la Rose-Croix.' He was the librettist of Erik Satie's *Le Fils des étoiles.*

Appendix C—Personalia

Pessard, Émile (1843–1917), a composer of light operas whom Debussy particularly admired in his early youth. He was a teacher of Ravel.

Peter, René, French journalist and dramatist who has written a valuable book about his friendship with Debussy.

Pierné, Gabriel (born 1863), French composer and conductor. A pupil of Franck and Massenet, he became conductor of the Concerts Colonne, where in 1910 he conducted the first performance of Debussy's *Ibéria*. He has composed several stage works and is a member of the Institut.

Régnier, Henri de (1864–1936), French poet and novelist who was friendly with Debussy and Pierre Louÿs. His work 'is a poetic evocation of the past, full of mystery and fantasy and written in a rather deliberately precious and archaic style' (Larousse).

Renoir, Auguste (1841–1919), one of the outstanding painters of the Impressionist school.

Rossetti, Dante Gabriel (1828–82), English painter and poet of Italian descent, founder of the Pre-Raphaelite Brotherhood. His *Blessed Damozel*, in a translation by Gabriel Sarrazin, was the text of Debussy's *La Damoiselle élue*.

Satie, Erik (1866–1925), a strange personality who seemed, above all, intent on attracting attention by his freakish acts. In his youth he was a pianist in a Montmartre café. He began to study composition seriously only at the age of forty, when he entered the classes of Albert Roussel and Vincent d'Indy at the Schola Cantorum. At the time of his death he was considered the *bon oncle* of the group of young French composers called 'Les Six.'

Sivry, Charles de (1848–1900), French composer of light songs and operettas and accompanist at the Cabaret du Chat Noir. He introduced Debussy to his mother, Mme Mauté de Fleurville (q.v.), who prepared him for the Conservatoire.

Tiersot, Julien (born 1857), French writer on music. Pupil of Massenet and César Franck. Has edited the correspondence of Berlioz.

Debussy

Toulet, Paul-Jean (1857–1920), a subtle and fanciful poet who became addicted to opium. He wrote a libretto for Debussy adapted from Shakespeare's *As You Like It.*

Verlaine, Paul (1844–96), a rare lyrical poet. Unable to restrain his passion for women and his addiction to drink, he lived the life of a debauchee. His young wife, Mathilde Mauté, whom he abandoned in England, was the daughter of Debussy's piano teacher.

Vidal, Paul (1863–1931), French composer of ballets and operas, conductor at the Opéra. He was an intimate friend of Debussy's at the Villa Medici.

Willy, pseudonym of *Henri Gauthier-Villars* (1859–1931), an amusing and caustic musical critic, who wrote in the *Écho de Paris* under the name of 'L'Ouvreuse du Cirque d'Été.' Married the charming writer Colette (the librettist of Ravel's *L'Enfant et les sortilèges*), in collaboration with whom he wrote several books.

Wyzewa, Teodor de (1863–1917), French writer of Polish origin who helped to found *La Revue wagnérienne.* With Georges de Saint-Foix he wrote an important work on Mozart.

Ysaÿe, Eugène (1858–1931), Belgian violinist, one of the great virtuosos of his time. Debussy's *Nocturnes* were originally intended for him, and his string quartet gave the first performance of the Quartet of Debussy.

APPENDIX D

BIBLIOGRAPHY [1]

Ambrière, F., 'La Vie romaine de Claude Debussy.' (*La Revue musicale,* Paris, January 1934.)

Antoine, A. 'Mes souvenirs sur le Théâtre Antoine et sur l'Odéon.' (Paris, 1928.)

Arconada, M., 'En torno a Debussy.' (Madrid, 1926.)

Aubry, G. Jean-, 'Claude Debussy et la musique française moderne en Angleterre. (*La Revue S.I.M.* March 1909.)

—— 'Some Recollections of Debussy.' (*The Musical Times,* London, May 1918.)

—— 'L'Œuvre critique de Debussy.' (*La Revue musicale,* December 1920.)

—— 'La Musique et les nations.' (Paris and London, 1922.)

Barre, A., 'Le Symbolisme.' (Paris, 1911.)

Bérys, J. de. See under Caillard, C. F.

Bonheur, R., 'Souvenirs et impressions d'un compagnon de jeunesse.' (*La Revue musicale,* May 1926; special number entitled 'La Jeunesse de Debussy.')

Boucher, M., 'Debussy.' (Paris, 1930.)

Bruneau, A., 'Musiques de Russie et musiciens de France.' (Paris, 1903.)

Brussel, R., 'Claude Debussy et Paul Dukas.' (*La Revue musicale,* May 1926.)

Caillard, C. F. and Bérys, J. de, 'Le Cas Debussy.' (Paris, 1910.)

Calvocoressi, M. D., 'Musicians' Gallery.' (London, 1933.)

Cardinne-Petit, L., 'En écoutant Pierre Louÿs.' (*Les Nouvelles littéraires,* Paris, December 22, 1934.)

Casella, A., 'Claude Debussy.' (*Monthly Musical Record,* London, January 1933.)

---

[1] The special publications of Debussy's letters are listed on page 272.

Debussy

Chennevière, D., 'Claude Debussy et son œuvre.' (Paris, 1913.)

Cœuroy, A., 'Appels d'Orphée.' (Paris, 1928.)

Cortot, A., 'The Piano Music of Debussy.' English translation by Violet Edgell. (London, 1922.)

Daly, W. H., 'Debussy: a Study in Modern Music.' (Edinburgh, 1908.)

Debussy, C., 'Monsieur Croche antidilettante.' (Paris, 1921.)

—— 'Monsieur Croche the Dilettante-hater.' English translation (anonymous). (London, 1927.)

Decsey, Ernst, 'Debussy.' (Vienna, 1933.)

Durand, J., 'Quelques souvenirs d'un éditeur de musique.' (Paris, 1924.)

Ellis, A. I., 'Stéphane Mallarmé in English Verse.' (London, 1927.)

Emmanuel, M., 'Pelléas et Mélisande.' (Paris, 1926.)

—— 'Les Ambitions de Claude-Achille.' (*La Revue musicale,* May 1926.)

Fábián, L., 'Claude Debussy und sein Werk.' (Munich, 1923.)

Gatti-Cassazza, G., 'Debussy.' (*The New York Times,* March 15, 1925.)

Gianturco, E., 'Claude Debussy.' (Naples, 1923.)

Godet, R. (see also under Prunières, H.), 'Claude Debussy.' (*La Semaine littéraire de Genève,* April 13, 20 and 27, 1918.)

—— 'Le Lyrisme intime de Debussy.' (*La Revue musicale,* December 1920 and January 1921.)

—— 'En marge de Boris Godounov.' Vol. II. (Paris and London, 1926.)

—— 'En marge de la marge.' (*La Revue musicale,* May 1926.)

—— 'Weber and Debussy.' (*The Chesterian,* London, June 1926.)

Gosse, Sir E. W., 'French Profiles.' (London, 1905.)

Gui, V., 'Debussy in Italia.' (*Musica d' oggi,* Milan, December 1932.)

Gysi, F., 'Claude Debussy.' (Zurich, 1926.)

Inghelbrecht, D. E., 'Souvenirs.' (*La Revue musicale,* December 1920.)

Indy, V. d', 'Richard Wagner et son influence sur l'art musical français.' (Paris, 1930.)

Jardillier, R., 'Pelléas.' (Paris, 1927.)

Appendix D—Bibliography

Klingsor, T., 'Les Musiciens et les poètes contemporains.' (*Mercure de France*, November 1900.)

Koechlin, C., 'Quelques anciennes mélodies inédites de Claude Debussy.' (*La Revue musicale*, May 1926.)

—— 'Debussy.' (Paris, 1927.)

—— 'La Leçon de Claude Debussy.' (*La Revue musicale*, January 1934.)

—— 'Souvenirs sur Debussy, la Schola et la S.M.I.' (*La Revue musicale*, November 1934.)

—— 'Sur l'évolution de la musique française avant et après Debussy.' (*La Revue musicale*, April 1935.)

Kurt, E., 'Romantische Harmonik und ihre Krise in Wagners Tristan.' (Berne and Leipzig, 1920.)

Laloy, L., 'Debussy.' (Paris, 1909.)

—— 'Le Théâtre de Claude Debussy.' (*La Revue musicale*, December 1920.)

—— 'La Musique retrouvée.' (Paris, 1928.)

—— 'Debussy.' (*La Revue des deux mondes*, Paris, July 15, 1932.)

Leblanc, G., 'Souvenirs.' (Paris, 1931.)

—— 'Maeterlinck and I.' English translation by Janet Flanner (London, 1932.)

Lépine, J. 'La Vie de Debussy.' (Paris, 1930.)

Liebich, L. S., 'Claude A. Debussy.' (London, 1908.)

—— 'An Englishwoman's Memories of Debussy.' (*The Musical Times*, June 1918.)

Liess, Andreas, 'Claude Debussy. Das Werk im Zeitbild.' 2 vols. (Strasburg, 1936.)

Lockspeiser, E., 'Debussy, Tchaikovsky et Mme von Meck.' (*La Revue musicale*, November 1935.)

Meck, N. F. von. See under Tchaikovsky.

Messager, A., 'Les Premières Représentations de Pelléas.' (*La Revue musicale*, May 1926.)

Newman, E., 'The Development of Debussy.' (*The Musical Times*, May and August 1918.)

Niemann, W., 'Die Musik seit Richard Wagner.' (Berlin and Leipzig, 1913.)

Oulmont, C., 'Deux Amis. Claude Debussy et Ernest Chausson. Documents inédits.' (*Mercure de France*, Paris, December 1, 1934.)

Perracchio, L., 'L'Opera pianistica di Claude Debussy.' (Milan, 1924.)

Peter, R., 'Debussy. Vues prises de son intimité.' (Paris, 1931.)

Pierné, G., 'Souvenirs d'Achille Debussy.' (*La Revue musicale*, May 1926.)

Prod'homme, J. G., 'Claude-Achille Debussy.' (*The Musical Quarterly*, New York, October 1918.)

Prunières, H., 'A la Villa Médicis.' (*La Revue musicale*, May 1926.)

—— 'The Youth of Debussy.' (*The Sackbut*, London, October 1926.)

—— 'Autour de Debussy.' (*La Revue musicale*, May, June and September 1934.) A detailed criticism of Léon Vallas's 'Claude Debussy et son temps,' incorporating notes by Robert Godet. The June and September numbers contain a rejoinder from Léon Vallas.

Rebois, H., 'Les Grands Prix de Rome de musique.' (Paris, 1932.)

Régnier, H. de, 'Souvenirs sur Debussy.' (*La Revue musicale*, May 1926.)

La Revue musicale. Special number entitled 'Wagner et la France.' (October 1923.) Other numbers listed under names of contributors.

La Revue wagnérienne. (Paris, 1885–8.)

Rolland, R., 'Musicians of To-day.' Translation by M. Blaicklock. (London, 1915.)

Santoliquido, F., 'Il dopo-Wagner: Claude Debussy e Richard Strauss.' (Rome, 1909.)

Setaccioli, G., 'Debussy è un innovatore?' (Rome, 1910.)

—— 'Debussy. Eine kritische-ästhetische Studie.' Translated from the Italian by F. Spiro. (Leipzig, 1911.)

Shera, F. H., 'Debussy and Ravel.' (London, 1925.)

Suarès, A., 'Debussy.' (Paris, 1922.)

Appendix D—Bibliography

Symons, A., 'The Symbolist Movement in Literature.' (London, 1908.)

Tchaikovsky, P. I., 'Peripiska s N. F. von Meck.' Vol. II. (1879–81; Moscow, 1935.)

Templier, P. D., 'Erik Satie.' (Paris, 1932.)

Ternant, A. de, 'Debussy and Brahms.' (*The Musical Times,* July 1924.)

—— 'Debussy and some Italian Musicians.' (*The Musical Times,* September 1924.)

—— 'Debussy and Some Others on Sullivan.' (*The Musical Times,* December 1924.)

Tiersot, J., 'Promenades à l'exposition universelle.' (*Le Ménestrel,* Paris, May 26, June 30, July 14, 1889.)

—— 'Un Demi-siècle de musique française. Entre les deux guerres.' (Paris, 1918.)

Vallas, L. (see also under Prunières, H.), 'Debussy.' (Paris, 1926.)

—— 'Les Idées de Claude Debussy, musicien français.' (Paris, 1927.)

—— 'The Theories of Claude Debussy.' English translation by Maire O'Brien. (London, 1929.)

—— 'Claude Debussy et son temps.' (Paris, 1932.)

—— 'Claude Debussy: his Life and Works.' English translation by Maire and Grace O'Brien. (London, 1933.)

Vasnier, M., 'Debussy à dix-huit ans.' (*La Revue musicale,* May 1926.)

Verlaine, Mathilde, 'Mémoires de ma vie.' (Paris, 1935.)

Vidal, P., 'Souvenirs d'Achille Debussy.' (*La Revue musicale,* May 1926.)

Vuillermoz, E., 'Autour du Martyre de saint Sébastien.' (*La Revue musicale,* December 1920.)

—— 'Claude Debussy.' (Paris, 1920.)

Walch, G., 'Anthologie des poètes français contemporains,' Vol. II. (Paris, 1927.)

Woolley, G., 'Wagner et le symbolisme français.' (Paris, 1934.)

Debussy

LIST OF DEBUSSY'S PUBLISHED LETTERS

To	Published in
Antoine, A.	'Mes souvenirs sur le Théâtre Antoine et sur l'Odéon,' by A. Antoine. (Paris, 1928.)
Aubry, G. Jean-	'Some Recollections of Debussy.' (*The Musical Times*, May 1918.)
	'La Musique et les nations,' by G. Jean-Aubry. (Paris and London, 1922.)
	'Debussy,' by M. Boucher. (Paris, 1930.) Facsimile.
Baron, E.	'La Vie romaine de Claude Debussy,' by F. Ambrière. (*La Revue musicale*, January 1934.)
Calvocoressi, M. D.	'Les Idées de Claude Debussy, musicien français,' by Léon Vallas. (Paris, 1927.) Facsimile.
Chausson, E.	'Correspondance inédite de Claude Debussy et Ernest Chausson.' (*La Revue musicale*, December 1925.)
	'Deux lettres de Debussy à Ernest Chausson.' (*La Revue musicale*, May 1926.)
	'Deux amis. Claude Debussy et Ernest Chausson. Documents inédits.' (*Mercure de France*, December 1, 1934.)
Debussy, C. E. (Chouchou)	'Terres latines.' Brussels, March 1936.
Durand, J.	'Lettres de Claude Debussy à son éditeur' (i.e. Jacques Durand). (Paris, 1927.)
Godet, R.	'Claude Debussy,' by Robert Godet. (*La Semaine littéraire de Genève*, April 20 and 27, 1918.) Fragments.
	'Le Lyrisme intime de Debussy,' by Robert Godet. (*La Revue musicale*, December 1920 and January 1921.) Fragments.
	'Dissonances.' Geneva, December 1923.
	'En marge de la marge,' by Robert Godet. (*La Revue musicale*, May 1926.)

Appendix D—Bibliography

To	Published in
Godet, R. (cont.)	'Autour de Debussy,' by Henry Prunières. (*La Revue musicale*, May 1934.)
Guéritte, T. J.	'Some Recollections of Debussy.' (*The Musical Times*, May 1918.)
Gui, V.	'Debussy in Italia,' by Vittorio Gui. (*Musica d' oggi*, Milan, December 1932.)
Hartmann, A.	'Claude Debussy et son temps,' by Léon Vallas. (Paris, 1932.)
Huvelin, P.	'Pour la musique française,' edited by Paul Huvelin. (Paris, 1927.)
Laloy, L.	'La Musique retrouvée,' by Louis Laloy. (Paris, 1928.)
Lenormand, R.	'Claude Debussy et son temps,' by Léon Vallas. (Paris, 1932.)
Louÿs, P.	'Correspondance de Claude Debussy et Pierre Louÿs.' (*L'Esprit français*, Paris, July to December 1931.) Catalogue d'autographes. Simon Kra (publisher). (Paris, December 13, 1928).
Malherbe, C.	*La Revue S.I.M.* (Paris, February 1910.)
Messager, A.	'Pelléas et Mélisande,' by Maurice Emmanuel. (Paris, Mellottée, n.d.) 'Claude Debussy et son temps,' by Léon Vallas. (Paris, 1932.)
Peter, R.	'Debussy. Vues prises de son intimité,' by René Peter. (Paris, 1931.)
Toulet, P.-J.	'Correspondance de Claude Debussy et Paul-Jean Toulet.' (Paris, 1929.)
Vasnier, M.	'A la Villa Médicis,' by Henry Prunières. (*La Revue musicale*, May 1926.)
Ysaÿe, E.	'Lettres inédites de Claude Debussy à Eugène Ysaÿe.' (*Les Annales politiques et littéraires*, Paris, August 25, 1933.)

APPENDIX E

To Raoul Bardac

BICHAIN, 31*st August* 1901.

DEAR FRIEND,

My delay in replying in no way means that I was untouched by the delicate attention of your letter. But here in Bichain, where I am sorry that we shall not see you, the minutes pass, one knows not exactly how.

I have the feeling of being at the other end of the world from Paris. The beastly fever that worries us all more or less, can't play havoc here, and there's no mistaking that the movement of the trees against the river-banks forms a counterpoint less poor than ours. . . . But the people are much less lovely than their setting. I needn't tell you that 'le geste auguste du semeur' [1] is quite forgotten and that when the angelus gently orders the fields to sleep you never see any one striking that solemn pose of the lithographs. [2]

What you tell me of X . . . [3] is most praiseworthy. One can never spend too much time constructing that special atmosphere in which a work of art should move. I believe that one should never hurry to write but leave everything to that many-sided play of thoughts—those mysterious workings of the mind which we too often disturb, prompted (though we may not like to admit it) by materialism and even cowardice.

Thank you for the Quartet. [4] I shall be much indebted to you and don't know how I can repay you. Anyhow you can always

---

[1] Line of Victor Hugo.

[2] Allusion to the well-known pictures of Millet, *L'Angélus* and *Les Glaneuses*.

[3] Work of Raoul Bardac.

[4] An arrangement of Debussy's Quartet made by Raoul Bardac.

count on me—for whatever that is worth, for I don't ever expect to become a big pot. I am far too unconcerned about my fellow-beings, which is incidentally the only way to choose between them.

I shall be in Paris about 10th September and am afraid of being worried by more people than usual. But if you will come and see me it will make me forget how tiring they are.

Affectionately,

C. D.

Sunday, 25th February 1906.

MY DEAR RARA,

Forgive my laziness! Well, 'regonflons des souvenirs d'hiver,'[1] as Willy would make Mallarmé's Faun say. And what a winter! Rain, the trees look like disconsolate widowers, and for a change they've put the flowers inside and the poultry outside. Vain-glorious people try to fill the void with symphonic descriptions. Well, we heard *Schéhérazade*[2] again. It doesn't improve with age. It reminds one more of a bazaar than of the Orient. And of course Chevillard[3] isn't a bit like the princess. . . . We heard too *Un Jour d'été à la montagne* by Vincent d'Indy. This kind of d'Indy is from beyond the Cévennes.[4] As I am not very well informed on this place, I can hardly speak of it. There seemed to be an immoderate use of the bassoon—and fancy having a piano. I thought they had pianos only in the mountains of Switzerland.

---

[1] Play on the word 'divers' in the line from *L'Après-midi d'un faune*:

'O nymphes regonflons des souvenirs divers.'

('On other memories, Nymphs, life's breath bestow.'

From the translation by A. I. Ellis.)

[2] By Rimsky-Korsakov.

[3] Camille Chevillard, the conductor.

[4] The implication here is that this is the old, authentic d'Indy. Allusion to the expression: 'C'est de derrière les fagots'—something genuine, and to the *Symphonie Cévenole*, a work that d'Indy composed twenty years earlier.

You didn't have any luck at the Société X . . .[1] But you have no reason to feel very resentful. First of all you weren't properly backed, and then you don't belong to any of the groups who are allowed to mess things up. You have time to prepare your play—so don't strike out on a bad line or one that might lead to nothing.

You are talented, but you can never be too aware of the long road ahead. You know how little respect I have for the parasite development which has too long bolstered up the glory of the Masters. With such a feeling there comes a keener sense of values and one may discover a melodic line more sensitive to design and timbre. Let your ideas breathe, for they can so easily succumb to the pretentiousness of form.

In a word, have patience! It is a major and even a domestic virtue which helps a great deal. But I don't want to spoil a fine day for you with this shower of moral and aesthetic considerations. What's the good? Aesthetics have really only a relative value and I'm afraid that morals have too.

The description of your days is delightful. You are right! It is better to let one's mind soak in the sun—like the flowers and the photographs—while one's nerves can still react.

Gather impressions. But don't hurry to note them down; for music has this over painting, that it can bring together all manner of variations of colour and light.[2] It is a point that is not often observed though it is quite obvious.

And then, from time to time forget music altogether. 'Practice makes perfect' is a schoolmaster's notion. And it is not in very good taste to badger those one loves the most [3] with constant requests.

Your mother has a wonderful cold. You know how opposed she is to all medicine, and that doesn't help matters.

Little Chouchou is going to have yet another nurse. The one

---

[1] Allusion to some songs of Raoul Bardac which were badly sung at a concert of this society.

[2] Debussy was no doubt thinking of paintings such as the series of Claude Monet (in the Musée de l'Orangerie in Paris) of a lily-pond at different times of the day. Music, he implies, is not bound to any particular *tone* of impression.

[3] Meaning musical inspiration.

she has at present says that her husband has been unfaithful to her. So she is going to find out the trouble for herself, which is not very wise and certainly not very economical.

I shan't speak to you of what I am doing. Although I have been writing very little, music offends my ear. The reason for that, we will say, is the colour of the sky.

Au revoir . . .

C. D.

To the Royal Philharmonic Society in London

CHÂTEAU DE PUYS, *27th August* 1906.

DEAR SIR,

Having been away from Paris, I have only recently received your kind invitation to conduct the orchestra of the Philharmonic Society.

Before replying I had to be sure of the date when *Pelléas* will be given at the 'Monnaie' at Brussels, for I have to go there and super-intend the rehearsals. I can now be free on the 16th or the 30th of May 1907, the dates suggested in your letter.

It remains for me to say that I don't speak English at all and fear that this may prove a hindrance at the rehearsals with your excellent orchestra. Apart from this fear I shall be very glad to be amongst you.

Yours cordially,

C. D.

In his reply, the secretary suggested that he should conduct *Pelléas,* apparently not realizing that it was an opera, and adds: 'As the Philharmonic Society is not in the habit of paying a fee to those distinguished composers who honour us with their presence, we hope you will allow us to offer you £15 to cover your expenses.' Debussy scornfully replies (on 24th September):

Pelléas et Mélisande is a musical drama in five acts which lasts $2\frac{1}{2}$ hours, so that it is not possible to give it at a concert. Furthermore, as it is likely to be given in London, this is an additional reason for avoiding any concert performance.

When you asked me to conduct the Philharmonic Society I naturally thought of some symphonic work. I am sorry there was this misunderstanding, but once again, not only is it impossible to give *Pelléas* at a concert, but the composition of the work is such as to make extracts utterly impossible.

The secretary's note appended reads: 'I wrote and said "quite so," and would he come and direct some symphonic work—no reply.' A final refusal was sent on 19th October.

APPENDIX F

ACHILLE-CLAUDE DEBUSSY

Manuscript memoir by Nicholas von Meck in the Tchaikovsky Museum at Klin (U.S.S.R.)

THIS adds a few details to the account of Debussy's association with the von Meck family in Chapter II. The reader will easily interpret for himself the opinions expressed and may make the necessary rectifications of dates and places by referring to the correspondence of Mme von Meck which I have quoted. Nicholas von Meck seems not to have had a great appreciation of Debussy's character. There is something disconcertingly patronizing about his remarks (especially in view of the fact that they were written in 1926), and indeed when Debussy went to Moscow in 1913 his boyhood friend was only able to say that he was 'a funny, fat, and empty little man.' On the other hand it is interesting to see that the song, *Ici-bas tous les lilas meurent,* by the brothers Paul and Lucien Hille-macher, is referred to as by Debussy, for this apparently means that the eighteen-year-old boy unscrupulously passed off this composition as his own. It was recently published under Debussy's name (see Appendix B). On the friendship with Alexander von Meck, M. Georges de Meck, his son, informs me that a collection of letters from Debussy to his father was lost at the time of the Revolution. The translation of this document from the Russian was kindly made for me by Countess Bennigsen.

In the year 1879 my mother, Mme N. F. von Meck, addressed herself to the Paris Conservatoire, requesting them to recommend her a pupil from the piano class who could teach my sisters music during the summer, accompany their singing, play four-hands with my mother and play in her trios and quartets.

The Conservatoire sent A. Debussy, who was then nineteen.

The little Frenchman arrived, dark, thin, sarcastic, and gave everybody amusing nicknames. For instance, he called our plump teacher 'petit hippopotame en vacances,' and we in turn nicknamed him 'le bouillant Achille.' He joined us in Switzerland, and from there we went to Italy and stopped in Rome. Once we walked past the Villa Medici, where the best students of the Conservatoire and the Academy of Arts [L'École des Beaux-Arts] reside for a year at the cost of the French Government. One of us, pointing to the villa, said to Debussy: 'This is your future home.' It was interesting to see how longingly he looked back on the Villa Medici.

From Rome we went to Florence, where we lived at the Villa Oppenheim, and from here, in October, Debussy returned to his studies in Paris. On leaving us he was very sad, and my mother had to comfort him, promising that in the spring of 1880 he would again return to us. He did join us the next year, in Moscow, and he spent the whole summer with us visiting various places and towns in Europe.

My mother considered Debussy a gifted musician, not only as a pianist, but also as a composer. He was a pupil of Massenet, and at that time his professor exercised a strong influence on him.

My mother acquainted him with Russian music and with Wagner. Of the Russians he got to know Tchaikovsky and all the members of the 'Kutchka,' Rimsky-Korsakov, Cui, Moussorgsky and Borodin.[1] Both Wagner and the Russian composers produced an unfavourable impression on Debussy, which was quite natural,

---

[1] 'All the members of the "Kutchka,"' but Balakirev is omitted. And we know that, in Moscow, Debussy did become acquainted with this composer. 'Dear friend, do you know Balakirev's songs?' writes Mme von Meck to Tchaikovsky (21st August 1881). 'I came across them recently, and they please me immensely. There is a picturesque element in them which appeals to the imagination. Not only do you hear a melody in them, but you hear it against a certain background.' Those are words which might have been written by Debussy himself; and indeed, it would not be surprising if Mme von Meck, who was apt to take her opinions from other people, got this one from her 'little pianist Bussy.'

since French music at that time was too near the music of the classical composers, and Debussy, following this tradition, did not react to all innovations.

But as he became better acquainted with Russian music he appreciated it, though by his French nature he was inclined to inter-pret it in a superficial and elegant manner. No doubt his acquaint-ance not only with Russian music and Wagner, but also with his contemporaries in other countries, widened his outlook and influenced his development. Of his compositions at that time his song, *Ici-bas tous les lilas meurent,* was frequently sung and played in our house by my sister Julia Pachulska [*née* von Meck]. The manuscript of this song was in the possession of my brother Alexander von Meck, who was in correspondence with Debussy for a long time.

Our prophecy in 1879 about Debussy's residence at the Villa Medici was fulfilled, for he finished his studies at the Conservatoire by obtaining the *Prix de Rome,* and having been assisted by my mother, went to Rome. In conclusion I may add that as a com-panion Debussy was a very pleasant, lively and even-tempered man, and we were always sorry when he left us.

When he returned to Moscow during the musical season of 1913–14, only my sister Sophia Galitzin [*née* von Meck], his former pupil, saw him. Debussy always remembered his sojourn with us with gratitude and pleasure.

N. K. MECK.

1926.

INDEX

ABRAHAM, Gerald, 136, 151
Albeniz, 185
Albert, King of the Belgians, 98, 150
Alheim, Pierre d', 48
Alkan, 10
Allan, Maud, 93, 183
Annunzio, Gabriele d', 92, 191–193, 203, 260
Antoine, actor, 85, 104
Après-midi d'un faune, L', 40, 48, 57–9, 63, 72, 89, 90, 93, 94, 125, 128, 160, 166–73, 179, 186, 201, 229, 231, 275
Arabesques, 133, 135
Ariettes oubliées, 119–23
Arosa, Achille-Antoine, 4, 5
Arosa, Paul, 5
As You Like It, 102–5, 107
Aubry, G. Jean-, 58, 89, 223, 231, 232
Auric, Georges, 230
Avellan, admiral, 54, 55

Bach, 28, 192, 193, 220, 234
Bailly, Edmond, 68, 87, 260
Bakst, Leon, 93
Balakirev, 16, 40, 280
Balcon, Le (*Cinq Poèmes de Baude-laire*), 115–18
Ballade (piano), 40, 136
Ballade à la lune, 10

Ballades de Villon, 91, 92, 130, [131
Balzac, 8
Banville, Théodore de, 10, 19, 25, 32, 166
Bardac, Emma, *See* Debussy, Emma
Bardac, Raoul, vii, 221, 274–7
Baron, Émile, 31, 32, 115
Barre, André, 34
Bataille, Henry, 95
Baudelaire, 35, 37, 115, 119, 124, 130, 131, 149, 231
Bax, Arnold, 232
Bazille, Auguste, 11, 12
Beardsley, Aubrey, 216
Beau Soir, 13, 111, 180
Bédier, Joseph, 102, 260
Beethoven, 10, 20, 28, 29, 44, 53, 114, 156, 160, 220, 223, 226, 234
Bellaigue, Camille, 80
Belle au bois dormant, La, 16, 111, 112
Benda, Georg, 204 [15
Bennigsen, Alexandra, Countess,
Bennigsen, Olga, Countess, viii, 279
Bennigsen, Count, vii, viii, 16
Berceuse héroïque, 98, 150
Berlioz, 10, 17, 27, 30, 35, 40, 44, 107, 113–15, 187, 188, 221, 228

282

Index

Bérys, José de, 88

Bizet, 17, 43, 140, 231

Bloch, Ernest, 228

Blondin, 78

Boîte à joujoux, 93, 134

Boito, Arrigo, 28

Bonheur, Raymond, 16, 41, 260

Bordier, J., 58

Borodin, 16, 17, 112, 221, 229, 280

Bossi, Enrico, 231

Bouchardy, Joseph, 52

Bourgault-Ducoudray, A., 58

Bourget, Paul, 19, 72, 111, 260

Brahms, 42–4, 232, 234

Brayer, Jules de, 47, 48

Brouillards (Préludes II), 150, 180

Bruneau, Alfred, 39, 63, 64, 69, 260

Busoni, Ferruccio, 231

Bussy, Counts de, 3

Bussy, Valentin de, 3

Bussy-Rabutin, Roger de, 3

Cabat, Louis, 261

Caillard, C. Francis, 88

Calvocoressi, M. D., 87, 88, 120, 217

Campanini, Cleofonte, 90

Canope (Préludes II), 150

Capell, Richard, 66

Caplet, André, 92, 93, 185, 261

Carraud, Gaston, 79, 86

Carré, Albert, 56, 78, 107, 108, 261

Casella, Alfredo, 66, 231

Castro, Guillem de, 48

Cathédrale engloutie, La (Préludes I), 149, 150, 165

Cendrelune, 60

Cerutti, 7

C'est l'extase (Ariettes oubliées), 119, 120

Cézanne, 46

Chabrier, Emmanuel, 29, 39, 42, 45, 49, 140, 230, 231, 261

Chamberlain, Houston Stewart, 60, 61, 261

Champfleury, Jules, 37

Chanson espagnole, 19

Chansons de Bilitis, 61, 62, 98, 122, 125–7, 131, 134, 182, 195, 205

Chapman, Henry G., 194

Charles, Duke of Orléans. *See* Orléans

Charpentier, Gustave, 63, 78

Chausson, Ernest, 39, 50–2, 54, 55, 57, 67, 191, 261

Chevaux de bois (Ariettes oubliées), 115

Chevelure, La (Chansons de Bilitis), 61, 127, 195

Chevillard, Camille, 86, 101, 261, 275

Children's Corner, 86, 134, 148, 149

Chopin, 7, 10, 72, 98

Chute de la maison Usher, La, 102, 106, 107, 188

Cinq Poèmes de Baudelaire, 40, 44, 53, 115–19, 134

Clair de lune (Fêtes galantes I), 122

Clair de lune (Fêtes galantes I, first version), 122

Clair de lune (Suite bergamasque), 122

Cocteau, Jean, 230

Cœuroy, André, 37

Cohen, Alexander, 166

Colles, H. C., 227

Colloque sentimental (Fêtes galantes II), 123

Colonne, Édouard, 218, 261

Combarieu, Jules, 81

Comme il vous plaira. See *As You Like It*

Comte, Auguste, 34

Coronio, Nicolas G., vii, 138

Couperin, 164

Cox, Nita, 91

Cui, César, 16, 39, 280

Damoiselle élue, La, 40, 49, 53, 57, 62, 70, 189–91

Danilchenko, cellist, 13

Danse, piano, 136

Danse bohémienne, 13, 133, 134

Danse de Puck (Préludes I), 149

Danse sacrée et Danse profane, 82

Danseuses de Delphes (Préludes I), 149

Darcours, Charles, 57

Daphnis et Chloé, 60, 61

Dargomizhsky, 226

Daudet, Alphonse, 3

De grève (Proses lyriques), 124

De soir (Proses lyriques), 124

Debussy. *See also* Bussy and Roustan

Debussy, Adèle (sister), vii, 4–6

Debussy, Claude-Emma (daughter), 84, 86, 148, 276

Debussy, Emma (second wife), 83, 84, 86, 95, 104

Debussy, Eugène (brother), 6, 66

Debussy, Lily (Rosalie, first wife), 73, 74, 77, 83–6, 95, 96

Debussy, Manuel - Achille (father), 3–5, 7, 8

Debussy, Victorine (mother), 4–6, 8

Degas, 36

Delibes, 10, 17, 18

Delius, 180, 216, 232

Delmet, Paul, 63, 70, 220, 222

Déroulède, Paul, 35, 40

Devil in the Belfry, The. See *Diable dans le beffroi*

Diable dans le beffroi, Le, 102, 105–7, 188

Diane au bois, 25, 27, 30, 32, 49, 108, 166, 188

Diaghilev, Serge, 93, 94, 186, 213

Dickens, 149

Doll's Serenade (Children's Corner), 148

Doret, Gustave, 57, 261

Dreyfus, 69, 216

Dubois, Théodore, 80

Dufranne, Hector, 78

Dujardin, Édouard, 36

Dukas, Paul, vii, 41, 87, 96, 111, 229, 262

D'un cahier d'esquisses, 82

Dupuis, Henri, 58

Durand, Émile, 10, 11, 13, 14

Durand, Jacques, 6, 7, 68, 70, 82, 83, 88, 90–2, 94, 95, 97–9, 102, 105–7, 163, 183, 185
Durand & Cie, viii
Dvořák, 226

Elgar, 91, 232
Eliot, T. S., 224
Ellis, A. I., 37, 166, 167, 275
Emmanuel, Maurice, 10, 17, 18, 20, 201, 204, 209, 226
En blanc et noir, 98, 134, 150
Enfant prodigue, L', 21, 49, 188, 189
Ennery, Adolphe Philippe d', 52
Épigraphes antiques, 98, 134, 150
Estampes, 82, 134, 138–41, 143, 185
Et la lune descend sur le temple qui fut (Images for piano II), 145
Études, 98, 134, 150
Éventail, L' (Trois Poèmes de Stéphane Mallarmé), 128

Fábián, Ladislas, 182
Fabre, Lucien, 36
Fall of the House of Usher, The. See *Chute de la maison Usher*
Falla, Manuel de, 140
Fantaisie, piano and orchestra, 49, 133, 143
Fantin-Latour, 36
Fantoches (Fêtes galantes I), 113–15, 122, 165
Faune, Le (Fêtes galantes II), 123
Fauré, Gabriel, 63, 83, 218, 230, 231, 262

Fées sont d'exquises danseuses, Les (Préludes II), 150
Ferronnière, Octavie de la. See Roustan
Fêtes (Nocturnes), 90, 141, 175, 177–80
Fêtes galantes, Set I, 19, 113, 122, 124
Fêtes galantes, Set II, 82, 122–4, 182
Feydeau, Georges, 66
Fille aux cheveux de lin, La (Préludes I), 149, 150
Flanner, Janet, 52, 67, 77
Flaubert, 32, 34
Flers, Robert de, 78
Fleur des blés, 13, 111
Flûte de Pan, La (Chansons de Bilitis), 127, 128, 165
Fontaine, Mme Lucien, 113
Foss, Hubert J., 225
Fragonard, 113
France, Anatole, 69
Franck, César, 10, 17, 58, 63, 69, 87, 135, 160, 191
Frères en art, Les, play, 74
Fromont, publisher, 70

Gaby, 71–3
Galitzin, Sophia, Princess. See Meck, Sophie von
Garden, Mary, 78
Gatti-Casazza, 108
Gauthier-Villars, Henri, 73, 266, 275
Gautier, Théophile, 37
Gavioli, 217

Gémier, actor, 104, 105

General Lavine-eccentric (Préludes II), 149, 150

Gerville-Réache, Mme, 78

Ghil, René, 37, 38, 262

Gide, André, 53

Gigues (Images for orchestra), 89, 93, 185, 186

Gil-Marchex, René, 143

Gilaiev, viii

Glazounov, 58

Gluck, 87, 103, 220, 221, 225

Godet, Robert, vii, 48, 49, 51, 55, 67, 73, 75, 81, 82, 84, 93, 100, 103, 106, 107, 227, 262

Goethe, 28, 43

Golliwog's Cake-Walk (Children's Corner), 148, 149

Goncourt brothers, 32

Goossens, Eugène, 232

Gounod, 18, 21, 22, 28–30, 36, 37, 42, 113, 188

Gray, Cecil, 225

Green (Ariettes oubliées), 121–3

Grieg, 7, 216, 217, 226

Grimshaw, A. E., 232

Guéritte, J. T., 89, 91, 231

Gui, Vittorio, 91

Guinand, Édouard, 189

Guiraud, Ernest, 10, 17, 18, 25, 44, 111, 226, 262

Hall, Elisa, 163, 164

Handel, 233, 234

Harmonie du soir (Cinq Poèmes de Baudelaire), 117

Hartmann, Georges, 70, 75

Hasselmans, Mme, 218

Hébert, Ernest, 26, 29, 30, 262

Heine, 25

Hellé, André, 93

Heller, Stephen, 10

Hillemacher, Paul and Lucien, 279

Hohenlohe, Cardinal von, 29

Hokusai, 182

Holst, Gustav, 232

Hommage à Rameau (Images for piano I), 145

Hommage à S. Pickwick Esq. P.P.M.P.C. (Préludes II), 149

Honegger, Arthur, 230

Hugo, Victor, 78, 274

Huysmans, J. K., 36, 38, 97, 262

Hypsa, E. Vincent, 112

Ibéria (Images for orchestra), 89, 91, 165, 185

Il pleure dans mon cœur (Ariettes oubliées), 120

Images, orchestra, 88, 89, 183–6

Images, piano, Set I, 88, 89, 134, 143–5, 183

Images, piano, Set II, 88, 89, 134, 143, 145–7, 183

Indy, Vincent d', 39, 49, 63, 87, 163, 191, 230, 275

Ingénus, Les (Fêtes galantes II), 123

Ingres, 26, 30

Ireland, John, 232

Isle joyeuse, L', 82, 134, 143

Iznoskow, Wladimir, 39

Jardins sous la pluie (*Estampes*), 112, 141, 180, 185

Jaurès, Jean, 69

Jet d'eau (*Cinq Poèmes de Baudelaire*), 117, 119

Jeux, 93, 94, 106, 107, 183, 186, 229

Jimbo's Lullaby (*Children's Corner*), 148

Jobert, Jean, viii

Jusseaume, 78

Khamma, 93, 183

King Lear, incidental music, 85, 107

Koechlin, Charles, 93, 180, 183, 262

Kufferath, Maurice, 57

Laforgue, Jules, 41, 215, 263

Lalo, Édouard, 10, 231

Lalo, Pierre, 86, 193

Laloy, Louis, vii, 7, 16, 46, 47, 81, 85–7, 100, 101, 142, 145, 228, 263

Lamartine, 68

Lambert, Constant, 225

Lamoureux, Charles, 36, 50, 62, 263

Lassus, Orlandus, 28, 220

Lavignac, Albert, 9, 263

Lawrence, D. H., 224

Leblanc, Georgette, 66, 75–7

Leclerq, Maurice, 87, 88

Lekeu, Guillaume, 39

Leoncavallo, 28, 217

Lépine, Jean, 17, 69

Lerolle, Henri, 55

Leroux, Xavier, 32, 263

Lhermite, Tristan, 128, 129

Liebich, Mrs. Franz, 90

Liess, Andreas, 225

Lisle, Leconte de, 149

Liszt, 8, 11, 29, 133, 142, 143, 226

Loeffler, Charles Martin, 228

Louis XIV, 129

Louÿs, Pierre, 41, 52, 56, 60, 61, 63, 68–70, 72, 125, 195, 222, 227, 263

Madrid, princesse des Espagnes, 10

Maeterlinck, 44, 51–3, 66, 75–80, 87, 193, 194, 197, 198, 200, 201, 212, 263

Magnard, Albéric, 39

Malipiero, Francesco, 231

Mallarmé, Stéphane, 19, 37, 38, 41, 57, 58, 94, 97, 121, 128, 166, 168, 201, 215, 228, 263, 275

Mallock, William Hurrell, 35

Mandoline, 113–15

Manet, 31

Manoury, Victorine. *See* Debussy, Victorine

Marie-Antoinette, 220

Marie, Gabriel, 57

Marmontel, Antoine-François, 9, 10, 12, 20, 263

Marot, Blanche, 62

Marty, Georges, 24

Martyre de saint Sébastien, Le, 92, 107, 191–3, 203

Massenet, 12, 13, 17, 18, 36, 37, 39, 52, 70, 111, 113, 122, 148, 163, 188, 190, 221, 222, 229, 280

Mauté de Fleurville, Mme, 7, 8, 264

Mauté, Mathilde. *See* Verlaine, Mathilde

Mazurka, 40, 135

Meck, Alexander von, 14, 279, 281

Meck, Alexandra von, 15. *See also* Bennigsen, Alexandra, Countess

Meck, Georges de, 279

Meck, Julia von, 12, 14, 281

Meck, Maximilian von, 14, 15

Meck, Nadezhda von, 11–17, 20, 111, 263, 279–81

Meck, Nicholas von, 15, 279–81

Meck, Sophie von, 14, 71, 281

Meck, Vladimir von, 16

Meissonnier, Ernest, 6

Mendès, Catulle, 48, 54, 61, 64, 79, 80, 94, 264

Mer, La, 82, 83, 86, 88, 89, 94, 179–85, 193

Merrill, Stuart, 41

Messager, André, 56, 78, 81, 83, 84, 105, 264

Meyerbeer, 30, 215, 221

Michelangelo, 30

Milhaud, Darius, 230

Millet, 274

Minstrels (Préludes I), 149

Missa, Edmond, 85

Monet, Claude, 46, 138, 176, 211, 231, 262, 276

Montépin, Xavier de, 72

Monteverdi, 225

Moréas, Jean, 32, 35, 264

Moreau, Gustave, 36

Moreau-Sainti, Mme, 18

Mort des amants, La (Cinq Poèmes de Baudelaire), 117

Mottl, Felix, 55

Mourey, Gabriel, 102, 164, 213, 264

Moussorgsky, 16, 40, 45, 47, 48, 115, 148, 151, 175, 212, 221, 226, 280

Mozart, 44, 79, 114, 203, 204, 207, 220, 225, 227, 234

Musset, Alfred de, 8, 14

Napravnik, Eduard, 16

Nerval, Gérard de, 37

Newman, Ernest, 94

Nijinsky, Romola, 94

Nijinsky, Vaslav, 93, 94, 186

Nikisch, Artur, 215, 218

Nocturne, violin and piano, 19

Nocturnes, orchestra, 59, 60, 62, 63, 73, 90, 173–9, 186

Noël des enfants qui n'ont plus de maisons, 99, 128

Nordau, Max, 80

Novello & Co., 70

Nuages (Nocturnes), 175, 176,

Nuit d'étoiles, 13, 111 [179

O'Brien, Grace, 5, 79, 84, 93, 163, 175, 193

# Index

O'Brien, Maire, 5, 79, 84, 93, 163, 175, 193, 214
Ode à la France, 100
Offenbach, 10, 31
Ojetti, Ugo, 66
Orléans, Charles, Duke of, 128–30, 193
Orphée-roi, 102, 103, 107

Pachulska, Julia. See Meck, Julia von
Pachulsky, pianist, 15
Pachulsky, violinist, 13, 14
Pagodes (Estampes), 138, 139
Palestrina, 27, 28, 192, 220, 234
Pantomime, 113, 114
Parry, Hubert, 71, 232
Pater, Walter, 228
Paysage sentimental, 16, 112, 180
Péladan, Joseph, 45, 264
Pelléas et Mélisande, 38, 40, 44, 48, 51–6, 59, 62, 64, 65, 70, 75–82, 84, 87, 90, 92, 102, 105, 108, 111, 123, 125, 128, 129, 133, 163, 180, 186, 188, 192–212, 230, 277, 278
Périer, Jean, 78
Pessard, Émile, 10, 11, 265
Peter, René, 69, 71, 73, 74, 87, 95, 107, 213, 265
Petite Pièce, clarinet, 164
Petite Suite, 133, 134
Philipp, Ignace, 58
Piccinni, 87
Pierné, Gabriel, vii, 6, 20, 24, 29, 91, 101, 265
Pizzetti, Ildebrando, 230

Placet futile (Trois Poèmes de Stéphane Mallarmé), 128
Poe, Edgar Allan, 34, 102, 107, 213
Poèmes de Baudelaire. See Cinq Poèmes
Poèmes de Stéphane Mallarmé. See Trois Poèmes
Poissons d'or (Images for piano II) 145–7
Poulenc, Francis, 230
Poulet, Gaston, 100
Pour ce que plaisance est morte, 129, 130
Pour le piano, 133, 134, 137, 138
Prélude (Pour le piano), 138
Prélude à l'Après-midi d'un faune. See Après-midi
Préludes, Set I, 91, 134, 149, 150
Préludes, Set II, 134, 149, 150
Primoli, Joseph, Count, 27
Printemps, for orchestra, 31, 32, 49
Promenoir des deux amants, Le, 91, 128, 129
Proses lyriques, 124, 125
Proust, Marcel, 41
Prunières, Henry, 4, 19, 29, 30
Puccini, 230
Puerta del vino, La (Préludes II), 149
Pugno, Raoul, 54, 218

Quartet for strings, 40, 57, 62, 89, 141, 151–63, 274

Rabbe, 32
Rabutin, Roger de, 3
Rameau, 101, 103, 145, 221, 234

289

Rapsodie, clarinet, 164

Rapsodie, saxophone, 163, 164

Ravel, Maurice, 87, 94, 113, 138, 140, 142, 143, 160, 230, 231

Recueillement (Cinq Poèmes de Baudelaire), 117

Redon, Odilon, 36, 86

Reflets dans l'eau (Images for piano I), 143–5

Reger, Max, 145

Régnier, Henri de, 41, 42, 52, 265

Renan, 34, 35, 40, 69

Renoir, 138, 178–80, 265

Resphigi, Ottorino, 231

Réty, Émile, 18, 211

Rêverie, 40

Reyer, Ernest, 215

Rimbaud, Arthur, 38, 97

Rimsky-Korsakov, 16, 40, 136, 138, 221, 229, 275, 280

Rodin, 94

Rodrigue et Chimène, 48, 49, 72, 79, 94, 188

Roger-Ducasse, 164, 229

Roger, Thérèse, 72

Roi Lear, Le. See *King Lear*

Rolland, Romain, 79, 88, 97, 211, 225

Roman de Tristan, Le, 102, 103

Rondeau, song, 14

Rondel chinois, 19

Rondels de Charles d'Orléans, 129, 130

Rondes de printemps (Images for orchestra), 89, 91, 112

Ronson, 78

Ropartz, Guy, 57, 58

Rossetti, Dante Gabriel, 49, 60, 66, 189–91, 265

Rousseau, Jean-Jacques, 201, 228

Roussel, Albert, 229

Roustan, Mme, 4, 5, 7

Rubinstein, Anton, 11, 13, 16

Rubinstein, Ida, 92, 191

Rubinstein, Nicholas, 11

Saint-Saëns, Camille, 7, 10, 29, 48, 58, 59, 63, 81, 111

Sand, George, 37

Sarabande (Pour le piano), 137

Sarrazin, Gabriel, 49, 189, 190

Satie, Erik, 45–7, 61, 97, 136, 201, 217, 230, 265

Saulaie, La (Willowwood), 60

Savard, Augustin, 26

Schaeffner, André, 229

Scherzo, violin and piano, 19

Schmitt, Florent, 229

Schönberg, Arnold, 128, 231

Schott, publisher, 13

Schubert, 44, 127, 132, 218, 220

Schumann, 9, 10, 124, 148, 234

Scott, Cyril, 66, 231, 232

Ségalen, Victor, 103

Ségard, Achille, 61

Serenade for the Doll. See *Doll's Serenade*

Serov, 39

Sévigné, Mme de, 3

Sgambati, Giovanni, 28, 29

Shakespeare, 28, 32, 102–5, 149, 212

Shelley, 32, 173

Signorelli, 30

Sirène Musicale, Éditions de la, viii

Sirènes (Nocturnes), 175, 179, 180

Sivry, Charles de, 7, 265

Smithson, Harriet, 107

Snow is dancing, The (Children's Corner), 148

Soirée dans Grenade, La (Estampes), 140, 141, 143, 185

Sonata, cello and piano, 98, 164, 165, 182

Sonata, flute, viola and harp, 98, 164, 165, 182

Sonata, violin and piano, 100, 164, 165, 182

Sons et les parfums tournent dans l'air du soir, Les (Préludes I), 149

Spinoza, 100

Spleen (Ariettes oubliées), 120

Stanford, Charles Villiers, 232

Stassov, Vladimir, 151

Strauss, Richard, 63, 90, 91, 222, 229, 231, 232

Stravinsky, 93, 165, 185, 224, 227–9

Suarès, André, 65, 100

Suite bergamasque, 122, 133

Sullivan, 70, 91, 233

Swinburne, 36

Symons, Arthur, 231

Symphony, partly published, 16

Syrinx, 164

Taine, 34

Tchaikovsky, 11–17, 134, 221, 232, 280

Templier, P. D., 45

Ternant, André de, 28, 29, 42–4

Texier, Rosalie. *See* Debussy, Lily

Thalberg, Sigismond, 215

Thibaudet, Albert, 168

Thiéberg, Maurice, 19

Thomas, Ambroise, 29, 187

Tiersot, Julien, 40, 55, 265

Toccata (Pour le piano), 138

Tolstoy, 32

Tombeau des Naïades, Le (Chansons de Bilitis), 125–7, 165

Toulet, Paul-Jean, 84, 91, 95, 103–5, 266

Toulouse-Lautrec, 46, 150

Tours, Berthold, 70

Trio, G minor, 14

Triomphe de Bacchus, Le, 16

Tristan. See Roman de Tristan

Trois Poèmes de Stéphane Mallarmé, 94, 128

Turner, Joseph, 179, 185, 231

Valéry, Paul, 35, 36, 41, 68, 81, 223, 224

Vallas, Léon, vii, 3–5, 14, 49, 98, 103, 111, 115, 134, 141, 163–5, 175, 214, 215

Vasnier, 19–21, 23, 25–7, 30, 31, 33, 44, 115

Vasnier, Mme, 18–21, 23, 25, 33, 71, 113

Vasnier, Marguerite, 20, 21, 23, 25, 33

Vasnier, Maurice, 23, 25

Vaughan Williams, Ralph, 232

Velasquez, 98

Vent dans la plaine, Le (Préludes I), 150

Verdi, 28–30

Verlaine, Mathilde, 7, 8

Verlaine, Paul, v, 8, 19, 22, 37, 38, 41, 82, 97, 113, 115, 119, 122–4, 130, 131, 180, 189, 209, 215, 266

Victoria, Tomás Luis de, 220

Vidal, Paul, 10, 17, 18, 24, 26, 29, 32, 266

Vieuille, Félix, 78

Villon, François, 91, 92, 128, 130, 193

Voiles (Préludes I), 150, 180

Voltaire, 69

Vuillermoz, Émile, 87, 191

Wagner, 8, 9, 17, 21, 22, 26, 27, 29, 35–40, 42, 44–9, 52, 54–6, 61, 63, 64, 71, 79, 83, 87, 90, 103, 116, 117, 119, 122, 132, 149, 168, 190–3, 209, 217, 221, 222, 224, 225, 229, 230–2, 280, 281

Watteau, 113, 143

Weber, 107, 221

Whistler, 41, 173

Wilder, Victor, 36

Willy. *See* Gauthier-Villars

Wolf, Hugo, 132

Wood, Henry J., 89, 231

Wordsworth, 180

Wyzewa, Teodor de, 36, 266

Young, Filson, 233

Ysaÿe, Eugène, 52, 53, 56, 57, 59, 60, 218, 266

Zola, Émile, 64, 69

Zuléïma, 25, 30, 32, 49

MADE AT THE
TEMPLE PRESS ❀ LETCHWORTH
IN GREAT BRITAIN